The Wisdom of the Whole

Linda Bark PhD RN MCC

Copyrights © 2011
By Linda Bark

All rights reserved.

Cover design by Alyssa Boisson
Illustrations by Bob Boisson
Layout and book design by Aleksandra Jelic

Printed in the USA on recycled paper

ISBN-10: 1463636679

ISBN-13: 978-1463636678

Library of Congress: 2011916025

Create Space Press
San Francisco, CA

Dedicated

*to
my mother and father,
Mae and Harold*

*to
my daughter and her family,
Laurel, Jim, Mackenzie, and Madison*

*to
my clients, students, and all those who have the courage
to take the next step in their growth and development*

Acknowledgements

It takes a village to write a book...or maybe to write this book...or maybe I love any excuse to create a village. Whatever the reason—and they are probably all true—I have many to thank. This book integrates years of learning how to help people make changes, so I want to thank some early teachers, such as Merla Olson in my nursing school, who taught me the most valuable lesson about trusting the process—that mysterious step-by-step movement that facilitates real truth when I am tuned into my deep knowing. My coaching is based on this principle. And Dr. Yi Wu at the California Institute of Integral Studies, who expertly guided me in the fascinating world of Chinese philosophy and told me that the familiar adage of "The journey of 10,000 miles begins with the first step" is more correctly translated as "The journey of 10,000 miles begins from the ground upon which you are standing." He validated the importance of my identifying and understanding my philosophy. This foundation informs every aspect of my coaching practice, is woven into this book, and also guides my life.

Another early teacher of mine is Rudolph Ballentine, now a retired holistic physician who is focusing on writing and training that updates Tantra for the 21st century. I worked with Rudy in the 90s—first to learn his holistic healing ways, as I sat with him in Pennsylvania and New York while he worked with hundreds of clients—and then he joined me as we helped start up holistic healing centers. I immediately recognized from my first contact with him at the California Institute of Integral Studies that he thinks from an integral perspective, and over the years I've learned a great deal from him about wholeness. He was the last to read the final draft (he's not an easy evaluator), and when he gave his enthusiastic thumbs up, I gave a big sigh of relief and felt ready to send it for final editing.

When I started in earnest to write this book, I thought I would finish in about three months. After all, I said to myself, I've been teaching this for years, so it should come easy. I further reasoned that the first draft of my dissertation took only a week because it was at the end of almost nine years of study and just seemed to pour out of me. I expected the same —but guess what? I was wrong. It's been a three-and-a-half year process that amazingly has kept my interest and enthusiasm. Part of the reason it took that long was because I wanted to walk the talk of life and work balance. There were parts of my life that I just wasn't willing to sacrifice to an intense writing process, and I have no regrets.

Just as I'm grateful to teachers who helped me formulate my ideas, the many steps publishing required brought many others whose help I must acknowledge. One is the number 6 California Zephyr, an Amtrak train, which I've often taken to visit my daughter and her family. I had 12 whole hours, and sometimes longer, that I could write—no interruptions, no phone, and a dining car for lunch and dinner. Another rather unusual thank you goes to the staff at the "Gold and Silver," a family-owned restaurant since 1956, located in Reno, Nevada. It was there that I'd meet with Bob Boisson, my illustrator, and we'd dream up and revise the illustrations. Oddly enough, this was the same place that I wrote my thesis some 30 years earlier when I was working on my Master's degree in life transition counseling and lived in the area. (I guess I was an early forerunner of a Starbucks customer.)

I mentioned meeting with Bob, and he is someone at the top of my list to thank. When I started this book, I realized I wanted lots of illustrations. I often think in pictures, so it seemed like a natural and efficient way to simplify and explain complex content. I wanted this book to be a combination of Rudolph Ballentine's *Radical Healing*—for substance, a kind of "coaching for dummies"—for being user-friendly and simple in format, and a children's book—for fun illustrations. However, there are reasons why all books do not have over 80 illustrations: cost, layout, and lots of work. But, I love the ones Bob produced, and only wish they could all be in color. I loved working with Bob on them because he's so talented, and some of these concepts were not easy to illustrate: intuition, Law of Attraction, or Archaic structure of consciousness, for example. He was my first choice when considering illustrators, and I'm so fortunate that he stayed with this winding production process in such a collaborative way. Akin and quite literally "a kin" to Bob is Alyssa Boisson, his daughter, who definitely inherited talent from her Dad and her mother, Carol. Alyssa is a very creataive graphic designer and created the book cover.

And while we're on the graphic part of this book, deep thanks to Aleksandra Jelic, who did the layout. I took this book to many designers, and they would shake their heads at the complexity of the manuscript and say this would take months! That was scary. But then through my "village" connections I found Aleksandra, who looked at the manuscript, and in her very calm, solid way said, "Yes, this will not be hard. I can do it in three weeks." I was elated and have found her to be patient, very competent, and fast. That "can do easily" attitude saved me many sleepless nights. I loved getting the emails entitled "Book Back" as she added page after page of content and illustrations and I could see the book growing chapter by chapter.

Next are manuscript readers to thank—those whose feedback and caring helped me in my writing process. It wasn't that I didn't know what I wanted to say, but I sometimes struggled with how was I going to say it and for whom. In the beginning, I really needed to find out if the basic idea of using Jean Gebser's framework even made sense to people. This structure had helped me and my students but would it make sense to a larger audience in book form, even with the help of illustrations? Feedback from many readers helped me keep in mind the coaches who were going to use it for learning and for practice. Special thanks to them: Diane Conrad, Peter Ennen, Cecilia Enquist, Judith Gruber, Sam Hanser, Mike Harris, Ginny Katz, David

Lazaroff, Alison Rose Levy, Michelle and Merrill Long, Alice Meisels, Michael Stratford, Susan Orr, Catherine Osterbye, Mary Perez, Judy Phoenix, Susan Quinzi, Jerry Reilly, Roz Reynolds, Pat Sennoff, Frances Spikes, Markie Stephens, and Duncan, Lisa, and Mathew Work.

Then I must acknowledge my "editorial staff." Early in the process I benefitted from people who could not only edit but who had taken my course and understood the framework and ideas. Susan Drouilhet and Kamron Keep helped immensely. Ruth Backstrom came along close to the end, to help pull things together. She came to visit for several days and was like a birthing coach who helped me with those transition panting, pushing breaths. Fall Ferguson stepped in toward the end, adding her valuable skills to help with the process. Hats off the all of them.

And of course, I want to thank Michele Chase, who was the knight in shining armor who came in at the very end and crafted, polished, and proofread this final version. It's no wonder she's won writing awards. When I called to see if she could take up the final thrust to completion, she said she was just finishing reading Jean Gebser's book! I was amazed. Very few people even know of Gebser, and fewer still have read his book. I knew her help at that juncture was perfect.

I certainly want to mention one of my staff members, Chandra Page, who has seen this book grow from a small seed to a full-fledged actual book. She's helped with numerous administrative tasks along the way, plus generally running the Institute in a methodical, practical, steady way that allowed me to focus on the book. Michelle Young Long, Kate Sadowsky, Nina Fry, Michelle Ninde, Beth Warshaw, Leslie Olsson, and Crystal Bayley also assisted with this process. To them, my thanks.

And to the participants in my coach training courses, who've helped me build the learning community over the last 20 years—my deep respect and acknowledgement. Although some of the contributors wrote something early on, most wrote at the end, and so the last month before the manuscript went for its final editing, I was receiving the contributions. Night after night, I would drive home softly crying—not from sadness but from such a full heart: full of so much love and admiration to see how they had integrated the principles or been supported by the concepts and to see how they put them out in the world. Even as I write this, my eyes tear up and I say thank you. . .thank you to the people who came and continue to come to this course, to learn together and then support one another as well as me. Thank you for that love, that respect, that partnering with others from their hearts. We see so much violence in the world at large, but this is the opposite—this is what prevents and heals the violence.

I also want to acknowledge my personal support system—my family and many friends, some of whom I want to especially thank, such as Marsha and Michael Joyce, Dea Daniels, with whom I co-created the Gebser framework for holistic healing, Gary Kaplan, and Darlene Hess. Also, Jay Perry, who was my first coach and also helped train me in coaching. Recently, working together in a coaching session, it took us three minutes to come up with the name for the book. He said, "In reading this book, it seems like it's really about the wisdom of the self." "Well," I said, "it is more than that, Jay. It's bigger. . .it's really bigger. . .it's about everything. . .It's about the wisdom of the "whole." And then we were both quiet, realizing that was the name of the book. I appreciate Jay for all his coaching, over many years.

Last, but certainly not least, are my clients, who allow me into their lives and trust me with their inner workings, who share what delights them, what scares them, and what comprises their working edge of new learning. Of course, I can't name them—which you, the reader, might be relieved about since that would make my acknowledgment list even longer. But to my clients: you know who you are. I treasure our partnership. I learn from it. It keeps me alive and growing. It helps me fulfill my life purpose. I thank each of you from the bottom of my heart.

Table of Contents

Introduction — 1
    It's about You First — 1
    The Whole Person Coach — 3
    It's All about Coaches Too — 5
    Are You Ready to Change Your Life? — 12

Part One—Overview of Approaches to Coaching — 15
    Sample Session 1A—Should I Change Jobs? — 17

Chapter 1—Welcome to Coaching — 27
    Coaching As a Partnership — 28
    A Deeper Partnership in the BCI Model — 29
    A Learning and Growth Approach Is Key in Coaching — 30
    Learning and Growth Areas Are Expanded in the BCI Model — 30
    Coaching Encourages Clients to Find Their Inner Voice of Wisdom — 33
    Clients Can Find Their Inner Voice More Easily in the BCI Approach — 33
    Coaching Is About Exploring the Unknown — 34
        Coaching Grid — 34
        All Squares Become Larger with the BCI Method — 36

Chapter 2—The Development of Coaching — 41
    New Times Generate New Ideas, New Approaches, and New Professions — 42
    Psychology and Coaching — 44
    The Impact of Organizational Development and Business in Coaching — 46
    Contribution from the Sports Arena — 48
    Coaching and Health Care — 48
    Nursing and a Coaching Role — 51
    Additional Coaching Influences — 52
    Cross-Fertilization — 53
    The Exponential Growth of Coaching — 53
    Coaching Is Still Developing — 54

Chapter 3—Coaching Structure and Competencies — 61
    Core Competencies of Coaching — 62
        Setting the Foundation — 63
        Co-Creating the Relationship — 68
        Communicating Effectively — 69
        Facilitating Learning and Results — 70

How the BCI Model Expands the Core Competencies	70
Putting It All Together	75

Chapter 4—Helping People Navigate Change — 83
    Holistic Approaches Support Change — 85
    Maps for Change — 90
        Bridges' Map for Change — 90
        Bark Coaching Institute Model of Stages of Change — 92
        Models of Change Facilitate Awareness — 94
    Coaching Readiness — 95
    Using Models of Change — 102
Sample Session 1B—Progress Interrupted! — 104

Part Two—The Toolkit — 109
    How Developmental Models Work — 110
        Archaic — 111
        Intuitive — 112
        Mythical — 113
        Mental — 114
        Integral — 114
    Accessing the Gifts of Earlier Structures — 115
    A Note About Coaching Tools and the Structures of Consciousness — 116

Chapter 5—The Mental Structure of Consciousness in Coaching — 121
    Sample Session 2A—"Help, I'm Falling Apart!" — 122
    Overview of the Mental Part of Coaching — 127
    Mental Tools for Assessment at the Beginning of Coaching Sessions — 130
        Assessing Learning Types — 130
    Mental Tools for Clarification and Awareness throughout Coaching Sessions — 135
        Critical Thinking and Decision-Making — 135
        1-10 Scale for Measurement — 137
        Choosing between Options: An Orienting Tool — 141
        The Pie Chart — 145
        Lists and Prioritizing — 146
        Observing and Working with Behavior Patterns — 149
    Mental Tools for Homework at the end of Sessions — 155
        Plans and Timelines — 155

Chapter 6—Coaching Tools from the Mythical Structure of Consciousness — 161
    Sample Session 2B—"I Want to Get Things Done!" — 162
    Tools Based Upon the Mythical Structure of Consciousness — 167

Mythical Assessment Tools	169
Personal Constitution	169
Vata, or Air-Like	172
Pitta, or Fire-Like	174
Kapha, or Earth-Like	175
Other Applications of Personal Constitution	178
Empowerment Language	179
Empowerment Sounds Like Having a Choice	179
The Language for Getting Needs Met	182
Communicating Needs and Wants	184
Mythical Tools that Facilitate Clarity and Awareness in the Middle of Sessions	188
Working with Story	188
Harnessing the Power of Imagery	193
Creative Dialog	197
Mythical Tools As Homework	203
Affirmations	203

Chapter 7—The Intuitive Part of Coaching — 209

Sample Session 2C—Up Against a Brick Wall	210
Overview of the Intuitive Part of Coaching	214
Intuitive Tools Used in All Sections of the Coaching Session	217
Walking the Talk	217
Being Guided by Intuition	221
Silence	227
Intuitive Coaching Tools that Facilitate Clarity at the Beginning of Sessions	229
Magic Wand	229
Intuitive Coaching Tools to Use in the Middle of Sessions: Working with Energy	231
Working with Body Energy	231
Working with Chakras	233
Connecting through Tapping	239
Working with Direction of Energy Currents	241
Working with the Breath	244
Group Energy in Coaching	247
Law of Attraction	250
Group Energy and Family Dynamics: Powerful Questions	254
Intuitive Tools As Homework	257
Drawing upon the Healing of Nature	260
Food and Nutrition: The Food, Mood, and Nourishment Log	263
Creating Rituals	270
Further Thoughts about Accessing the Intuitive	272

Chapter 8—The Archaic Part of Coaching — 277

- Sample Session 2D—The Sacred Friday — 278
- Overview of the Archaic Part of Coaching — 281
- Archaic Coaching Tools for Clarity and Awareness During Sessions and As Homework — 284
- Meditation, Prayer, and Contemplation — 285
    - Being in the Now—the Present Moment — 287
    - Working with a Sense of Life Purpose or Meaning — 289
    - Compassion — 290
    - Working with the Three Faces of God — 293
- A Few More Comments about Drawing from the Archaic — 295

Chapter 9—The Integral Structure of Consciousness — 299

- Sample Session 2E—Putting It All Together — 300
- Overview of the Integral Structure of Consciousness in Coaching — 308
- The Four Quadrants of an Integral Approach — 313
- Powerful Questions for Aspects of Ourselves Described by the Quadrants — 318
- The Integral Coach in the BCI Model — 322
- The Integral Coach in Action — 325
    - For Use All the Time — 325
    - For Use in Assessment — 327
    - For Use at the Beginning of Coaching Sessions—Where Does Your Client Want to Go? — 328
    - Tools for Use in the Middle of Sessions — 330
    - Tools for the Ends of Sessions (Homework) — 335
- Some Final Comments — 337
- Coaching Graduates Work Integrally — 337

List of Contributors

Ginny Katz, MS, MSS—*Coaching in Kindergarten*	32
Marian Boileau, RN, BSN—*Trusting the Unknown?*	36
Bhaskar Banerji, MA—*A Pain in the Neck*	37
Laura Boone, BS, MBA—*Veterinary and Dental Coach*	38
Nicole Florez, MA—*Health Coaching*	49
Mary Elaine Southard, RN, MSN, APHN-BC, Diploma in Clinical Homeopathy, DNP (student)— *What Kind of New System Will We Build?*	50
Estelle Brodeur, MS, PMHCNS-BC, ACC—*Therapy and Coaching*	67
Karen Sanders, MSN, RN, AHN-BC—*Coaching the Phoenix Nurses*	78
Beth Warshaw, MA—*Is Group-Coaching As Effective As Individual Coaching?*	79
Kate Sadowsky, MA—*Avatar Association and Behavioral Change*	80
Teresa Corrigan, RN, MA, BCB, CLYT—*A Full-Spectrum Approach to Surgery Coaching*	86
Sally Arnold, RN, MA, AHN—*From Contemplation to Preparation for Action*	103
Laurel Wachtel, BS—*Changing One Aspect Changes the Behavior Pattern*	154
Rachael Friedman, MD—*Baby Steps to Create Health*	157
Susan Friedman, BSN—*Empowerment for Patients*	186
Susan Spoelma, MBA, MSN, RN, NEA-BC, DNP (student)—*Organizational Leadership*	187
Mike Harris, Certified Coach—*The Power of Stories*	192
Linda Chiofar, RN, MSN, HN-BC—*Imagery in Coaching*	196
Catherine Osterbye, BS, MS—*Archetypes and Sub-Personalities in Dialog*	199

Mary Perez, RN, Reiki Master—*Teaching Self-Care by Caring for Myself*	218
Michelle Long, MA—*Support for Moms*	219
Cynthia Lester, M. Ed.—*Accessing Intuition*	223
Dawn Preisendorf, MA—*Intuition Makes for Extraordinary Coaching*	224
Markie Stephens, MHR, BSN, RN—*Calling on the Angels*	225
Lisa Leum, BA, RN—*Energetic Support for the Dying*	246
Suzanne Koivun MSN, RN, CCAP, CCAPT, Reiki Master *Equine Assisted Coaching and Subtle Energy*	247
Darlene Hess, PhD, AHN-BC, PMHNP-BC, ACC—*Manifesting Your Goal*	252
Kamron Keep, RN, BSN—*Aromatherapy as An Adjunct to Coaching*	258
Ruth Backstrom, PhD—*Facilitating Sustainability*	261
Barbara Hannelore, BA, MHE, MT—*Women in Harmony with Nature*	263
Dea Daniels, RN, CWW—*Healing and Nourishment*	264
Paula Szloboda, RN, NI, MA, MBA, Therapeutic Chef—*Health Education and Health Coaching, the Dynamic Duo!*	268
Fay Daley—*A Closer Walk with God*	286
Merla Olsen, RN, PhD-ABD—*Meaning Comes from How We Live*	290
Roxanne Taracena—*The BCI Approach in Action*	338
Judith Gruber, MSW, LCSW, CCET—*Money As an Integral Issue!*	339
Kathy Moehling, RN, AHN-BC, ND, LCPC, LMT—*So Many Applications for Coaching Tools!*	340
Steve Friedman, DDS—*Coaching Tools for Service in a Dental Office*	342

Introduction

Hello! Welcome to this conversation about coaching. I'm happy you're here!

It's about You First

Let's start by looking at who you are and what you hope to get from your investment in this book. If you're a professional who helps others to lead flourishing, happier lives, this book will help you become even more effective. Besides theory, you'll learn many practical tools and techniques to use personally and professionally every day. In my experience, nurses, social workers, nutritionists, bodyworkers, yoga instructors, doctors, coaches, teachers, occupational therapists, psychotherapists, massage therapists, personal trainers, and physical therapists have found the approach presented here to be especially useful. But the list doesn't stop there. Even if you're not currently a member of the helping professions, you'll see many applications to everyday situations.

If you're interested in learning about affecting change for yourself, this book is also for you. People who've used these methods have repeatedly found that the powerful questions and exercises can be applied to all areas of their personal lives—career, relationships, work/life balance, sense of purpose, or health.

2 INTRODUCTION

You can use this book as a companion text for my coaching course, or you can use it as your primary teacher at this time, given its fun and easy design, playful illustrations, interactive exercises, and generous spaces for your note taking. In classes trainees have opportunities to practice and to share their experiences, and here you'll also find many stories of how coaches are using this approach. I also model coaching sessions between clients and myself, just as I would do in classes. When reading the stories and sample sessions, please imagine yourself in one or both roles and consider how you'd engage. You'll find a toolbox full of practical and time-tested possibilities and many appealing questions for your own exploration, presented in boxes throughout the text. However, as you'll see, coaching is more than just a set of skills: coaches need to walk their talk.

I've created this book so that you can participate—it's a conversation between you and me. Coaching is an interaction, a partnership between coach and client. I teach my classes so as to model this, and I thought it would be wonderful for you to have a similar experience. I invite you to experience these coaching tools firsthand as yet another facet to your learning and absorbing this very effective model, called BCI, for Bark Coaching Institute. I would also love your feedback so that this book and my model continue to evolve based upon all of our experiences. Please send your ideas and comments to wisdomofthewhole.com. And thanks!

The Whole Person Coach

So what's this way of coaching that creates a new level of success and fulfillment? Great question! I'm glad you asked. The BCI Approach combines holistic and integral perspectives. *Holistic* is a term you've probably heard before, relating to seeing from a whole body, mind, and spirit perspective. This is a broad vision, but still doesn't include everything relevant. By adding an integral viewpoint, the picture becomes even more rich, comprehensive, and telling. The term *integral* might not be as familiar to you as the term holistic. Integral refers to the whole, total, or complete perspective: foreground, background, side ground, up ground, down ground, all around ground, and all the aspects of a situation, person, or event. Each "separate" part is treated as interconnected with all the others.

Intriguing? But you may be asking, "Why do we have to come from this very big picture?" Another good question! For much of the last century, our thinking process has tended to be linear and analytical; we've created specialized bodies of knowledge, and we've focused on discrete components. As the field of coaching has developed coaches have often taken on a mental, logical perspective that's served coaching well. In fact, taking a mental perspective is the framework of the coaching model presented in this book. However, just as other disciplines are discovering that they need a larger foundation, coaching for the 21st century requires a more complete picture of wholeness that allows taking advantage of all types of holistic and integral approaches to facilitating change. We have many options available to us; why not try them when we and our clients are interested?

We've sharpened our skills of discernment and differentiation; however, now we're beginning to realize that besides understanding the parts of a system in detail, we need to grasp how all pieces fit together so we can truly appreciate how things work in their totality. We can see signs of this developing awareness across the globe. In international politics, we're discovering that military and diplomatic solutions together create more powerful results than either approach alone. In the corporate world, interdepartmental collaboration is replacing the "silo" management system—a model characterized by a lack of communication or shared goals. Environmental challenges and building sustainability scream out for a comprehensive, holistic, and integral perspective. And currently we all recognize the dire need for change in a troubled global financial system based on fragmented, piecemeal policy. Understanding how things fit together is critical; seeing the whole picture not only gives us more clarity for reaching our goals, it may also be crucial to our survival, individually and as a species.

But even though this holistic and integral approach may sound promising, you might think that considering all these pieces would make things too complex and complicated. In reality, the process usually becomes easier. Why? Because with such an approach all things are already connected, so working with them just follows the natural, realistic flow of things.

Needless to say, as a society we aren't yet especially skilled at how to create, weave together, and act from multiple perspectives, but that seems to be our task at hand. As a species, we're in a huge and rapid change process, and the ways we thought and acted in the past, and even in the past decade, often no longer work. Albert Einstein once said something to the effect that we can't solve problems by using the same kind of thinking we used when we created them. We need to step outside of the familiar, try new things, and explore multiple perspectives.

There's good news—we're learning how to come from our wholeness at a fairly rapid rate. With many of us expanding and integrating a whole picture perspective with effective action in the world, we're contributing to a greater whole—our collective wisdom. What you and I learn helps all of us—perhaps your learning makes it slightly easier for the next person, and perhaps I'm able to grasp something with a bit less effort because of another who came before me. In this way, I truly believe we all are connected and growing together. Bravo!!!

And that, in essence, is what this book is all about: using and integrating multiple ways of knowing and being to create happier, healthier, more successful, and fulfilling lives, individually and together. Of course, the focus is how to do it in coaching, but the concepts are relevant to other areas as well. Learning and applying the principles described in any arena of human experience helps our species' development.

Knowing how to explore this big picture in coaching by using a multitude of powerful ways of being and thinking is the purpose of this book.

So how can we actually do this in coaching? Imagine that you're an investigator for a jewel robbery. If you speak with a couple of people, you have an idea of what happened. But if you talk to more people, you can really put the pieces together and apprehend the thief! Now, a coach is not usually trying to find out who stole the diamonds, but *is* an investigator in some sense. The coach is in a dynamic partnership with clients who are moving toward a new goal—toward a new place in life—toward a new level of health and wellness—toward new ways of being and living. The more the coach can listen and ask powerful questions that speak to the essence and multifaceted aspects of the situation, the more the coach can help clients sense the whole picture. This is the real power of the BCI Model. From this more complete picture, clients can put together better plans and actions that are going to lead to real and lasting change and success. The clients' decisions will be more authentic, efficient, and accurate because they're aligned with more parts of themselves and of the situation. False starts or directions are usually eliminated, saving time, energy, and sometimes money. Both the client and the coach feel a real sense of fulfillment by being involved in this worthwhile partnership.

It's All about Coaches Too

The BCI Approach is not only about looking at the clients' big picture. The coaches also come from their whole selves, in context. My students and clients often ask me about my own journey—how I arrived at where I am now, how I embraced a holistic and integral perspective, personally and professionally. I think it's important to know the paths others have traveled; it helps to put their wisdom and your learning in context. So with that in mind, here's my story.

In my youth, I always wanted to be a nurse. My heroine was the fictional character Cherry Ames, and I read all the books about her. The series portrayed her in different types of nursing with such titles as Cherry Ames—Flight Nurse, Army Nurse, Chief Nurse, Cruise Nurse, Mountaineer Nurse, Dude Ranch Nurse, Department Store Nurse, and Jungle Nurse! I grew up in Harvey, Illinois, a quiet suburb of Chicago, and her adventures fascinated and inspired me. As I later discovered, her stories mirrored my truth of evolving roles and career options—a path that has kept nursing alive and vital for me throughout my professional life. Whenever I felt the need to work in a new way, I investigated the possibilities, and if what I found seemed sound, I asked, "Why not?" Eventually, I would discover that others wanted to join me in new, groundbreaking adventures. This always felt wonderful!!! And this is exactly what happened when, as a forerunner in my field, I started a private practice in nursing in 1970.

In 1977 I switched from being the nurse to being the patient. I experienced my own health crisis, and in the process I discovered alternative approaches and a holistic model for healing. In my mid thirties, I'd been diagnosed with osteoarthritis and could barely walk. Desperate for healing, I decided to investigate new directions. Just poking around one day in a health store in Reno, Nevada, I saw a booklet entitled, *You Can Heal Arthritis*. I quickly picked it up and read it from cover to cover right there in the aisle. That was my introduction to this strange new world of holistic healing—a world and philosophy that didn't match what I'd been taught in my excellent but conventional nursing education.

I soon learned about toxins and body/mind/spirit approaches to health and healing, and decided to spend a month at Bernard Jensen's health ranch in Escondido, California. My plan was to undertake a water fast to eliminate toxins from my tissues and, in the process, hopefully reduce my arthritis. Coming from an extensive background in nursing, I felt suspicious of this strange approach, but my desire to heal overcame my resistance. Weeks before the fast, I was instructed to begin an elimination diet, giving up meats, sugars, and carbohydrates, and only to eat vegetables. I did well with the regime, but as I drove toward the ranch across Nevada and California, I kept thinking about not eating anything for two weeks. Would I die? I had my car. I could always escape. To assuage my anxiety and fear, I went from one Dairy Queen to the next, eating hot fudge sundaes all along the way. It was really fun! Fortunately, I confessed upon checking in at the ranch—no doubt because they asked directly about my compliance with the preparation and because I'm such a poor liar. Of course, for my own health and safety, they then decided I needed several more days of preparation before beginning the water fast.

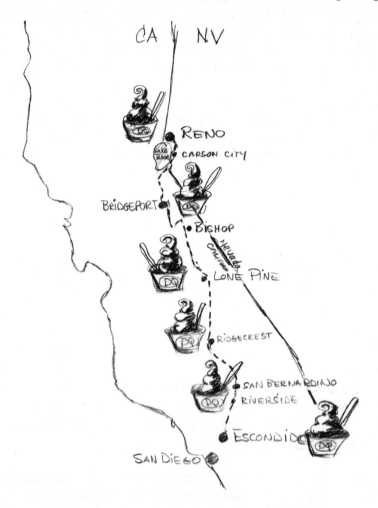

At the ranch, I attended many classes, read books on healing, took short walks, and wrote in a journal. Do you have any idea how much time and energy is spent in the eating process? I didn't—and I discovered lots of extra time! I watched other guests experience what was called a "healing crisis." It didn't look fun—people seemed to get sick. I decided I wasn't going to have a healing crisis, but my strategy didn't quite work (surprise!), and I soon learned about a healing crisis at the cellular level. After the first several days of water fasting, I began to feel really good—on top of the world even—and then slowly over a period of several hours, I began to feel as if I were coming down with the same flu I'd experienced several months before my fast. This only lasted part of a day, and then I returned to my feeling-good place, which I much preferred. Several days later, I had a severe headache reminiscent of the encephalitis I had experienced five years earlier, and for which I'd taken massive doses of penicillin. During the two days of healing-crisis headache, I could taste penicillin; if you've ever tasted it, you know it's not to be confused with any other taste—and not a pleasant one. I felt like it was coming out my pores, my skin, and especially—for some reason—my tongue.

Through my reading, I discovered more about healing crises. Constantine Herring, a founding force in homeopathy, devised a theory to help patients determine if a symptom was part of a healing process or an indication of further deterioration of their health. He developed four laws of the curative process. He proposed that first people heal from the inside out. That seemed to make sense to me. I knew from my nursing experience that abscesses need to heal from deeper to more superficial levels and then finally at the skin level. Second, he said our healing proceeds from the more important organs to those of lesser importance. I could buy that. Third, Herring stated that we heal from our most recent illness back. In other words, we heal illnesses in the reverse order of their origin. Lastly, he explained that we heal from the top of our body downward.[1] I wasn't so sure about the last two of Herring's "Laws of Cure," but when I looked back over at my own experience, I discovered that my healing crises had exactly followed the patterns described by this theory. I was amazed.

The fasting process changed my life. Today I wouldn't recommend water fasting, as I now know that there are kinder, gentler ways to cleanse the body. However, the joint swelling and pain disappeared, and I couldn't ignore the improvement in my symptoms. Upon my return home, I explored bodywork and several other holistic approaches.

When I began to integrate what I'd learned through my experiences as a patient with what I did in my nurse role, I began an enormous amount of reevaluation about healing. As I wheeled patients off to surgery to have a tendon cut or some part removed, I couldn't help thinking that there were additional ways of healing. Would these other methods help my patients too? For me, it was not either/or, but rather both/and. I wanted to know if these alternative and holistic healing modalities could be helpful in addition to the traditional Western medical approach.

After this period of reassessment, I decided that yes, I wanted to bring more healing options into my work. With the support of the Medical Director at my VA Hospital, we brought in a Feldenkrais practitioner, and our patients began to work with this trained professional to learn new neuromuscular movement. (One example of Feldenkrais work is the "reeducation" of a frozen shoulder so that it functions more normally and a patient might be able to avoid surgery.) Patients began to have new and expanded health care options. I also taught a holistic nursing course for the staff so that they could see how a body/mind/spirit approach could

8   INTRODUCTION

As I wheeled patients off to surgery, I couldn't help wonder about other healing options.

revitalize their own sense of wellbeing and their nursing practice. They began to act personally and professionally from this more whole perspective that improved their health and gave them new tools to use with their patients.

I was hooked on seeing the whole picture and incorporating multiple ways of healing. This worked, *and* that worked, *and* that worked, *and* that worked. When I had a particular challenge, I realized it was connected to another issue that was part of some other history, *and, and, and*. "The knee bone is connected to the ankle bone. . . ." Holistic healing worked. I saw this in my life and in the lives of my patients. Hungry to learn more, in 1990 I found all roads leading to the California Institute of Integral Studies in San Francisco. It was here that I would learn about integrating East and West, North and South—bringing together all ways of healing and thinking—seeing the whole picture—learning about an integral approach.

As part of my graduate work exploring multiple healing options, I led medical tours to China for the Institute of Noetic Sciences, New Dimensions Radio, the California Institute of Integral Studies, and my own company. Eventually, I decided I wanted a longer opportunity in China to discover firsthand how to help Westerners—myself included—understand and use Traditional Chinese Medicine, a healing system based on energy or qi. I knew that the Chinese patients had access to both Chinese and Western medicine; how did they decide which one to use? In some instances, they combined both systems. How did that work, and how were the two synthesized? I was bursting with questions, and so beginning in 1997, I spent over one-and-a-half years in southern China. Throughout that time, I discovered even more questions and also found some answers.

During my graduate studies in the early 90s, I became clear that part of my life's work was to integrate different healing systems and that working in and with holistic or integral healing centers would be a natural next step for me. With many years of conventional and holistic/integral nursing experience behind me, combined with organizational development training, I knew I'd found a meaningful purpose and became a consultant in this field. I'd seen how multiple approaches were combined in China. How could what I learned there transfer to centers in the United States? Holistic healing centers were popping up everywhere, and patients were seeking and spending their own out-of-pocket money for complementary and alternative medicine.

My healing center model actually called for an orientation that I'd practiced for many years: not just expert consultant/practitioner but also holistic and integral coach. I'd often found that people were overwhelmed when told by an "expert" to change their lives in order to improve their health. Exercise, nutrition, stress reduction, and overall life balance were frequent goals, but many people didn't know where to start or anything about complementary and alternative healing. I discovered that at this stage of their journeys a partnership model inspired people to take small but meaningful steps toward their goals. Coaching as a profession was in its inception; when I discovered it and later experienced it, I realized "this is what I do. I've had a coaching perspective all this time, and it's based on the holistic/integral orientation that brings such powerful healing." I sought coach-specific training. I had a name for my approach. I found myself again pioneering a new role in nursing. I thought that Cherry Ames and I could write a new book: *Cherry Ames, Health Coach*. Yet at the same time, when I was starting up healing centers, I couldn't find health professionals trained in a holistic and integral model, let alone in coaching. Feeling that this orientation was absolutely essential in healing centers, I decided to train others in my holistic and integral coaching model.

Besides training the health coaches, I also worked on areas such as business plans, healing environments, programming, and staffing. At that time people thought there was a recipe for centers and would ask me questions such as, "How many massage therapists, or chiropractors or naturopaths or coaches or nurses or doctors should we have?" and "Which programs should be developed?" They expected some kind of cookie-cutter process, just as we sometimes expect a clear-cut one-size-fits-all approach when we address health challenges. However, I knew that successful centers are not developed from a standard recipe. Each one needs to grow organically from its context, from the local proponents of a holistic approach, and from the needs of the community. A healing center in California would have different programs and staff than one in the Midwest.

I also knew that the organization's culture is key to the ultimate success of the center. Another level of "healing center" had surfaced for me—that of the internal culture. How did the practitioners work with each other? Was it more than a hallway filled with specialists? Did they know, trust, and experience one another's work? Did they engage in client conferences to learn together how to view the whole picture while respecting each unique perspective? How did practitioners and administrative staff treat each other and handle issues like emotion, power, and inclusion? Was blaming encouraged, or were wrong turns dealt with as creative learning opportunities? How were salary scales decided? What were the explicit and implicit values—and did the mission statement jive with what was happening on a day-to-day basis? And perhaps most importantly, did the healing culture empower staff, practitioners, *and* clients?

The physical structure and culture of a healing center need to reflect its underlying approach to health and healing, but I also knew that just as important is how each individual staff member or practitioner demonstrates it in how they practice, including how they take care of themselves. You could say that each person is a center for healing—each is at the center of healing—and how self-healing for the staff happens or doesn't happen is an essential part of the success of a center. "Physician heal thyself," the proverb says. Empowering clients must become a natural extension of how those offering healing empower themselves.

Partnership is at the heart of each aspect of successful healing centers, and a coaching approach enacts this very well. Centers I helped develop needed coaches/guides/navigators to help clients get in the door—for instance, explaining "What is this holistic approach about anyway?"—and they needed coaches to assist clients on their healing journey as they explored the new avenues day to day. I found that the coaching focus on partnership, learning, maps for change, active listening, powerful questions, direct communication, managing progress, and accountability were extremely effective in developing healthy cultures in the centers. Coaching also helped staff and practitioners with their own growth and healing. My path at the turn of the century focused on coaching—both developing my own coaching practice and teaching others my coaching model.

Three aspects of a center promote healing and growth:
the physical structure, the group culture, and staff self-care.

By now, of course, I knew that seeing the whole picture worked. However, in the process of fine-tuning my trainings, I realized I needed a conceptual framework to house these various methods—something like a file cabinet with different drawers to help people classify all the different approaches to healing. It was too confusing and overwhelming to aim to "do it all." So in 2002, I asked a very close friend and colleague, Dea Daniels, to team up with me to develop a healing matrix. We'd taken a class from Rudy Ballentine and Lorie Dechar, entitled "The Alchemy of Healing." Here we were introduced to Jean Gebser's book, *The Ever-Present Origin*, in which he described five structures of consciousness or ways of perceiving that stretched from the beginning of human existence on into the future.[2] Dea and I applied this framework to create our conceptual file cabinet—and classified and organized different methods for healing. As I continued to work with this unfolding system, I also began to use it to categorize coaching tools. Eventually, this structure became the organizing framework for the BCI Model, and the foundation for this book.

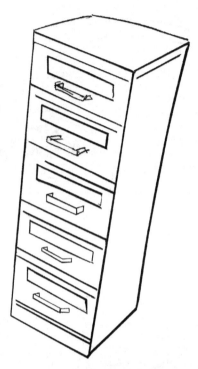

I needed a conceptual framework to house all the various methods—something like a file cabinet with different drawers to help people classify all the different coaching tools.

Are You Ready to Change Your Life?

As much as I could I've modeled this book after what happens in my coaching trainings. It's divided into two parts—a structure that moves from overview to details and applications. In Part One you'll get a sense of what coaching is and how it developed, as well as the general contours of the Bark Coaching Institute Model. I'll talk about some current issues in the field. Part Two introduces you to the BCI Approach in more detail, with chapters 5 through 9 detailing techniques that apply the conceptual framework. More particularly, each chapter articulates how various structures of consciousness (described later) apply to coaching. In each chapter, you'll have a chance to consider applicable tools and *powerful questions* that arise out of a particular structure of consciousness.

So that you can see how coaching works in practice, I've included examples of coaching sessions crafted from my coaching experience. Two are in Part One, and others open the chapters in Part Two. Just as you might experience in class, you'll find me repeating important points from time to time, occasionally in chapter summaries. Also, throughout the book, graduates of my coaching courses share their stories of how they use the model both personally and professionally. I have moved the footnotes to the end of the chapter for easy reference.

You might feel inclined to begin with the first chapter to learn about coaching in general and this new model in particular, and then continue sequentially through the text for a more detailed account. Alternatively, you might find it fun to go through and read sample coaching sessions and the stories from graduate coaches to see the BCI Model in action before digging into the "nuts and bolts" of why and how to do it. Please find the way that works best for you.

The illustrations in the book are often generic so they can refer to a man or a woman, which will allow you to picture yourself on the page. You can use them to imagine yourself as the coach or the client. Enjoy jumping into the pages to enrich your experience.

---

[1] Rudolph Ballentine, *Radical Healing: Integrating the World's Great Therapeutic Traditions to Create a New Transformative Medicine* (Honesdale, PA, Himalayan Institute, 2011), 341-346.

[2] Jean Gebser, *The Ever-Present Origin.* Translated by Noel Barstad (Athens, Ohio: Ohio University Press, 1985).

Part One

We're all aware that we have access to a lot of information that used to be known only to professionals, including material on how to direct and manage our lives. We can easily find out about many approaches and techniques. Have you ever wished you had a partner to help you sort through the quagmire of methods that might be useful for you in your own life and professional practice? The depth and breadth of my education and training has allowed me to integrate many different coaching approaches and frameworks. Some address the "being" of coaching, or the philosophy and foundation of coaching, and some speak to the "doing" of coaching, or the actual tools and approaches. This multidimensional approach makes the BCI Model unique and offers several advantages.

First, different approaches build upon one another and reinforce accurate perception and learning. If the same information comes from more than one place, it tends to be more truthful and more believable. For instance, if I'm exploring my sense of purpose, and feedback from my body, my heart, and my mind all points to the same goal, I'm more confident that I've discovered a correct path. Similarly, when I travel and am trying to find my way to a destination, if one person gives me directions, I might follow them with some trepidation, and might or might not arrive. However, if each person I ask says something similar, and each adds some details that I find even more helpful, I can proceed with confidence.

Second, different approaches potentiate each other. The total effect is more than the sum of the parts. Not only do different approaches offer a variety of windows through which to view a goal and the steps to reach it, integrating them often brings a shift or "ah ha"—a whole new picture develops as a result. This adds ease and speed to the process of change.

As you'll read about in chapter 1, since coaching is a partnership, when the coach and client use a variety of perspectives, the partnership can become deeper—the third benefit of this integrative method. Think of when you meet someone and find out that s/he grew up the same place you did. Suddenly you feel like you know that person. You might discuss potential common friends and experiences. When I coach from a body, mind, and spirit perspective, my client and I can connect in many ways. For instance, we might go beyond the mental viewpoint and include a heart-centered exploration, since this opportunity is included in the method. Perhaps I might be picking up body sensations as we talk, and if my client is interested, I can share the feelings with my client. This somatic resonance is another way for us to deepen our relationship.

When I'm using my whole person and my client is using as much of their whole person as they're aware of or comfortable using, we have more territory to explore than when the coaching is focused on one or two approaches. Coming from a wide perspective, clients learn about and listen to their inner voices. They have more receivers listening to more parts of themselves. This facilitates faster, easier, authentic and aligned change. It may eliminate false starts or directions, saving time, money, and energy.

Coaching evolved in part as a response to a need to draw more of our psychological awareness into our behavioral repertoire, as we discuss in chapter 2. In the 1960s, radical cultural and social changes created a fertile ground for the growth of coaching that transcended the expert model and created more of a collaborative and partnership approach, with potential for self-growth and development. Coaching was shaped by cutting-edge psychology of that period and continues to have an interactive relationship with it. Coaches see their clients as capable and having great interior resources of knowledge. This creates a respect that promotes empowerment and success. Humanistic psychology views people as good and able to draw on inner wisdom.

Coaching also stands on the shoulders of many other disciplines, such as business, sports, and nursing. Working collaboratively and addressing one's critical voice are elements from these fields. Philosophy and the social sciences have informed coaching as well.

Although coaching is beginning to look like a profession, with numerous schools, publications, and professional organizations, it's still in its infancy. What remains to be defined includes an agreed upon definition of coaching, a body of knowledge that can be called coaching, and research to identify evidence-based practices. Certification and licensing are coming to the forefront of the industry and will help solidify this evolving field of service.

Core competencies are being developed for the field, and you'll find out about those in chapter 3. These are based on grounded theory, evidence-based practice, and critical thinking. In chapter 4 some of the theory behind coaching is presented, including Prochaska's stages of change, Bridges' maps for change, and my own version for voluntary change. The BCI Approach also draws upon the conceptual framework of Jean Gebser, who looked at structures of consciousness over time and identified five major mutations: the Archaic, the Intuitive, the Mythical, the Mental, and the Integral. I've introduced these structures of consciousness, or ways of thinking and being, as a method of organizing the many ideas and techniques I introduce. In Part Two you'll find specific coaching tools that arise from these structures and approaches—ones I've found extremely valuable in my twenty years of coaching practice.

Before beginning chapter 1, take a look at this sample coaching session that will be referred to throughout Part One. As you do, you might like to jot down any questions and observations.

Sample Session 1A—Should I Change Jobs?

"I feel like I don't know where I'm going, and that bothers me! I need to change jobs, but I don't know what kind of job to move into. I'm usually very good at getting myself where I want to go, but right now I have no idea where that is. I'm not sleeping, and I just feel so much pressure! I'm now at my wits end," says Sandra.

"I hear the angst in your voice and the stressful situation you're experiencing," I say to her. "It feels like a thoroughbred racehorse at the starting gate, nostrils flared, right front hoof pawing the ground, ready to go but not able to move forward. The horse really wants to run, but the gate hasn't opened yet, and the horse can't even see the finish line. Is that what it feels like?"

"Yes, that's it!" Sandra exclaims, adding, "I feel like I should be making a big change in my career but I don't know where to go. It's even more confusing because one part of me says that

I shouldn't change a thing, that I really do have a good job. It pays well, is close to my home, and I have seven years of seniority. But I just feel bored all the time! I'm doing a good enough job, but I know I'm not doing what I could do if I were really interested in the work. I keep telling myself that I should be happy and content with this job, especially with the economy being so wobbly. Half my friends think I should stay, and half think I should leave. My husband—we've been married for twenty-five years—supports any change I want to make because he sees how I'm struggling with this issue. My kids are grown and doing their own thing and they're behind me as well. I'm very lucky to have that kind of understanding."

I say, "You do have wonderful support, and I understand how confusing this is for you. What is the most important place you want to get to today by the end of our session?

"I want to understand these different parts of me and why I can't move forward like I usually do," she says.

"And how would you know that you accomplished that understanding?" I inquire.

"That's easy. I wouldn't feel so stressed. I could take a deep breath." she says.

"What would be the best way to learn about these different parts?" I ask.

"I don't know. I've tried to reason this out for months now, and I'm driving myself, my family, and my friends crazy and getting nowhere, so I guess I'll try something new—in fact, that's why I called you for a session. Do you have an idea of how to get clearer about this?" Sandra asks.

I say, "Well, I do have a tool that I sometimes offer to clients that might be useful, would you be open to experiment a little bit? The process is somewhat directive at times but I will be sure to keep you in charge of the call as much as possible."

Sandra states, "Yes! I am so ready to move. Where do I go?"

"Okay. So, first travel to another place in the room, and since we're having this phone conversation, I'll also stand and move to a new place in my office as a way of partnering with you and discovering these places with you. Remember, this is just an exploration. Tell me when you're at the new location," I request.

"Okay, I'm standing on a small area rug," she relays.

"Perfect," I say. "Now in this place, could you imagine that you're the part of yourself that you described earlier—the part that is logical, feels your current job is just fine, realizes that you earn a good salary, enjoys the close proximity of your job to your home, and finds your job a stable port in changing economic times?"

"Yes, this exercise seems a bit strange, but I can do it, and quite honestly, this place does feel very familiar. I like logic, and it's worked well in my life. It's predictable."
I further inquire, "What kind of body sensations can you feel as you stand on the area rug and explore this part of yourself?

"I don't feel anything except in my head." Sandra relays.

"Okay, great. What do you notice in your head?" I inquire.

"Well," she says tentatively as if she is straining, "it's busy. . .very busy. . .gears grinding. . .in a good way. . .things fitting together, and one thing moving the next. I see the gears working smoothly, and it's pleasurable but pretty busy. Lots going on. I realize that I ignore other parts of my life, like exercise and eating right, but I don't want to look at that now.

I ask, "Okay, so if you don't want to look at that, then what do you want to look at?"

"Hum," she says after a minute, "As strange as this seems, I want to go back to my head. I feel like my head is glowing! I don't know what that means." She pauses and begins to laugh, "Maybe I'm radioactive! I understand the 'active' part of radioactive. That describes me to a tee," she emphatically says quickly, and then in a softer, slower voice, she adds, "I don't know about the 'radio' part."

I find her words intriguing but wait in silence to see where her thoughts take her. I am fascinated by her image.

Slowly she speaks, "I guess the radio part is about me broadcasting my thinking to the world. I'm known for my good ideas and especially my follow-through: this seems like the place they're generated from—my head. I think I see this as a gift I can share with people. Hum. . .maybe I'm making this up, but now I feel my heart area warm up. The word that comes to me is 'meaningful'. These things seem less clear than what I know about my mind which is very full and busy. She starts to laugh again. I hope that there's enough oil so those gears keep working. . . .I'd better keep taking my fish oil. I hear that's food for the brain, and now I understand it—oiling the gears." She laughs again.

I laugh with her and ask, "Meaningful is a powerful word. Do you want to explore that more, move to another part of the room or explore in a different manner?"

She takes a minute before she speaks. "I certainly feel like I know my head more than any other part of me, and it's a good part. I really value it. I guess I got a glimpse into my heart and the word 'meaningful' but I am ready to leave this place. Where do we go next?" she inquires. "How about moving to another location in the room that represents the part of you that thinks you should change jobs?" I ask.

"Oh, I don't know. I don't like that part. I wish it would go away!" she says emphatically.

"You're in charge of our session. Do you want to go to some other location, do you feel finished moving around the room, or is there something else you want to talk about?" I question.

"Well, if I stop now, I don't think I'll learn about this other part, and it's so insistent, it doesn't let me rest, so if I don't do it now with your help, I don't think I'll be able to sleep again tonight. And I'm really getting tired of this—quite literally," Sandra says.

"Fine," I say. "Go to another place in the room, and let's investigate that second part of you." Sandra comments, "All right, I'll move over here by the window."

"Okay, I'll move by my window as well. So to reiterate what you stated earlier, this is the part of you that's very loud and wants to be heard, that keeps you awake at night and that feels you need to change your job. Now that you're there, what does this feel like?" I inquire.

I feel like I'm that racehorse and think that I have to get someplace. I feel boxed in. I'm very powerful but don't have a mouth. I can't talk. I don't know why I can't speak," she says with a louder, more pressured tone.

I say, "Intriguing. What else can you report?"

"All I can say is that I feel big. I feel powerful. I feel like I'm held in place. I feel a bit frantic. This does not feel good," she says forcefully.

"What do you want to do about that feeling?" I ask.

After a minute of silence, she says that she wants to imagine pushing down the sides that are holding her. I encourage her to do that.

"Whew," she exclaims, "that feels better. I don't know how this worked, but now I have a voice.

"What would you like to do now?" I ask.

"I want to talk!" she states excitedly, "I have a lot to say. I have places to go and things to see. This is what will keep me young and purposeful. I feel like I can finally breathe, and that's a big relief. I still feel very big and powerful. I especially want to say that there's no way to get rid of me. I'm here to stay. I can be roped off, but I won't give up. I have the tenacity of a bulldog and the power of a horse!" She begins to laugh. "That's a really strange looking animal—a bull dog horse! But that's how I feel in this spot in the room."

"What else would you like to feel or say?" I inquire.

"I really feel my legs. They feel strong, very strong, and my jaw feels tight. I'm clenching it, and what immediately comes to mind is a recent problem. I went to my dentist because I thought that I had some cavities, since my teeth were hurting. After a through exam, she said the cause of the problem was that I was beginning to grind my teeth, and that was the reason for my pain. She said if it continued, I could have a night guard for my mouth so I couldn't grind my teeth. I don't want this to continue. It hurts, and I certainly don't want to wear that contraption in my mouth."

I say, "Okay. You're very clear about that. Now is there anything else that you want to examine from this place in the room?"

"No," she says quietly," but what's the good of this? It seems like I have two very good parts of me. Both seem clearer from my visit to them, but what do I do now? They seem like an apple and an orange. I don't know how they could get along."

"Those are great observations and questions. Where do you want to go from here?" I query.
"I do want to see how they could cooperate with each other. After all, they're both parts of me and now I see that they've been at war, and neither of them will give up. They're equals, and I don't want my teeth worn down to nubs as they battle on. I finally get the picture. This is a big relief. My shoulders actually relaxed. Now I know what's been going on, but the question remains, how to stop the conflict?" she says soberly.

"Well, would you like to keep moving to other places or do you have a different idea of how to proceed from here? It seems like your question is 'how can these two get along'? Is that accurate?" I ask.

Sandra says, "I don't know the answer or even how to find out how they could get along, but what I do know is that I want to sit down because I can think well when I do. I want to go to my favorite chair," she states.

We each move to a chair and I inquire, "Sitting in this new place what comes to you?"

"Well, I think the two parts of me should sit on the opposite sides of a table, like in mediation, and we should help them talk to each other," she responds.
"Okay, what happens next," I ask.

"At first they have problems sitting down, but as the minutes go by and we continue to invite them to come together and talk, they finally sit down. We tell them that they're each strong and experts in their own right. They really like hearing that! They seem to relax a bit as they find out that neither of them is in trouble. I ask the question—'How could they get along?' They just sit and stare daggers at each other, and neither says anything. You and I decide to go into a huddle to figure out what to do. So now we're in the huddle. What should we do?" she asks.

I say, "Would it be helpful take a deep breath and see what ideas arise?"

She agrees that is a good idea and we each take a long breath. I ask, "Now what comes up for you?"

She says slowly, "I wonder if I have the right question: how they can talk to each other. Yes, yes, that goal is the problem. They've just met, and already I'm asking them to get along. Maybe they need to get to know each other better. How could we do that?"

"Good question," I respond, "What idea do you have?"

"Hum," she says. "Maybe they could introduce themselves to each other, you know, the way people get to know each other. Where they are from and what they do. Something like that."

"Great idea. Tell me how it goes," I reply.

"Okay, I ask them to do that, and it works pretty well. They're very cautious with each other, but they do at least begin to talk. I think that's as far as they can go today. It's a beginning, and that's a lot better than being at war. I feel more relaxed about this situation. I think my teeth will be happier too!"

"Alright, you've increased the understanding and you're relieved...so what's going to take this from understanding to being something real and practical for you? It could also be fun," I say.

"Well, something does come to me, and it might seem rather foolish, but this was my thought. I could just revisit the scene where they're talking and eavesdrop. I think I'd feel some relief to still see them at the table and continuing to talk," she says with delight and some shyness.
"That sounds great," I say. "Let me explain a little bit more about coaching homework. If you

do your homework, that's wonderful, and if you don't, that's wonderful too because then we explore why you didn't do it—from a learning perspective—not from blame. Results are about feedback, not failure. If you don't complete your homework or fieldwork, we might have several questions to explore: was it the right homework, is this the right direction, or what interfered with you completing the fieldwork? Does that make sense?" I ask.

"I never thought about homework as feedback. When I hear 'homework', I feel like I'm in school, but this doesn't feel like school. You don't act like my teacher because you're not teaching me what to do or telling me what I should do. I think you're helping me explore my beliefs and ideas. 'Fieldwork' sounds better to me. I could more easily think about it being feedback," she explains.

"Great," I say, "and I'm glad that you have a sense of my partnership with you to help you get where you want to go. I completely understand that you don't know where that is at this point, but I want to be next to you, figuratively speaking, as you discover your direction. I think you made a good step today, finding out more about different parts of yourself. I really look forward to talking with you next week. A fieldwork plan is usually detailed, observable, and measurable. Is there some time in your schedule that your eavesdropping would fit in, or do you want to do it spontaneously during the week, or is there some other way you want to add this to your week?"

"I could do it in bed before I fall asleep each night. I'm usually pretty tired, and I don't know how much time I could dedicate to it, but I could try," she states.

I say, "Often I encourage clients to underpromise when selecting fieldwork. Small steady steps usually promote lasting change. It is the steady, forward-moving turtle that wins the race, not the rabbit that makes inconsistent, variable progress. I also sense a strain in your response. What seems to work the best is something that feels fun and easy and very reasonable. Something that energizes you. Something that you could even look forward to doing."

"I just don't know if this will really help me, but I'll give it a go and maybe just say that I'll do it twice. As I think about it again, I guess I should do it in the morning with my first cup of coffee. I usually take a little time for myself at that point. Yes, that feels better," she admits.
"Wonderful," I say. "I look forward to your report on your fieldwork experience. Now that we've come to the end of our forty-five-minute session, was it what you expected?"

"Not really. I thought you'd help me think things through more and I'd come up with an answer, but I suppose this has been going on for almost three months. . . .Well, really, I guess it's actually been longer than that. It was almost a year ago at my birthday that I began to feel uneasy about my job. So I don't really think something like this could be changed in forty-five minutes. In fact, if it had, quite honestly, I don't know if I'd trust it. The whole part about picking something small and the imaging experiment are very different for me, and I don't know if it will help, but actually I do feel more relieved, even now, so something did happen, even if I can't understand it. I think I can sleep tonight, and for that I'm very grateful."

"I'm delighted that you might be able to rest, and I really appreciate your courage in trying new approaches. I look forward to talking to you next week, no matter what results you have with your eavesdropping fieldwork," I say and we both laugh. We make our arrangements for our next conversation and then hang up.

In her second, follow-up session the next week, I found that her teeth grinding had almost completely stopped, she was sleeping night after night, and she saw these changes as significant progress arising from our one session together. She was beginning to tune into new parts of herself in ways that she never had before, and although this was novel and at times awkward, she found it very useful. After months of feeling stuck, she found she was making fast progress. For these reasons, she signed up to become my client. Tune into a later coaching session with Sandra, presented at the end of Part One. Find out how some unexpected events moved her along her path toward dealing with her career transition.

Have you ever had a dilemma like Sandra's? What helped you move toward your goal?

Chapter 1
Welcome to Coaching

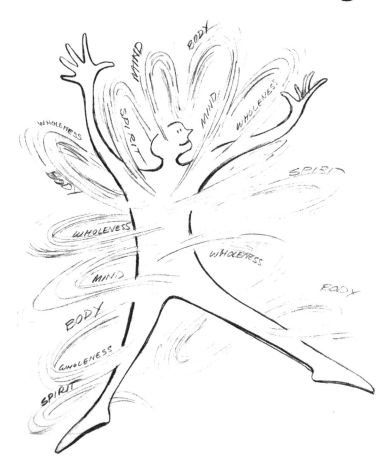

I'm curious if the coaching session with Sandra (Sample Session 1A) held some surprises for you. In how the coach "moved with" the client as she somatically enacted the process of standing for different sides of herself and listening to them, you can see an emphasis on *coaching as partnership*. You can notice how the coach didn't provide answers but a skillful series of questions and techniques for tapping into what the client feels and knows. This in turn is based on an assumption that no generic "right answer" exists, but that *coaching is a learning process*, for all involved. Through it *clients are encouraged to find their own inner voice* that tells them what's best for them, which often requires *exploring the unknown*. Let's look at each of these in turn, before going on to the next chapter, which outlines some structural phases of coaching sessions.

CHAPTER 1: Welcome to Coaching

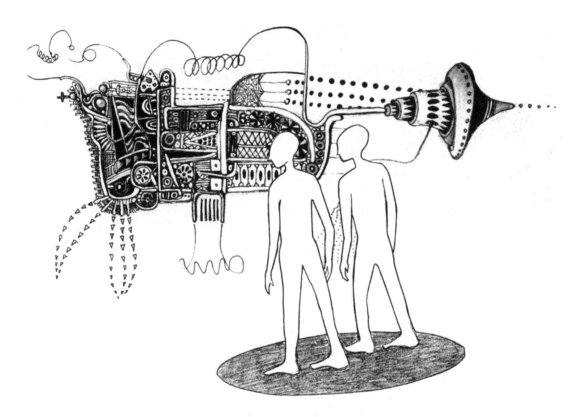

Coaching As Partnership

This illustration represents the relationship between the coach and the client. Notice that the coach and the client are next to each other, in partnership looking at a particular situation—this one is very complex. They are side by side, but if you observe closely, the coach is next to and slightly behind the client. This mirrors the principle that the client is in charge—directing the session. The coach is following the client's lead and going in the direction the client wants to pursue. The coach doesn't interact as an expert knowing all the answers but instead is skilled in supporting movement without leading. This figurative position, with the coach *next to and slightly behind*, allows the client to move at a self-determined pace and in a self-determined direction. In this partnership relationship, the coach is actively using many skills, such as deep listening, powerful questioning, co-creating plans, and supporting accountability. The client is listening to self for what resonates as "right," becoming aware, making decisions, creating steps toward goals, taking actions, evaluating progress, and celebrating success. You could see this process with the coaching example of Sandra (Sample Session 1A). I followed her lead, whether it was exploring her warring parts or learning to listen to her body and inner voice. I was not the expert who knew what she should do.

Most helpers are much more familiar and comfortable with the expert role in which the helper leads the client. That was true of me in the beginning, but then I learned that the coaching role supports very powerful results. Like most professionals, I was educated to be in the expert role, paid to do so, and valued for this skill. Learning to work in partnership usually requires additional training, as shifting to a role in which we are not leading is harder than it may sound. But like me, you'll come to find it natural and productive if you practice.

A Deeper Partnership in the BCI Model

We usually think of partnership as two people acting in concert. However, the BCI Approach expands the scope of the coaching partnership to include body, mind, and spirit, and many different types of perspectives. I'm helping my clients identify and integrate (partner with) more parts of themselves, to see more options, and to consider new possibilities. That healing partnership restores a sense of wholeness from which whatever issues they bring can be addressed. I'm able to help my clients come to wholeness because I've brought that sense of respectful partnership to all aspects of myself—I'm using more parts of myself to work with more parts of them.

I'm listening and acting from that expanded and deeper sense of wholeness. As I become very present and focused on my clients, I may notice that my throat becomes tight or I start to have the same kind of pain in my head that they're experiencing. I'm listening with my body and picking up signals that they may or may not notice. Sometimes I feel that my throat is becoming ticklish or tight and ask if that is the case with my client. I may lose energy or experience the nervousness that my client is describing. My spirit may feel deflated. I may feel lost and confused. I have skills to become aware of these feelings, experiences, and sensations, to observe or witness them, then to integrate them in how I give feedback or ask powerful questions, and then release them. Often my awareness leads to my clients understanding something from a fresh perspective and facilitates a helpful step toward their goals.

This deep partnership relates to the "being" part of coaching rather than the "doing" part of coaching. Again, I'm not for one and against the other: both are important. The "doing" part of coaching is vital and refers to using tools, asking questions, setting agreements—the active, observable part of coaching. The BCI Model for coaching is loaded with different tools and approaches. The "being" part of coaching is more subtle and more difficult to describe. It refers to the way I am when I'm coaching, the philosophy that informs my practice: the respect and admiration I feel for my clients; the sense of honor I feel as they deeply and sincerely share their vulnerability, progress, and struggles; the pure excitement and happiness I feel when they're delighted with a new accomplishment; the unconditional love I feel toward them as another person on the planet wanting to do good things with their lives. I took a graduate course on Chinese philosophy from Dr Yi Wu, an esteemed and extraordinarily wise teacher, who said that how we translate the old proverb of "a journey begins with the first step" isn't really accurate. He explained that a more correct translation is "a journey begins from where you are standing." I'll never forget his comment; for me, the "being" of coaching is formed by the place I'm standing—my philosophy of coaching.

I'm not saying that other coaches don't act from this place as well, but my method of coaching includes body, mind, spirit, and more, so it promotes this deeper connection, encourages open discussion of it, and facilitates growth in all of these areas. More of me connects with more of my client, which allows for deeper connections through more points of contact. This deep partnership facilitates learning.

A Learning and Growth Approach Is Key in Coaching

Curiosity is the hat the coach wears. Because coaching is based on a learning and growth model, whatever comes up becomes input for looking systematically at what works and what needs to be changed. Coaches are curious about what they hear, feel, see, sense, and notice. Curiosity also helps the coach stay out of judgment and blame, which hinder the change process. Coaching is about learning and always being curious to see how things are connected and how they affect each other. For example, how could a client become clearer on the reality of a situation? What steps lead to which goals? What rewards a new way of acting? Can the sequence of the steps be changed? Can a new reward be introduced? An approach based on curiosity and learning can make coaching effective and fun. This learning approach feels lighter and helps the client stay more empowered. This may seem like a simple factor, but it's part of what makes coaching different from consulting, where the helper is the expert.

As Sandra said, at first this learning approach felt strange to her, but as we worked together over time, she really came to appreciate it and to discover how these skills could be used in other areas of her life. A learning approach is user friendly for both coach and client, as what they are doing together comes to transcend failure, leading to the places where they find the real source of their happiness.

Learning and Growth Areas Are Expanded in the BCI Model

When my clients and I explore more aspects of their being and surroundings from numerous perspectives, we find much more to be curious about, much more to learn, and much more to enjoy. The map is expanded—becoming not just about one person, but maybe the whole town, ancestors, the country, the world, or the universe.

Curiousity is the hat the coach wears.

Imagine looking through different windows to assess a situation, put together a plan, or evaluate progress. Some windows look out on actual scenes, and others on created ones. I love offering my clients an opportunity to wave an imaginary magic wand and see new options in a situation. I delight in seeing how they could physically portray a situation, tell a story, draw a picture, dance a new idea, sing a feeling, create dialog around a theme, assess the impact of their sense of purpose on a situation, ask for help, collaborate with others, talk to the place something lives in their body, reach into their deepest knowing, come from an energetic perspective about it, and/or meditate on a situation. From this expanded model, creativity and curiosity can flow freely for me as the coach and for the client. Expanding learning areas helps expand my client's awareness and growth.

As you saw with Sandra, not everyone feels comfortable working in all these ways, although usually when they experience the benefit of looking at change from a broader picture, they like it because it works. When Sandra stopped grinding her teeth, she could see the value of dealing with parts of herself that were fighting under the surface. I always invite the use of a tool and never insist that it should be applied. My clients are the bosses. They decide how the session goes. I can make requests but they're always in charge. My clients feel completely free to say no—completely in charge of deciding to agree with the request. This means that they're not agreeing from a sense of duty, obligation or a need to please me, their coach.

This learning approach can be used at any age. Read here about the teacher who shows kids how to be coaches.

Ginny Katz, MS, MSS
Coaching in Kindergarten

I'm a kindergarten teacher and spend my days with five- and six-year-olds. When they're in an argument, and really in all aspects of their lives, they're used to having adults intervene, and to counter this I spend part of my year allowing them to ask powerful questions to learn how to arbitrate their own disagreements.

One way I help them build the coaching skill of asking powerful questions is by having a rotating role that is called "The Coach." They take this role *very* seriously and, like other jobs, they practice being the coach for one week when it's their turn. This means that they all have this responsibility several times during the year. Here's how it works.

Someone yells, "I need The Coach," and the coach has permission to stop whatever s/he is doing and go to the kindergartener who calls for the coach. The first thing the coach does is ask, "What happened?" and then listens to each person involved. Often a child will want to interrupt another during the telling of the quarrel, but the coach is very good at learning to say, "No interrupting, I'll listen to you next."

For example, let's say that two children are in the block corner, and Jack knocks Stephanie's tower down. After they each tell their version of what happened, the coach asks, "What would make this better?" The children talk it over and might decide to start all over and build something brand new together. Before the coach leaves, the coach often says, "Do you want to shake hands?" and they usually do. The coach also looks directly at each kindergartner and says, "Are you all right?" and listens to the answer. If there is still a problem, they call me, but ninety-five percent of the time, they solve it themselves.

I model and teach the coaches how to ask the other kindergartners what will solve the disagreement rather than have the coach decide the answer because that just repeats the expert role rather than teaching them a coaching role. This can take much of the year, and sometimes a couple of children don't learn this partnership role. They continue to tell the children how to solve the conflict. The good news is that most can demonstrate the coaching role by the end of the school year in June.

Other coaching tools I use several times a day are silence and taking a breath. Sometimes a kindergartner will ask to do them or want the whole class to relax using those approaches. We do little mini-meditations that help the kindergartners ground and center. I take those breaths with the students, and they help me, and my staff members, too!

Coaching Encourages Clients to Find Their Inner Voice of Wisdom

A coach can help uncover the client's inner voice of wisdom by asking powerful questions: "What would cause you to feel more congruent with your deepest truth?" "When you tune into your inner knowing, what becomes clearer?" These are just two of the questions that can come up on a journey of change that facilitates profound awareness. Once the client's inner voice of wisdom is found, it can become a compass for showing how to move forward in ways that are authentic for the client. A number of things may prevent us from hearing our inner voice:
- relying on others as experts more than we really need to;
- relying only on our mental awareness;
- relying on the "shoulds" or conditioning of our past or parents;
- paying too much attention to pragmatism (for example, expected results);
- being too outer directed and trying to please others;
- having too little confidence in our own inner wisdom;
- not having a clear way to ascertain the validity of our intuition;
- not being able to access our intuition or inner knowledge.

Clients Can Find Their Inner Voice More Easily with the BCI Approach

I've found that because the BCI Approach is multidimensional, we can almost always find a channel for tuning into clients' voices. Clients can use all types of verbal and even non-verbal methods to discover and clarify that inner expression, which builds confidence and familiarity with each level of inner knowing that they can access. Being able to access that inner voice of wisdom also helps people to embrace multiple facets of themselves that seem to be in conflict. They can integrate aspects of themselves and find a broader path that honors multiple needs simultaneously. Sandra (Sample Session 1A) was able to learn how her teeth grinding reflected the inner conflict between her logical voice and her sense of purpose by using a dialog tool. And multiple tools often magnify each other such that answers come more easily and quickly and feel more authentic and satisfying.

Coaching Is about Exploring the Unknown

Coaching Grid

It may seem paradoxical to emphasize both finding the inner voice of wisdom and exploring the unknown, but the process of exploration is the path to finding that wisdom, and even then, clients find that what they know is always evolving. So what exactly do we mean by "the unknown"? What happens when we think of it almost as a location?

One way to understand the coaching arena is to look at an illustration of two squares resting on top of another two squares. The left top square (1) represents what the client knows but the coach doesn't. The right top square (2) depicts what they both don't know. The bottom left (3) stands for what they both know, and the bottom right (4) corresponds to what the coach knows but the client doesn't know. Inspiring, significant, and substantial change happens in a session when the coach and the client are exploring in the space of Square 2: where neither of them knows. It makes coaching interesting, exciting, and always a new adventure. The vitality lives here. They are walking together into unknown territory and seeing what new idea, perspective, awareness, and action can arise from powerful questions, deep listening, and direct communication.

Square 1 What the client knows but the coach doesn't know.	**Square 2** What neither the coach nor the client knows.
Square 3 What the coach knows and what the client knows.	**Square 4** What the coach knows but the client doesn't know.

If the coach goes to Square 4, s/he has turned into a consultant: the expert, the information giver. Does this ever happen when I work with my clients? Yes, it does. Sometimes my client will ask me a question about a resource; other times, a way forward or an idea comes to my mind that seems "perfect." I need to be very careful about my "great ideas." If I tell them to my clients, they may lose the opportunity to discover their own "great idea," which really empowers them to feel successful. And quite honestly, my "great idea" is usually great for me but not always so great for my clients. They come up with things I never think of, and *how* they express their ideas, their assessment about something, or their right next step is most powerful for them.

My goal is to spend as little time as possible in Square 4 because it doesn't serve my client as well as us spending time in Square 2. If I'm spending more than two percent of my time there during a session, I begin to feel uneasy. My business coaching is the exception to this guideline. Since my private practice started in 1970, I've done significant organizational start-up and development. I'm willing to share what I've learned, and the amount of time I spend in Square 4 as the consultant might be between twenty and sixty percent.

However, in life-coaching staying out of Square 4 is easier said than done. I was trained as an expert, and for many years I was paid based on this role, which felt comfortable. To shift to Square 2 was unsettling. If I wasn't the expert, why would people want to pay me? What value could I provide? Where were we going to end up in that unknown land of Square 2? Yikes! However, I found that Square 2 is where the juice is—where powerful coaching happens. Over time, I was able to trust it more and more. And what I discovered was that it was easier! It's very hard to be an expert for someone—I don't know everything. Changing to the coaching role of asking masterful questions, listening deeply, and using direct communications was a big relief. I've noticed that in coaching trainings, as students really learn to trust the outcome of being with their clients in Square 2, some actually change their physical posture. Several have said that it feels like a big burden has been lifted off their shoulders, and they sit and move differently.

Another advantage of staying out of Square 4, or the expert space, is that giving advice and/or information to a client doesn't always work. Sometimes patients are told to change their eating and lifestyle. At times, they might want more information about how to do this, but usually what's most helpful is a step-by-step coaching approach. It's helpful for them to decide what to change first, and yes, sometimes a bit of information from Square 4 is helpful, in moderation. I recently went to a new health care provider and he gave me about fifteen things to change. Granted all of them were adjustments that would have improved my health, but I left his office feeling disempowered and overwhelmed. Even though I decided to focus on two changes, and did accomplish those two, I didn't feel successful at my next visit. I wished he could take my course and learn coaching! I did ask him to suggest only one thing at a time, and now I'm feeling more successful because I can fully follow through on that one change and make it a lasting transition.

No matter what kind of coaching I'm doing, I want my client to feel empowered. As described in Sample Session 1A, Sandra and I were working in the second square for most of the session. I certainly didn't know how things would work, and she was definitely in new territory. This is what makes coaching alive, fun, and successful and why Sandra wanted to become my client. She was a stranger in a strange land, and being willing to stay with the unknown was producing the results she wanted but hadn't been able to get by herself. She wanted a partner to go with her.

> *How often have you been given advice that either didn't work or didn't feel good? Can you think of times that you've been well meaning but the advice you gave someone else just didn't have the effect you had intended?*

All Squares Become Larger with the BCI Method

Though the coaching area—Square 2—is where we hang out in sessions, the result of focusing on the unknown is expanding the known. Often my clients ignore parts of themselves that have valuable information, or, like Sandra, they stick with one way of assessing a situation. By drawing on different perspectives, new ways of thinking, body wisdom, energetic momentum, or subtle inner direction, and using a wide variety of tools or approaches, what was unknown becomes known and valued.

Marian Boileau, RN, BSN
Trusting the Unknown?

Last week I graduated from the coaching course, and my big takeaway is realizing the magic that happens when I partner with my clients. It's fascinating to participate in a client's journey to change through accessing their own wisdom, especially because I've worked hard to learn to trust the unknown as I face it in myself and in the coach's role. I learned about Square 2 early in my training, but I'd become a little scared when my client and I started into that unknown place. Maybe part of my reluctance was being afraid of crossing a boundary into therapy. I wondered if my client would start feeling angry or sad and what I would do. I've learned that although coaching doesn't limit the focus to feelings as therapy often does, feelings do come up and are helpful indicators of what is working and what needs to change. I've had many experiences of painful feelings transforming when both of us can hold a space for not knowing and trust the process.

Bhaskar Banerji, MA
A Pain in the Neck

Sometimes I have to struggle with my Consultant Gremlin. A man came for some bodywork, as he was experiencing a lot of pain in his shoulders and neck. I suggested that we try some wellness coaching first, and he agreed. We started off with him relating his life struggles. I could tell that he was quite stressed, and so at some point during his meandering monologue I interjected and asked him to rate his stress on a scale of one to ten. He rated it at a seven. My gremlin thought it was closer to a nine, but I kept my mouth shut and decided it was best to go with the client's perceptions and let the client drive the process.

Then I asked him "what could you do to bring it down a notch, say to a six?" He said he would read before going to bed. Once more my gremlin thought "what a useless response." He should be meditating, it screamed. Once again I decided to keep quiet and trust the coaching principle that the client knows the best course of action to take (even if he's not aware of it yet).

Then I asked him how many times a week would he commit to this new activity, and he said that every night he would read before retiring. This I thought was over-committing, and that he would be setting himself up for failure, but my client didn't think so and refused to budge from his ambitious position. I suggested we could go with that for now and if he wanted to change it after a few days, he could give me a call and let me know. Sure enough, he called midweek and asked if we could reset the action goal to three times a week, as he was having a hard time hitting the initial target.

When he came in for the next session, I started by asking him how things were going. He said his neck pain had entirely disappeared! Really? Immediately I was all ears. What happened? He said he had quit his job! At some point during the week he realized that every time his supervisor screamed at him he would tense his neck and shoulders, and that over the years that behavioral response had resulted in the development of chronic pains. No screaming supervisor, no pains—it was as simple as that!

So now that his health problem had been resolved I asked him if he'd like to focus on anything else. He said yes, "I'd like you to teach me how to meditate." I could hardly believe what I was hearing. By trusting the coaching process and keeping my Consultant Gremlin in check, I'd made a space for the client to realize of his own accord that meditation is what he needed if he were to keep his stress levels down in the long run and gain the necessary clarity to move in the direction of wellness. This was a very important lesson for me in trusting the coaching process and an incident I often remind myself of prior to starting a wellness coaching session.

Laura Boone, BS, MBA
Veterinary and Dental Coach

For the past fourteen years I've been working with dental and veterinary teams as a "consultant." After years of wondering why I wasn't seeing long-term results, when I started working with Linda I realized that there's a huge difference between consulting and coaching. Consultants will tell you what to do and then leave. A coach will inspire and ask great questions to help you discover and own your goals so that the forward momentum continues.

After being coached for many years, I gradually began using the techniques and tools that Linda used with me, with my clients. One example is suggesting that they create visualizations of where they are now and where they want to be, asking them what that looks and feels like. I might create a life-like scale of numbers from 1 to 10 on the floor and ask a specific goal-related question for clients to enact by physically standing by that number and also by experimenting with walking slowly towards their goal, thinking about the journey, their feelings, and how it would impact their life if they really met their goals. For future work with them or during another segment of the session, I would create a gap analysis worksheet and realistic checklist of what needs to happen.

I now see how to merge the consulting and the coaching role. The results have been astounding. I've often received trips and rewards for being the most successful coach in my company. My clients have benefited as well, learning that increasing the bottom line of profit only comes from increasing collaboration, teamwork, the development of a healthy culture, values-driven practices, and good communication—all principles of coaching.

---

[1] I first learned about the Johari Window exercise in the 1960s in a nursing psychology class. It was designed to help people with communication and relationships by providing an opportunity for people to explore their blind spots. Then many years later, at a training workshop in Beijing, China in 2007, I heard about using a modified Johari Window concept in coaching. (Eva Wong and Lawrence Leung, *The Power of Ren: China's Coaching Phenomenon*. Singapore: John Wiley & Sons, Asia, 2007). My latest reference for coaching based on the Johari Window framework is an article in *The International Journal of Coaching in Organizations*, Issue 3, 2009, pp. 73-96. It's by William Bergquist. The article effectively explores the second-quadrant referred to in my book as a place ripe for exploration since it influences the dynamics of the other three squares.

Chapter 2
The Development of Coaching

Before I present the many holistic and integral coaching tools in Part Two, I want to provide a context for coaching. Having an idea of the ways that coaching evolved, where it is now, and where it's headed provides a needed foundation to understand the practice, the field, and the upcoming chapters.

Coaching has developed a client-empowered model—clients are seen as capable of being self-aware. That's really different from a more authoritative, dependent-on-the-"expert" paradigm, with clients who don't follow instructions judged as "non-compliant" and/or wrong. Instead of indicting a client who didn't follow through with some agreed upon action step, a coach would take a client-centered perspective: "Does my client understand the action step? Is the idea a good fit with the client's culture or values? From the client's perspective, what would be the right next step? Does the proposed action match the person's current capacity for engagement? And how can I, as a coach, listen even more deeply to discover what's truly going on for my client?" This humanistic approach not only feels good to both clients and coaches but is a reason coaching is rapidly growing as a profession.

Michael Stratford, a coach to Fortune 500 executives, trainer of thousands of coaches worldwide, and renowned author, sums up this perspective when he says that the client is all of these:
- unique and whole,
- intelligent and a problem-solver,
- capable of focus, follow-through, and accomplishment,
- an adult and personally accountable,
- imaginative and creative,
- acting from his/her own sense of order and organizing principles,
- willing to be a learner,
- clear,
- resilient,
- competent in the work,
- able to provide for him/her self,
- strong, talented, and brave,
- able to act from his or her own inner compass and unique vision, dream, or goal.[1]

Imagine how it feels to be partnered by someone operating from this belief system! How did coaching arrive at this point of view?

New Times Generate New Ideas, New Approaches, and New Professions

In the United States, coaching developed in an environment of significant cultural changes. There are eras when the call for change is so great that new ideas must emerge to meet the needs and challenges of the shifting times because the old ways just no longer work to address the problems and issues. Such is the story of coaching, which came into being during and in response to such an evolutionary moment. Marilyn Ferguson, who wrote about the pioneers of that period, stated this.

> A leaderless but powerful network is working to bring about radical change in the United States....In the beginning, certainly, most did not set out to change society. But they found that their lives had become revolutions. Once a personal change began in earnest, they found themselves rethinking everything, examining old assumptions, looking anew at their work and relationships, health, political power, and "experts," goals and values.[2]

In the 1960s the counterculture movement spawned new initiatives and phenomena as varied as sensitivity groups, EST/Landmark, team building, humanistic psychology, Eastern spiritual traditions, open marriages, childcare centers at work, the Haight-Ashbury drug scene, bra burning, and civil rights. These new ideas required not only a new way of being—they also called for a new way of *being together*. Collaboration, partnership, and the notion of shared power began to challenge the reigning authorities, both ideological and actual. You can see how this laid the foundation for the coaching model.

These expanding cultural paradigms, combined with an increasing national prosperity, created environments rich with time, money, and inspiration to invest in personal growth and self-exploration. In the US and the UK—the two countries where coaching initially surfaced—gross national income increased 367 percent and 360 percent respectively, for the twenty-year period from 1975 to 1995.[3]

Along with the socioeconomic changes, versions of coaching sprung up in different places, as you'd expect when change is desperately needed. Two early United States pioneers—Laura Whitworth in California and Thomas Leonard on the East Coast—didn't know about each other, and both thought they had discovered coaching.[4]

Vicki Brock's substantive dissertation, entitled the "Grounded Theory of the Roots and Emergence of Coaching" describes coaching lineages. For her research, Brock used extensive literature resources as well as interviews with 170 prominent individuals in the coaching field. According to Brock:

> A major lineage emerged from the Erhard/Flores large group awareness trainings (LGAT) and psychology. Erhard managed the delivery of the training, and Flores created the content of the movement. A second lineage involved Tim Gallwey and Laura Whitmore. Several of the largest and oldest coach training schools, as well as the several professional organizations came out of these lineages. Coach U, Coachville, and professional organizations of the International Coach Federation (ICF) and the International Association for Coaching (IAC), were created by Thomas Leonard, who was a "descendant" of the Erhard/Flores lineage. Laura Whitmore founded the Coach Training Institute and helped found and lead other professional organizations.[5]

Despite the variations in coaching techniques, shared foundations of this budding new discipline have been identified, as you can discover in chapter 3.

Psychology and Coaching

Humanistic psychology has been a main influence on coaching.[6] Let's look at two psychologists whose theories form the foundation of coaching: Abraham Maslow, who synthesized theories about needs, and Carl Rogers, who presented information about drives, defenses, and a client-centered approach.[7]

In the 50s Abraham Maslow presented his *hierarchy of needs*. He integrated research on motivation and produced a pyramid model that had five levels.

From the bottom up they were listed as 1) physiological needs, such as hunger and thirst; 2) safety; 3) belonging and love; 4) esteem; and 5) self-actualization. He argued that a person needs to satisfy first-level needs before moving to the next level, and on upward.[8] Coaches help clients to identify their needs, and these sequenced stages add clarity to the process. The hierarchy also helps coaches identify who is a coaching client. If a potential client requests coaching but is dealing intensely with the three lower-level needs, s/he might be referred to other professionals, such as social service providers or therapists. At least that's what I was taught. However, one of my former trainees— Grady Nobles—applies the BCI Method in her work with homeless patients in Oakland, California, even though we might presume that her clients are working with very basic needs. In an article written about a course I taught at the Alameda County Medical Center she says this:

> For me, the idea of establishing small goals to work toward a desired behavioral change has been very helpful. I learned to partner with the patient and identify reasons behavioral changes are difficult. Let's say I want the patient to do something like keep his medical appointments. When I think about possible obstacles I imagine remembering when the appointment is and having transportation to get to that appointment. But when I partner with my patients, I hear that they might not have clean clothes to wear or a place to shower.[9]

Remembering the emphasis on setting small steps toward a goal, as well as trusting clients to know what they need, Nobles helped patients deal with problems at the most basic level.

Other pivotal work for the development of coaching was presented in the early 50s by Carl Rogers, a clinical psychologist.[10] He saw people as basically good, with motivation and drive embedded in a life force he called the *actualizing tendency*. He agreed with Maslow that people must first fulfill basic needs and directed his work toward clinical practice, explaining that we have a need for positive regard that doesn't always get met. Our parents may be conditional about giving love: loving us only if we repress anger or if we excel in some arena. As a consequence we might adopt that perspective and only like ourselves if we receive all "A"s in school, for example. He calls this our *idealized self* in comparison to our real self. The more the two are different, the more suffering and anxiety we experience and the greater our tendency to develop defenses to reduce anxiety. We can use denial—for example, a student somehow doesn't find out her or his grades. We might use rationalization—helping us put blame on someone else or to reinterpret the situation, thereby holding onto the ideal self. Our hypothetical student may say that the teacher is not fair or the class was poorly taught.

These dynamics were the basis for Rogers' client-centered clinical approach. Since he believed that people were good and had natural drives to develop and self-actualize, his method was one of support and facilitation. He likened the therapy process to helping someone learn to ride a bike. In the beginning, you might help them balance and move forward, but at some point you have to let go so they can ride. You can't learn to ride a bike for them. Congruency or genuineness, empathy, and respect, were the cornerstones of his advice to student therapists. He felt that the therapeutic relationship based on these qualities would help heal the client no matter what other techniques were used.[11] These are basic tenets of coaching as well.

Additional psychological specialties have been incorporated into coaching practice. Cognitive-behavioral tools can help identify behavior patterns and aid clients in changing their thoughts and actions.[12] For instance, if a client wants to quit smoking, coach and client together can examine the client's behavioral patterns. What are the triggers and rewards for the client's smoking? How might the client generate equally or even more satisfying rewards with different, healthier behaviors? Transpersonal techniques are also brought in, allowing access to a sense of self beyond the individual and adding intentionality to the concepts of coaching.[13] For instance, I often ask clients how their life purpose links to a particular aspiration because when they see a connection, their motivation and commitment to their goal increases. Psychoanalytic psychology contributes an in-depth understanding of human dynamics to coaching.[14] Looking at drives, controls, limiting beliefs, dreams, images, "Freudian slips," and free association or flow of thinking are part of the coaching process.

Coaches who use psychological tools need to untangle them from the pathology model they might be embedded within—a framework for dealing with disease.[15] The shift from defining a client's issue as an opportunity and not as a problem is one example of a positive, proactive stance versus coming from the disease model. Coaching takes a health and growth perspective, and psychological tools need to be employed in a way that speaks to normal development and learning. The "what's right" approach of coaching emphasizes successes past and present as well as effective action in the present to facilitate positive change now and for the future.

A newer specialization—*Positive Psychology*— has been popularized by psychologist Martin E.P. Seligman, and it looks at what makes people happy, their strengths and positive traits, and how they can prevent negative, meaningless lives.[16] Seligman, a former president of the American Psychological Association, suggests that we look at what's right with people and not just at what's wrong with them so that people and communities can thrive. This orientation appeals to coaches, and some are beginning to use this approach along with the accompanying tools from positive psychology.[17]

One last approach to mention is the *Psychology of Coaching*. According to the University of Sydney in Australia, which claims to be the first world-based coaching psychology unit, this new field in psychology "involves the application of the research, theory, and practice of the behavioral science of psychology to the enhancement of life experience, work performance, and personal growth of normal (non-clinical) populations."[18] This program is described as a blend of counseling, clinical, and organizational psychology.

The Impact of Organizational Development and Business on Coaching

The business world has also strongly influenced coaching, especially the areas of organizational development, management, and leadership.[19] One way to trace this impact is to notice the subjects of business publications. Thirteen coaching articles focusing on management and training were published between 1937 and 1960.[20] In 1955, the *Harvard Business Review* was the first professional journal to publish a peer-reviewed paper on coaching.[21] These initial sowings in the corporate setting found fertile ground in the next three decades, and the profession of coaching began taking root. Gradually, organizations modified their operating styles away from bureaucracies that stifled autonomy, creativity, and innovation. They'd been relying on control and predictability but changed to environments that were increasingly humane, socially responsible, and open to new inputs and ideas. Many of the principles used to bring about these changes influenced coaching. For instance, relating management and leadership skills to bottom line outcomes contributed to the planning and accountability orientation of coaching. Two consultants who've worked with re-visioning the business world have also informed the development of coaching. The first is Peter Senge, an innovative organizational consultant and author of *The Fifth Discipline: The Art and Practice of the Learning Organization*.[22] His early publications were on the forefront of holistic and integral thinking in the 1990's, and he continues to challenge organization to play a positive role in global issues such as sustainability.[23]

Senge identified five components of learning organizations. The first is *systems thinking*, which is the ability to look at a situation via the big picture and see all the pieces connected in a dynamic process. When applying this type of thinking, a manager with an underperforming and inefficient employee would question the employee's training and comprehension of the task and look at availability of required resources. In other words, the manager would examine the coordination of the whole task without moving to blame and judgment of individuals. Action would be taken to make changes in that linked structure. Coaching adopted this learning approach to change.

Another element of learning organizations involves *personal mastery*. This refers to the ongoing effort of an employee to work earnestly in the pursuit of personal growth and development. Employees managed with this approach are encouraged to see situations realistically and to create meaningful personal visions. Walking the talk or showing by example is the way this approach has been added to coaching.

Interest in *mental models* is also a feature of learning organizations. These include beliefs, worldviews, and operational dynamics that shape each person. Senge encouraged employees to "turn the mirror inward, learning to unearth our internal pictures of the world, to bring them to the surface and hold them rigorously to scrutiny."[24] This is at the heart of coaching.

Senge felt that building a *shared vision* based on individual inquiry was a vital part of working toward a desired goal. His clients had meetings—not about reading the senior-management-created vision statement to the employees, but rather presenting opportunities for entire companies to co-create a set of goals and values that inspired commitment and alignment.[25] Recognize coaching's emphasis on partnership?

Creating shared vision results in *team learning*, which builds on both mental models and shared vision but then goes a step further. Team learning refers to the practical day-to-day work of a team of people learning to work together in ways that promote a healthy culture and desired goals. It's accomplished by engaging an ongoing dialog centered around two questions: "What is working?" and "What can be changed to work better?"[26] These are powerful questions that can be used in most coaching sessions.

The second influential consultant is Peter Block, a leading organizational consultant working with top companies internationally, and the author of several best-selling consulting books. His best known is *Flawless Consulting,* first published in 1980 and still widely used internationally.[27] This book was described as the most influential book in organizational development over the past forty years.[28]

Block advises consultants to ask themselves if they are being authentic with their clients. His approach has been based on consent and connectedness rather than the patriarchal dynamic of mandate and force.[29] He questions the whole idea of changing people and "getting them" on the same page. His ways are connected to coaching because he models and teaches partnership and collaboration.[30]

Contribution from the Sports Arena

Insight from the sports arena has also been brought into coaching. Tim Gallwey published *The Inner Game of Tennis*[31] in the early 70s, before sports psychology existed or there was much focus on mental preparation for athletic performance. Against predictions that the *Inner Game* would have a small audience, book sales took off; over one million copies sold, and the book was translated into several languages. In 1975, Harry Reasoner filmed a woman in her 50s who'd had no previous tennis-playing experience. After twenty minutes of instruction using "inner game" techniques, the woman could play tennis reasonably well, even though her training had included no technical instruction. This film brought national attention to the "inner game" methods.[32] Readers soon realized that the "inner game" addressed not only how to play tennis but also how to do one's best in any endeavor.[33]

Gallwey says that his approach stems neither from Eastern philosophy nor from a right brain/left brain learning system but truly evolved from his interest and experience in teaching people how to play tennis.[34] Through his teaching encounters he observed that his students had a critical voice, which he named Self 1, and that it strongly affected the progress of learning and success. He called the part of the self that has to hit the ball Self 2. He began to understand that as disapproving self-comments diminish and the trust in potential to do well increases, tennis skill and mastery flourish. He realized that he had the same experience as his students. He said that Self 2 is able to experience a mire of feelings that can be brought up in all facets of life. He said that "Self 2 is like an acorn that, when first discovered, seems quite small yet turns out to have the uncanny ability not only to become a magnificent tree, but, if it has the right conditions, can generate an entire forest."[35]

Coaching and Health Care

Beginning in the spring of 2009, the health care system was pushed to move wellness and health promotion to the forefront—a trend in perfect alignment with coaching. In a long interview by Daniel Redwood with Wayne Jonas in the Spring issue of the *Washington DC Pathways* magazine, Jonas said this:

> The Wellness Initiative for the Nation (WIN) is a groundbreaking set of health policy proposals calling for a paradigm shift in the direction of wellness, prevention, health

promotion and integrative practices. . . .Among WINs key components is the creation of a greatly expanded wellness and prevention infrastructure, *training thousands of full-time community-based "health and wellness coaches"* to work full-time on "chronic disease prevention and health promotion through comprehensive lifestyle and integrated health care approaches with specific demonstrated effectiveness."[36]

Below are comments from two BCI graduates who apply the model in health coaching.

Nicole Florez, MA
Health Coaching

The health coaching profession is gaining greater visibility and has now hit the mainstream. As a health coach for one of the top medical organizations in the nation, I've seen the increasing demand for this service as the benefits are profound and the impacts so powerful. It's a paradigm shift for the health profession to recognize that people are the experts on their own lives and have the ability to use their innate wisdom to identify what's needed to move towards greater health.

The power of coaching to facilitate transformation can be seen on a daily basis at my job. For example, one memorable patient of mine had been grappling with an emotional eating problem that was crippling her ability to enjoy food and eating. Through assessing her current stage of change and using intuition, reflective listening, and open-ended questioning, my patient was able uncover the root of her emotional eating and identify an actionable step to support her goals when she was confronted by her biggest trigger—cookies.

With the support of coaching, she came to identify that pausing, breathing, and visualizing her "best healthy self" before she decided whether or not to grab a cookie could help her move forward and break her old pattern. Furthermore, she discovered that strict deprivation and negative self-talk were not serving to unleash the positive changes she was pursuing. Coaching gave her the space and opportunity to explore, and ultimately, choose the direction that worked best for her and her life. This patient reported that her experience with health coaching transformed the way she experiences food—for the better.

Health coaching works because it's tailor-made for people's unique lives and circumstances. It's good work and important work—and given our collective health care crisis, it's surely not going away!

Mary Elaine Southard, RN, MSN, APHN-BC, Diploma in Clinical Homeopathy, DNP (student)
What Kind of New System Will We Build?

As we create this new network of health coaches to improve the health of our nation, several things need to be considered so that we not only build a large system but one that operates in a new way. Two factors are key: support and self-care for the staff, and building healthy organizational cultures. Basically this speaks to the coaching principles of respect for ourselves and each other and walking our talk.

I work as a health coach in a large insurance company and at times my job can be overwhelming. If I don't take care of myself first, I can't do anything for my clients. This really makes a difference in how I approach things. Otherwise my work is too energetically depleting. This is a core principle in coach training and was reinforced by one of the adjunct faculty in the Bark Coaching Institute who talked about his training in medicine. During one rotation he was really tired and decided he needed some time outdoors. He went and lay on the grass in the sun for ten minutes. When he came back, the attending doctor said sternly, "Where have you been?" He responded that he'd been taking care of a patient, and the doctor relaxed. He didn't mention that the patient was himself, but that short break revitalized him, which allowed him to finish his rounds. I often think about that example and remember that no matter how busy I am, I need to take that break or stretch for my own wellbeing.

Another factor in being successful in my position involves the culture of organizations. I work in several different clinics, and one especially has a wonderful culture where staff are friendly and supportive to each other and the patients. My whole body relaxes as I enter the clinic. I know that my time there will fly by and I'll be extremely productive. The team is collaborative and they really care about the patients. Time there is the high point of my week, and I hope that the success of this clinic spurs management in other centers to investigate the impact of this healthy culture.

In early 2010, I became involved in a national group of health and wellness coaching stakeholders which is co-creating definitions, standards, guidelines, and certification for a health and wellness coaching profession and role. We agreed about the urgency of the need, given that seventy percent of health care costs relate to lifestyle-based diseases, many preventable.

Together as the National Team we are crafting a certification process for health and wellness coaching based upon a vision of patient empowerment, disease prevention, and wellness.

At this early point in developing the process, many questions are being debated, such as the following:
1. Should standards and certification be determined for a separate professional role called *health and wellness coach*, as distinguished from general coaching certification?
2. Should there be two levels of health and wellness coaching: one serving clients who want to work on lifestyle issues, such as prevention of disease, and the other offering services to those with chronic or acute disease?
3. What are the prerequisites to take the certification test?
4. What certifying body should stand behind the certification process?
5. How will this certifying process be funded?
6. What is the landmark study that will look at the efficacy of this type of coaching, and how will it be funded?
7. How will health and wellness coaching be integrated into government programs since it is mentioned in the new health care bill?
8. What other kinds of reimbursement issues for health and wellness coaches will arise?

As you can see, much work remains, but the National Team's commitment to transforming health care remains strong. Some of the team members are nurses, and like me, they aspire to create a consortium of professional organizations that can collaborate in establishing common ground in setting standards and guidelines for health care professionals who want to practice a health and wellness coaching role. Nursing is the largest profession (2.6 million) and many members are embedded in the National Team that's working to move toward a national certification.[37]

Nursing and a Coaching Role

Nursing, especially holistic nursing, also supports coaching philosophy and practice, and some observers believe the future holds an ever-greater partnership between the two fields.[38] Below is an excerpt from a White Paper presented at the National Team Summit Meeting about health coaching that took place in September, 2010, in Boston.

> Nursing has always utilized knowledge from a wide variety of sources to achieve the best possible outcomes for clients. Coaching has emerged within nursing as one way to structure client interactions in a manner that enhances client-nurse partnerships. Based on the awareness that coaching is a separate and distinct competency, it is not to be confused with teaching, consulting, or directing others towards predetermined goals established by the nurse or others; thus, an innovative and creative Holistic Nurse Coach model of care has evolved. Nursing has taken the lead in establishing a holistic model of coaching—one designed to fully engage clients in self-care and the management of health care practices and outcomes.[39]

A Holistic Nurse Coach model of care addresses the need and desire of many health care providers to move away from a focus on disease management and towards ways to more effectively assist clients in living healthy, fulfilled, and productive lives that are compatible with and informed by the client's personal values, choices, and preferences. Health and wellness coaches from many backgrounds are needed to launch and implement a new approach to health care. As nurses collaborate with those who are developing the role, standards, and scope of practice for health and wellness coaches, it is important to recognize that coaching is a professional nursing competency within the scope of practice of professional nursing, and many nurses have already incorporated coaching into their professional nursing practice.[40]

Holistic Nurse Coaches bring an integrative perspective to coaching. A holistic framework created and developed by numerous nurse scholars provides a model for working for the whole person. The inclusive perspective of Holistic Nurse Coaches recognizes the biological, psychological, social/cultural, transpersonal, and energetic components of individuals. This perspective leaves space for openness and "not knowing"—the gateway to where new knowledge resides.[41] Erickson views this broad outlook as "integrative knowing,"[42] "a bringing together of multiple ways-of-knowing, integrating and creating new knowledge."[43] Many nurse coaches utilize a holistic, integral model of coaching that includes structures of consciousness as a way to frame coaching interactions.[44]

The code of ethics of the American Holistic Nurses Association also supports a whole picture perspective, referring to body/mind/emotion/spirit aspects, as well as concern for the ecosystem and environment.[45]

Additional Coaching Influences

Many other disciplines contributed to the foundations of coaching. Adult development, education, and transition theory offered learning types, stages of change, readiness, transformative learning theory, and reflective practices, to name a few. The communication and language disciplines supplied tools for clarifying questions—methods such as non-violent communication, which focuses on "I" messages, or statements expressing individual needs, and Neuro-Linguistic Programming training, a system that classified, modeled, and duplicated effective results of top communicators.[46]

Coaching has also looked to philosophy as a basis for practice. Examples include tenets borrowed from Eastern philosophy, such as living in the present moment, many different types of spirituality, and other aspects of philosophy that see reality as a choice.[47]

Coaching draws on a wide range of additional influences, such as those of the social sciences: cultural anthropology, economics, political science and sociology.[48] Self-help and elements of 12-step programs have also been integrated into coaching.[49]

At this point, seeing this long list of coaching's contributors, you might be wondering, "As a coach how can I possibly master all these areas?" Good news—it's not necessary to achieve expertise in each of these fields. The core competencies and coaching masteries, covered in the next chapter, distill the essences. However, now that you now better understand the history of coaching and the ideas that shaped it, you can consider what you already know and can do because of your expertise in contributing fields. When clients ask you how coaching is different from something else—for instance therapy—you can talk about how it's different and yet how it's a particular application of wider principles.

Cross-Fertilization

Different coaching specialties draw from diverse sources, with much overlap. For example, life coaches work with individuals who want to make changes - often in their personal lives - creating healthier lifestyles, improved relationships, an increase in confidence, or for assistance in completing a project. Business coaches specialize in facilitating change in the business environment, from entrepreneurial to corporate levels. However, the techniques used in life and business coaching aren't static and exclusionary but flow back and forth across the specialties. For instance, life coaches incorporate management concepts, including goals, timelines, performance, feedback, and motivation in their coaching repertoire. Likewise, the humanistic principles embedded in life coaching bleed into the corporate world, as business coaches work with their clients on sense of purpose, work/life balance, intuition, and personal growth. And both business and life coaches can use the "inner game" approach when dealing with the inner critic—that judgmental voice that influences success and achievement, regardless of the goal.

The Exponential Growth of Coaching

From 1990 to the present, the coaching profession has burgeoned. Now when someone says they're a life or business coach, in many countries across the globe people know what that means. This wasn't necessarily true twenty, or even ten, years ago. Certainly, popular media exposure has helped bring coaching to the public eye. The proliferation of coaching schools, professional and popular literature, and professional organizations have all contributed to this exponential growth. For example, the number of coaching schools has increased from 3 in 1995 to at least 273 in 2008.[50] An organization of schools, called the Alliance for Coach Training Organizations (ACTO), was created in 1998.[51] Professional organizations have also increased—from 0 to 16.[52] Similarly, coaching magazines and journals grew in number from 0 in 2000 to

11 in 2008.⁵³ And at the 2008 International Coach Federation convention in Montreal, Canada, over 425 coaching books were for sale.⁵⁴ Hundreds of schools now offer many different types of coaching education—in person and through teleclasses over the phone. Colleges and universities are also beginning to offer coaching programs. Some require on-site training.

Holistic and Integral Coaching is a growing area, and in fact the International Coach Federation added a new category called Body, Mind, Spirit Coaching for presenters at the 2008 Montreal Annual Convention. I googled "holistic coaching" and found 275,000 results—and 280,000 results came up for integral coaching.⁵⁵

Coaching Is Still Developing

Although coaching is beginning to look like a discipline—with schools, literature, a body of knowledge and organizations—the field is still cohering as a profession. Remember, it's only existed in any substantial form for approximately twenty years. Like other disciplines that have become professions, coaching is evolving. Nursing and massage therapy are other examples of professions that have undergone the growing pains of coming into their own.

A discipline requires a body of knowledge specific to its practice and differentiating it from other professions. This is especially true for coaching because with so many disciplines comprising its foundations, the lines distinguishing it from other professions can be blurry.⁵⁶ At this writing, no clear definition of coaching has been agreed upon by all parties. Some of the questions still under consideration are these:

- *Beyond being an expert in coaching, should coaches be professionally trained in the area of concern clients want to focus on?* According to Brock, her interviewees were about equally divided: half thought coaches should be experts in the fields of practice and half felt that this was not necessary.⁵⁷ Being an expert can facilitate how the coach operates in at least two ways. First, coaches can use their knowledge of the field to inform their powerful questions. For example, if I'm a health coach working with a client who's diabetic, and know that eating fiber with sweets reduces blood sugar spikes, I might ask when my client eats sugary foods. Second, since I'm aware of this fact, I might ask my client if s/he wants me to switch out of a pure coaching role and into the consulting role and inform my client about this interaction.

- *Who directs the session?* Although the International Coach Federation (ICF) and the International Association of Coaches (IAC) state that the client is in charge of the coaching session, some feel that the best interaction is one in which the client is in charge some of the time, but that the coach can, when appropriate, switch roles and become a consultant offering information and suggestions. This distinction can be a fine line. For example, in health coaching, an employer, insurance company, or doctor may give incentives to the health coach for improved client outcomes, such as lower blood sugar levels or the reduction of blood cholesterol. Do incentives from a third-party payer compromise the coaching agreement between coach and client? If the coach and client are working toward the same agreed-upon (and third-party sanctioned) goal, this may present no problem. But what if a client wants to work on something besides the lifestyle changes that affect blood sugar?

- *Should coaches be licensed?* Currently, anyone, regardless of training (or lack of it!), can be a coach. According to the most recent International Coach Federation (ICF) survey, 83 percent of clients report that they expect a coach to be certified.[58] Several professional organizations, as well as some coaching schools, certify their students. In my mind, unless the school is part of a stand-alone certifying organization like ICF, schools that certify their own students have a conflict of interest. Professions such as consulting don't have licensing regulations. Some wonder if licensing is an essential step in establishing professional credibility. There are advantages and disadvantages. Benefits include a clearer definition of services and understanding by the public of what to expect and how to hold coaches accountable for quality services. A disadvantage is that the standards for practice can decrease creativity and add an air of unnecessary fear to practicing. Who is the best body to regulate the profession is always an important question that needs to be addressed on a road to credentialing and licensing.

- *What is the role of research in coaching?* The need for research is paramount if coach-

ing is to be taken seriously.[59] But what kind of research is needed? Evidence-based practice in coaching has grown considerably since 2003.[60] The phrase *evidence-based practice* refers to the conscientious integration of best research evidence with clinical expertise and client values and needs.[61] It originated in the field of medicine and is considered to have developed from the establishment of the "Cochrane Reviews," an electronic database that consists of systematic reviews in various health care fields.[62] The teams that publish systematic reviews must make decisions about what to include. What constitutes the best evidence?

Often the best evidence is thought to result from empirical research, which means a *quantitative* approach to research (involving numerical measurement of an objective, reducible, cause and effect universe). However, not all practice easily or appropriately lends itself to quantitative research methods. Too much dependence on systematic reviews, which are based upon quantitative approaches, may limit the use of other effective approaches to problems and situations.

Qualitative research methods are not based upon quantitative measurements but work with meaning, assuming that it's socially and historically constructed.[63] Instead of counting or measuring, participants might be interviewed. Evidence-based practice ideally includes both kinds of methods. According to Darlene Hess, a preeminent innovator and researcher in integral nursing education, "It is easy to forget about things that do not appear in a research paper and it is hard to learn how to think about things that are not evident in the data but are important."[64] For example, what worldview was used to ask the original research questions in the first place? The focus can eliminate important considerations not evident when reading the research conclusion."

Published research and systematic reviews are important sources of evidence for practice, but they're not the only evidence, and can't be relied upon exclusively. It's also important to consult the evidence of what clients say and what happens in sessions, especially if the research findings conflict with the client's values or needs. For instance, research may show that a particular approach is useful in dealing with a life challenge, but if the client is not ready or interested in exploring that avenue, the coach needs to meet the client in the area of permission.

It's important too, to understand that knowledge is acquired in a variety of ways. Coaches can lean on theories that have been tested in the varied disciplines discussed earlier in the chapter and still come from a coaching role. Often, new theories are generated by using proven models and combining them in new ways. Other ways of knowing include coming from tradition, authority, trial and error, personal experience, role modeling, intuition, and reasoning.[65]

- *How do we apply a mixture of skills, models, and theories from different disciplines and have anything other than a haphazard and unsupported mish mash?* Might coaching be denigrated in the way naturopathy sometimes is—as offering significant benefits but having no cohesive theoretical base? Or are coaching and naturopathy both examples of integral disciplines that have a philosophical foundation that encompasses the whole picture of the client with many possible interventions?

---

[1] Michael Stratford, Masterful Questions: Getting to the Heart of the Matter: Master Coach Series, Vol. 3 (Laguna Hills, CA: Creative U Publishing, 2003), 86.

[2] Marilyn Ferguson, The Aquarian Conspiracy (New York: Putnam Publishing, 1980), 23-24.

[3] Vikki Brock's PhD dissertation is titled *"Grounded Theory of the Roots and Emergence of Coaching."* The 693 page document (this includes appendices and references) is an extraordinary research on the history of coaching. www.nobco.nl/files/onderzoeken/Brock_Vikki_dissertatie_2_.pdf Unpublished Dissertation, 17. She is in the process of publishing a book based on her graduate work.

[4] Ibid., 314.

[5] Ibid., 422-424.

[6] Ibid., 32. Dianne Stober and Anthony Grant. Editors, *Evidence Based Coaching Handbook* (New Jersey: Wiley and Sons, 2006), 29. Perry Zeus and Suzanne Skiffington, *The Coaching at Work Toolkit* (Sydney, Australia: McGraw Hill, 2002), 8.

[7] Brock, *Grounded Theory*, 40.

[8] Peter Senge, *The Fifth Discipline: The Art and Practice of the Learning Organization* (NY: Doubleday, 1990), 347.

[9] Sandy Keefe, "Holistic Coaching: It's All about the Small Steps,"*Advances in Nursing* vol. 3, issue 8 (2006): 12.

[10] Brock, *Grounded Theory*, 173 talks about individuals such as Rogers, Maslow, and Perls, trained in psychology and contributed to the creation of what was known as the *Human Potential Movement* and how the movement contributed methods and process to the developing discipline of coaching.

[11] The complete model is explained in Carl Roger's book *Client-centered Therapy* (NY: Houghton Miffin Company, 1961). *On Becoming a Person* (NY: Houghton Miffin Company, 1961) and *A Way of Being* (NY: Houghton Miffin Company, 1980) are other classic references for Roger's humanistic approach.

[12] Brock, *Grounded Theory*, 36-39.

[13] Brock, *Grounded Theory*, 178.

[14] Brock, *Grounded Theory*, 35-36.

[15] Brock, *Grounded Theory*, 36.

[16] Brock, *Grounded Theory*, 66-67 and Dianne Stober and Anthony Grant, Editors, *Evidence Based Coaching Handbook* (New Jersey: Wiley and Sons, 2006), 219-253.

Chapter 2: The Development of Coaching

17. Online you can find lists of positive psychology questionnaires, including the Attributional Style Questionairre (ASQ) by Martin Seligman. I'm including links to some on the website associated with this book.
18. www.psych.usyd.edu.au/coach/ Accessed on April 24, 2011.
19. Zeus and Skiffington, *Coaching at Work*, 7.
20. Brock, *Grounded Theory*, 164.
21. Brock, *Grounded Theory*, 164.
22. Cited in footnote 8. I found this book soon after it was published and have used these sound principles for work with groups and organizations and even individuals for many years.
23. Steven Prokesch, "The Sustainability Supply Chain" *Harvard Business Review—the Magazine* (October 2010), 1-3.
24. Senge, *Fifth Discipline*, 9.
25. Senge, *Fifth Discipline*, 9.
26. Senge, *Fifth Discipline*, 150-159.
27. Peter Block, *Flawless Consulting* (Hoboken, NJ: John Wiley and Sons, 1999).
28. Peter Block, *The Answer to How is Yes* (San Francisco: Berrett-Koehler Publishers, Inc., 2002), 201.
29. Personal conversation with Peter Block, San Francisco, CA July 14, 2002.
30. Block, *The Answer to How is Yes*, 171-183.
31. Timothy Gallwey, *The Inner Game of Tennis* (Random House, NY, 1974).
32. Ibid., viii.
33. Ibid., vii.
34. Ibid., xiv.
35. Ibid., xv.
36. Cleveland Chiropractic College, "Wellness Initiative for the Nation: Interview with Wayne Jonas, MD," *Health Insights Today* vol. 2, issue 2, (Spring 2009), www.healthinsightstoday.com/articles/v2i2/jonas_p1.html. In using this link, there is an underline after jonas that is masked by underlining this reference. Be sure that you use jonas_pl.html when looking for this quote. Parts of the WIN approach has been accepted into health care reform.
37. You can look up the most current Bureau of Labor statistics online.
38. Darlene Hess, Linda Bark, and Mary Elaine Southard, (September 25, 2010). White paper: Holistic Nurse Coaching. *Summit on Standards & Credentialing of Professional Coaches in Healthcare & Wellness*. Paper presented to National Credentialing Team for Professional Coaches in Healthcare, Boston, MA. Retrieved from www.wellcoach.com/images/WhitePaperHolisticNurseCoaching.pdf.
39. Ibid., 7.
40. Ibid., 3.
41. Barbara Dossey, "Integral and Holistic Nursing: Local to Global" In Barbara Dossey and Lynn Keegan, *Holistic Nursing: A Handbook for Practice 5th Edition* (Sudbury, MA: Jones & Bartlett, 2008), 23-24.

42 Helen Erickson, Editor, *Exploring the Interface Between the Philosophy and Discipline of Holistic Nursing: Modeling and role-modeling at Work.* (Cedar Park, TX: Unicorns Unlimited, 2010).

43 Ibid., 65.

44 This book was quoted in the White Paper. See footnote 38.

45 Mariano, Carla, *Holistic Nursing: Scope and Standards of Practice* (Silver Springs, MD: American Holistic Nurses Association, 2007), 120-121.

46 Brock, *Grounded Theory*, 448-450 and for a reference for NLP see www.nlpcoaching.com/whatnlp.html accessed April 24, 2011.

47 Ibid., 95-110, literature review of influence of various types of philosophy on coaching.

48 Ibid., 23.

49 Ibid., 52.

50 Ibid., 1.

51 For more information about this organization you can find material online.

52 Brock, *Grounded Theory*, 1.

53 Ibid., 1.

54 I personally counted the number of coaching books in the bookstore at the International Coach Federation Annual Convention in Montreal, Canada in November, 2008.

55 I googled these words on February 11, 2011.

56 Zeus and Skiffington, *Coaching at Work,* 10-12.

57 Brock, *Grounded Theory*, 254-256.

58 www.coachfederation.org/includes/docs/GCAS-8.doc The ICF Global Consumer Awareness Study was released on January 27, 2011. Site accessed on May 29, 2011.

59 Zeus and Skiffington, 317-318.

60 Brock, *Grounded Theory*, 257.

61 Stober and Grant, *Evidence Based Coaching Handbook*, 4-6.

62 Carol Macnee and Susan McCabe, *Understanding Nursing Research: Reading and Using Research in Evidence-Based Practice* (Philadelphia: Lippincott, Williams & Wilkins, 2006). This approach to research was shared with me by Darlene Hess, a nurse consultant, educator, coach, and experienced nurse practitioner.

63 John Creswell, *Research Design: Qualitative, Quantitative, and Mixed Methods Approaches* (Thousand Oaks, CA: Sage Publications, 2009).

64 William Neuman, *Social Research Methods: Qualitative and Quantitative Approaches* (Boston: Pearson Education, 2003), 458.

65 Nancy Burns and Susan Grove, *Understanding Nursing Research: Building an Evidence-Based Practice* (St. Louis, MO: Saunders Elsevier, 2007).

CHAPTER 3
Coaching Structure and Competencies

The coaching principles introduced in chapter 1 are at the heart of the BCI Approach: coaching as partnership and as a learning and growth process through which clients are encouraged to find their own inner voice by exploring the unknown. This coaching model is closely aligned with credentialing processes in the United States and doesn't contradict professionally-agreed-upon standards and values. Instead I'm enhancing the effectiveness by overlaying holistic and integral perspectives and techniques.

… CHAPTER 3: Coaching Structure and Competencies

Core Competency Skills of Coaching

I've already mentioned two of the largest associations whose mission is to provide guidelines and standards for coaching: the International Coach Federation (ICF) and the International Association of Coaching (IAC).[1] Along with other smaller associations, they've identified definitions, core competencies, roles for the coach and the client, and skills for coaching.
The ICF defines coaching as follows:

"Coaching is partnering with clients in a thought-provoking and creative process that inspires them to maximize their personal and professional potential."[2]

The IAC describes coaching in this way:

"Coaching is a transformative process for personal and professional awareness, discovery and growth."[3]

Each of these organizations has identified specific proficiencies. The IAC has nine Coaching Masteries:
- Establishing and maintaining a relationship of trust.
- Perceiving, affirming and expanding the client's potential.
- Engaged listening, which involves full attention to nuances, including that which is present but unexpressed.
- Processing in the present, with full attention on the client and from a perspective of mind, body, heart and or spirit, as appropriate.
- Expressing—the coach's effective communication.
- Clarifying.
- Helping the client set and keep clear intentions.
- Inviting possibility.
- Helping the client create and use supportive systems and structures.[4]

Both organizations specifically address ethical issues common to other helping professions, including these:
- Respecting differences among people, including age, race, religion, sexual orientation, disability, and socioeconomic standing.
- Acting with integrity toward clients, colleagues, and self.
- Establishing clear roles and boundaries for the coach and client, as well as sponsor, if applicable (i.e. third party who may pay for coaching, such as an employer or insurance company).
- Truthfully representing training, qualifications, and benefits of coaching.

- Respecting different approaches to coaching.
- Defining clear agreements in regards to compensation and billing arrangements.
- Being aware of personal issues that may interfere with coaching, and taking appropriate action.
- Conducting research proficiently and honestly.
- Handling client records and information confidentially.
- Referring clients appropriately.
- Avoiding conflicts of interest.
- Reporting to the appropriate authorities if a client discloses that they are of danger to themselves or to others.

These organizations also provide coach certification as a valid assurance that clients will receive excellent coaching services.[5]

I've been certified as a "master coach" (the highest level of credential) by the ICF, and I tend to turn to the competencies used by the ICF when teaching the BCI Model. The following discussion is based on the eleven basic competencies promulgated by the ICF, which are divided into four phases or steps, though, as you can imagine, use of the skills is overlapping and discursive.[6]

Setting the Foundation   Communicating Effectively
Co-creating the Relationship   Facilitating Learning and Results

Phase one involves *setting the foundation*. Practical aspects include establishing a meeting schedule, setting fees, and agreeing on the logistics of the sessions. Once that overall *agreement* is determined, coach and client create a specific agreement for each coaching session, such as the length and focus. When we talk about this phase in trainings we go over *ethical guidelines* as well as defining the roles of the coach and the client.

Setting the foundation also includes differentiating coaching from other professions, such as consulting or educating, which we talked about in chapter 1. Clients and coach trainees often wonder how coaching is different in goal, orientation, and practice from therapy, so it's worth a small digression here.

Historically, coaching developed in the sixties when people began to be interested in self-actualization, and the concerns of healthy people actualizing more of their potential became a new niche. It grew out of the business and personal growth venues. A new type of client emerged: people who wanted a particular type of guidance that didn't fit into the traditional therapy model. These clients wanted to address their current levels of performance and develop greater effectiveness in their current lives, rather than focusing so much on healing past experiences and traumas. While therapy focused on helping clients become more functional in the world, coaching addressed the desires of healthy people to optimize their levels of success.

As the field of coaching matured, it grew to overlap with the field of therapy. Therapists began to use coaching in their practice and coaches began to use their techniques with a wider range of clients, including homeless people, health-challenged clients, and others who were not necessarily interested in self-actualization. Yet there remains distinct differences between how therapy is done and coaching is delivered. The categories include the following:[8]

1. focus of attention;
2. time orientation;
3. types of conversations;
4. ways of relating;
5. client characteristics;
6. process itself.

Focus of Attention—Coaching conversations focus on goals, unutilized potential, solving problems, and developing critical skills necessary for a successful life. Coaches help clients find their own motivation to function at their highest capacity. Therapy, on the other hand, tends to be more retrospective, attempting to resolve past pain and eliminate dysfunctional symptoms and behaviors. The overlap in these two orientations is that both attend to developmental issues and focus on gaining knowledge. In therapy, knowledge, in the form of insight regarding the past, is used to heal past wounds. In coaching, knowledge, in the form of analysis of the present, is used to link increased awareness to more constructive actions.

Time Orientation—The approach in coaching is to attend to the here and now of events and their possible effects in the future. Although coaches may delve into the past as a guide for dealing with the present and future, they are more oriented towards dealing with a person's current circumstance. They spend less time than a therapist does in dealing with the past. In therapy, much attention is given to the past as a vehicle for repairing past traumas. The heart of therapy rests in analyzing the past and repairing old wounds.

Types of Conversations—Coaches tend to play a more active role in conversations with their clients; they share more of their own observations and suggestions. The coach is often more self-disclosing, and the relationship is less formal and bounded. The topics tend to be more action-related, and coaches start with the assumption that the client is whole and an expert in their own life situation. The client may lack clarity or experience certain obstacles, but they also have an intuitive sense of what's needed that a coach can help them tap into.

Therapy sessions, on the other hand, tend to be less defined and more rambling, with clients making connections between past experiences and current problems. The therapist stresses attending to feelings and encourages emotional processing of new material that may be unearthed. The overlap between the two is that both use inquiry methods, deal with boundary issues, promise confidentiality, and resist giving advice.

Ways of Relating—Therapists who've done both coaching and therapy all say they expect more from their coaching clients. Their therapy clients tend to be in crisis mode and therefore in a lower functioning state. They also say they tend to talk more in coaching and maintain looser boundaries between client and themselves than they do with their therapy clients. Since there's less of a stigma related to coaching, they're more able to acknowledge their relationship with their clients outside of their coaching. Therapist coaches also report feeling like they have more latitude with coaching; have more of a partnership, and can be more actively engaged with their clients. Their conversations with coaching clients are more action-and goal-oriented, and they are more self-revelatory.

With their therapy clients they have more rigid boundaries and use transference to help clients recover from past stresses. The idea of having dual relationships with the therapist is strictly discouraged. Furthermore, in therapy, all encounters are strictly face-to-face, except under extenuating circumstances, whereas in coaching, many clients interact totally over the phone. Therapists are viewed as healers or experts in their field, rather than as partners, as they are in coaching.

Client Characteristics—Certain clients need more than coaching because they need to deal with past issues in order to become functional enough to benefit from coaching. Clients who are suicidal, have deep depression, anxiety attacks, alcohol or drug addiction, personality disorders, or paranoia are better suited to a more therapeutic orientation. However, sometimes coaching complements therapy by helping people deal with the active concerns in their lives. For example, a homeless person might receive therapy to deal with the emotional baggage that they carry around, while working with a coach to help them strategize ways to improve their immediate circumstances. Clients for whom mood is a predominant concern may not be good candidates for coaching. Low affect, high levels of chaos, and an inability to take action or move forward would be characteristics that suggest the need for therapy. Any situation where the client is expecting their helper to be overly responsible is not a good situation for coaching. It's important that coaches learn to recognize the signs of clients whose problems are not suitable for coaching. They need to recognize the symptoms that should necessitate a referral to a therapist.

Process Differences—A coach works to help clients perceive solutions to obstacles, to learn new interpersonal skills, and to implement the best choices. The aim is clients increasing their capacity to be effective and to reach their goals. While it's understood that we're all human and that we have many failings, coaching also assumes that we have a much greater capacity for success than we usually imagine. An important role of the coach is to help clients stretch their imaginations to match their latent potentials. Envisioning a goal and clearly delineating the process of achieving it is a large part of what separates successful people from those who are not successful. Anticipating obstacles and designing solutions is another important ingredient in moving towards a goal. A skilled coach also helps clients learn to build on their strengths and compensate for their weaknesses so that they spend more of their time experiencing their own personal power and less time floundering in a state of frustration and despair. Simple adjustments can have huge payoffs for clients, and the art of coaching lies in finding such points of leverage. Over time small adjustments can accumulate and people can reach a tipping point where a mediocre level of achievement can be ratcheted up to a much higher level of accomplishment.

Good therapists help their clients achieve higher levels of wellness so that functioning in the world is not quite so overwhelming. They can slowly take clients from a place of despair or desperation to a place of confidence and greater self-awareness and self-control. They also can help their clients reduce their level of discomfort and actually extinguish negative symptoms over time. In coaching, clients know they're in charge, but in therapy, the clients learn that they can be in charge. In coaching, the process is co-created, and in therapy the therapist interjects interchanges that help clients feel more in charge of their lives.

Both therapy and coaching attempt to empower clients and give them more confidence, more skills, greater awareness, and a greater capacity to deal effectively with their lives. These two fields also help to inform each other. The field of therapy helps coaches to remember that change takes time and is a process that involves our mind, our emotions, and our physiology. We need to be patient, to not be afraid to explore the depths of a client's thinking, and to not expect change overnight. The field of coaching reminds therapists that people have a great potential for growth and for actualizing unimaginable things and that they have powerful personal insights into what they need most to make the changes they need to make.

A number of my students who are therapists have benefitted from adding coaching to their repertoires or changed roles from therapist to coach.

Estelle Brodeur, MS, PMHCNS-BC, ACC
Therapy and Coaching

After working as a nurse in various settings, then as a public mental health therapist, and next as a designer of stress management education groups for corporate health care employees, I wanted to move into a different conversational framework that embraced all of my professional experiences, that was grounded in health and possibility, that would facilitate client choices around positive life changes, and one where I could learn an expanded repertoire of tools to help clients move in directions they most wanted.

I was curious about whether this kind of practice existed. I was already an experienced group facilitator, educator, and therapist, and knew I wanted to use my current knowledge with both individuals and groups. I believed in the process of effective psychotherapy, having been both provider and consumer. Even so, I wanted to move into a different way of serving clients who were ready to take action and enhance their lives. I wanted to work with those who declared a vital desire for personal or professional change, and were ready to "get down to business." Through the years, I was aware of many who didn't fit criteria for mental illness yet wanted to live more fully, wanted to use their talents and skills more, wanted more courage and self-confidence, wanted to communicate to family and co-workers more effectively, wanted to increase their ability to manage stressors and take better care of themselves, to widen their circle of support, play more, and challenge beliefs holding them back.

I wanted a slightly different role as a change agent. Many of us go into therapy in search of an expert, and even though I believe wholeheartedly that this is often in the best interest of the client, I wanted to take a stance in which I could follow the client more than lead. A colleague recommended the Bark Coaching Institute. Since the theme of coaching seemed to keep cropping up, I paid attention and called Linda, and after talking to her, I knew I wanted to learn more. Two years later, after completing coach training, working with clients, being personally coached, starting my business, and becoming certified with the International Coach Federation, I knew I'd found the strong foundation I was looking for.

Although my background as therapist affords me a certain comfort level while listening to others' emotions, as a coach I can also help clients shift feelings during the session—since emotions are at the heart of change. Coaching is based in the present—that is, conversations are based around what the client wants to shift now around an emotion or thought, rather than continuing to work through past hurts, resentments, traumas, or "fixing" problems.

68   CHAPTER 3: Coaching Structure and Competencies

Setting the Foundation
Co-creating the Relationship
Communicating Effectively
Facilitating Learning and Results

The second phase of effective coaching, according to the ICF, relates to *co-creating the relationship*. Establishing *trust and intimacy* with the client is essential, achieved in part through offering a safe, supportive environment where respect and trust can flourish. Following through with commitments, acting open-hearted, providing support, championing new behaviors, and asking permission before moving into sensitive areas, also work together to help create this outcome. Exhibiting a coaching presence is also important in this phase.

Let's look more deeply into this idea of *coaching presence,* which refers to the "being" part of coaching—something I consider just as important as "doing." It's difficult to define, but clients know when that sense of presence is there and when it's missing. When it's present, they feel heard, seen, felt, and understood. Coaching presence refers to the subtle skill of listening intently and also of "holding the space" for the client—for instance by allowing time for the client to express herself or himself, even when they're groping. The coach listens intently to the client but doesn't become so absorbed that s/he loses the "outside" perspective to reflect and question.

Remember Sandra (Sample Session 1A) saying she felt like I was on her side even though she barely knew me and wasn't even able to see me because we were talking on the phone? She was referring to our partnership and the slow and steady building of trust and intimacy that was developing from my being present with her, my reflective listening, and my questions that helped her move to new places within herself.

CO-CREATING THE RELATIONSHIP

Setting the Foundation   **Communicating Effectively**
Co-creating the Relationship   Facilitating Learning and Results

The third phase involves *communicating effectively,* and here you'll find three very important skills: active listening, powerful questions, and direct communication. Each is a vital skill in coaching and reflects the coaching presence I previously discussed. In trainings these are practiced until they become natural, and you might try them out in your daily interactions as well as noticing how you respond when others do and don't use these skills.

Active listening is the coach's ability to hear what is and what's not being said and to summarize, paraphrase, or mirror back what the client is expressing to ensure clarity and to support clients as they explore. What's an example of active listening? Imagine Nancy, a client who's talking about her relationship with her boss. She states that she's been passed over for raises and promotions and that her work is not praised. She says that she has the smallest office, which doesn't even have a window. Her coach may say, "Oh, it sounds like you're not feeling valued," and Nancy then would agree or disagree with the coaching summary. Another example is my listening to Sandra's opening description of her situation in Sample Session 1A. I responded with a paraphrase that included an image about a horse pawing the ground.

Powerful questions are developed through active listening and help clients expand, reframe, and rethink. They're typically open-ended—powerful for shifting perspectives and for uncovering hidden ones. I know when I've asked a masterful question when my clients say, "That's a good question," and take a while to come up with an answer because they need to go deeper or to completely reconsider a situation. What does a powerful question sound like? One of my favorites is, "What is your life organized around?" Throughout this book you'll find some powerful questions you might try out as you develop your own style and repertoire as a coach. I hope you're also exploring these questions as you seek to become more aware of yourself—in this way your whole self becomes your most reliable tool!

> *How would you answer the question of "what is your life organized around?"*

Direct communication is the last skill under the heading of communicating effectively. The coach's clear and direct speech models good communication and also builds an honest and trustworthy relationship. The coach uses clear, non-sexist, non-racial, non-technical language and comes from a place of non-judgment, and these stem from a basic respect for the client. Metaphor, analogy, and honest feedback also enhance clear communication.

Setting the Foundation   Communicating Effectively
Co-creating the Relationship   **Facilitating Learning and Results**

The fourth phase relates to *facilitating learning and results*. These skills include helping the client create awareness, designing actions, planning, goal setting, and assisting the client in managing progress and accountability. These skills are key in the coaching process and help differentiate it from some other professions, such as therapy, which is not as directly action oriented.[7]

Often the coach provides a container or listening space as the client integrates multiple sources of information, facilitating, and tracking how things build toward the client's "ah ha" moment—that new way of looking at something—that new *awareness* that will lead to action. The skills we looked at previously are the catalyst for this shift: establishing a firm foundation, co-creating the relationship, deep listening, and powerful questions can all help lead to that new awareness. When the client has a new way of perceiving something, s/he moves into *designing new actions* and *setting new goals*. These steps create new *progress*.

Accountability is another aspect of coaching that clients appreciate, and it aids in getting results. In coaching, accountability is usually played out in the client selecting homework, fieldwork, or an assignment to accomplish before the next session. When clients know that their coach remembers their commitments, it makes a difference in their follow-through. This is a positive kind of accountability that helps clients hold their attention on what's important to them. Of course, it's important for the coach and the client to agree on a style and type of accountability for their relationship, ranging from checking in at the next session, to something like sending the coach an email, or calling the coach after a step is completed. So often clients don't notice their progress. They finish one goal, and it's off to the next, with not a moment of celebration or a pat on the back. Spending time on a reviewing progress is a wonderful part of coaching where coaches and clients can see how far clients have come.

How the BCI Model Expands the Core Competencies

The skills and areas in the phase of setting the foundation don't vary much, no matter which coaching approach you might adopt. But the BCI Approach enriches the other three phases, given its holistic and integral orientation. Let's look at this a bit now, with Part Two giving specifics.

The second ICF core competency, co-creating the relationship, speaks of the coach being present for the client. My model deepens how we understand relationship and presence to include being present in multifaceted ways—from a holistic (body, mind, and spirit) perspective, as well as an integral one (the total and complete picture). As a coach, I'm with my client using my whole self and a big picture orientation that offers my client the opportunity to meet me with their whole self and complete picture.

The BCI Model also profoundly impacts the third category of core competencies, including the skills of active listening, powerful questions, and direct communication. I'm not only *present* from a holistic perspective but *actively listening with my whole self*, which means that I'm able to notice changes in energy and body signals. Sometimes I actually feel what my clients are describing. Sharing this somatic resonance with my clients sharpens and expands their awareness. This deep listening brings in meaningful intuitive insights that inform my powerful questions. The depth and breadth of body, mind, energy, and spirit approaches allow for opportunities to look through a variety of different windows, which catalyzes new perspectives. Often seeing a situation in a new way changes options, solutions, and actions.

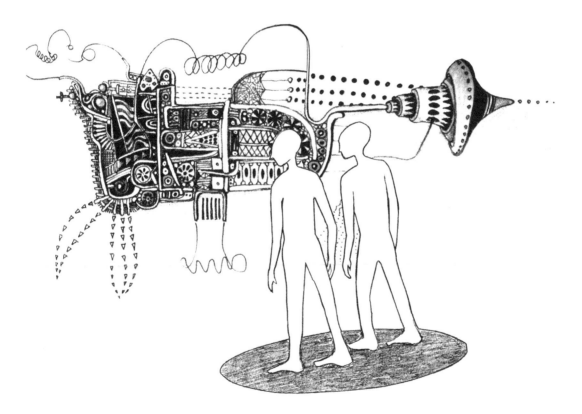

Remember the illustration at the beginning of chapter 1, with the coach and the client as they look at a very interesting and complicated situation represented by the complex object in front of the coach and the client?

72   CHAPTER 3: Coaching Structure and Competencies

Since this model offers so many multiple perspectives, the client may want to move up close and look at one part of the situation to see if some clarity and understanding can be gleaned.

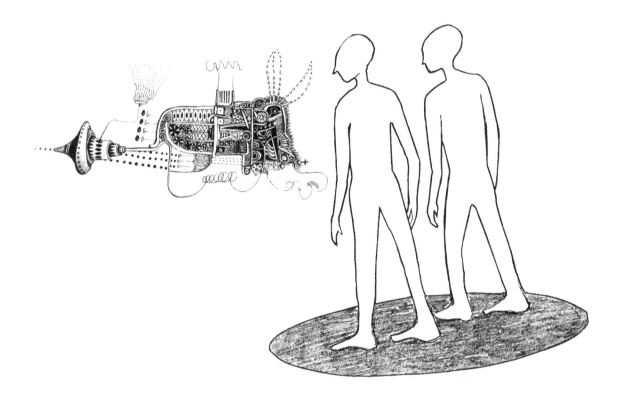

Perhaps the client wants to step back from the situation and look at things from a distance.

74   CHAPTER 3: Coaching Structure and Competencies

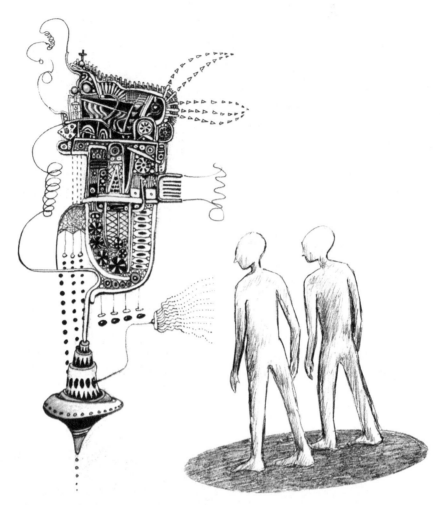

The coach might ask the client to view this situation from a completely new orientation.

The request might facilitate the "ah ha" moment when the client realizes that the entire circumstance is created by the top-like "generator," which is now pictured correctly at the bottom of the situation and causes the rest of the circumstances. The "generator" might represent a hidden attitude, a held belief, or an old behavior pattern that creates the rest of the picture. For example, taking this new orientation, a client might understand how the critical internal voice causes so much stress and disease in her or his life.

The expansion of choices, decisions, and opportunities available in the BCI Method constructively influences learning, action and results—the fourth core competency.

Putting It All Together

Although the core competencies are presented as though they're steps, I prefer to use them as a checklist of skills coaches must master, rather than a session guide that tells you what to do first, what to do next, and so on. They're the basic stages, but the overall path sessions tend to follow is more flowing and much simpler. A coaching conversation that takes place over time is basically about finding out where clients want to go—or *what* is the goal—and *how* they are going to get there within a certain timeline (*when*). I want to know what kind of *support* clients might need and if there are any anticipated *challenges* on their journey to their goal. After these questions are considered, the client can select a next step.

Both process outcomes and product outcomes result from good coaching. A process outcome for Sandra, in Sample Session 1A might be learning to listen to her inner voice better and to integrate conflicting parts of herself, while a product outcome would be finding a new and better job that's more aligned with her true purpose in life.

In some coaching sessions, my client wants to look at the little picture, like how to clean up a messy desk. After success in that realm, s/he might switch to the big picture and realize that having more order overall would bring peace and satisfaction, in which case the focus changes. Other times, my client might want to look at his or her whole life (the big picture) and select a small piece to change. Let's say that my client wants more peace of mind and thinks that would be accomplished if life were more orderly, so s/he selects cleaning a desk as a way to start.

76 CHAPTER 3: Coaching Structure and Competencies

BIG PICTURE

LITTLE PICTURE

Again, this new way of coaching uncovers more to explore and process. The generative power of the holistic and integral approach expands what can be included in the big picture, including a greater number of inner and outer parts. I hope you're looking forward to Part Two, where you'll find specific questions and exercises to use when appropriate.

In the next chapter we'll look at the elements of change, the last piece we need to overview before getting into techniques. Perhaps you're already imagining where and when coaching might be helpful for you and for people you know. Before we talk about change, take a look at the many ways graduates of my program have applied what they have learned. You may be surprised about the wide application of this model as you read about the variety of coaches and their many types of clients. What they're doing is always very interesting!

Coaching works with many different people and has many applications.

Karen Sanders, MSN, RN, AHN-BC
Coaching the Phoenix Nurses

I call them the "Phoenix Nurses" because they come back from the ashes. They're nurses who make poor clinical or non-clinical decisions, which results in suspension of their nursing licenses or being placed on probation. Nurses always face ethical dilemmas in work and must decide what to do, and sometimes they choose poorly. In my state, when a nurse is reported to the nursing board for violation of the Nurse Practice Act, s/he must attend a course on ethical-legal decision-making. I'm one of approximately thirty nurses in our state who teaches and coaches these nurses who've lost their licenses or are on probation.

Although I'm a department head in my hospital, managing seventy-five employees, and use my coaching skills frequently, my work with the Phoenix Nurses requires my best coaching skills. The results of suspending a nursing license can have cataclysmic financial, emotional, and professional impacts on nurses' lives. I've even worked with nurses who have moved into a downward spiral and become homeless.

Our initial meeting is very intense. I ask the nurse to tell me what happened, and s/he usually feels bad and cries during the first session. My heart goes out to anyone in this situation, especially because the poor decision was often made when they were very stressed, overworked, or tired. Perhaps they cut a corner when disposing of a narcotic or didn't go to find that second nurse for help during a very stressful time in a nursing unit. Other times the situation is more complex, related to addiction or some kind of fraudulent behavior.

Whatever the situation, I find myself using several coaching skills I learned in training at the Bark Coaching Institute. One of the most fruitful powerful questions I use in exploring feelings from a holistic perspective is, "Where do you feel that in your body?" In particular, I use this when we're dealing with issues related to re-entering the workforce, which requires job interviews. Many of these nurses have great anxiety about how to tell future employers the story of how they came to lose their licenses and then to explain the lessons they have learned from these experiences. I ask them to use a "0 to 10" scale, with "0" equaling "no stress," and "10" equaling "maximum stress," and to talk about where this stress is located in their bodies. I ask powerful questions to help nurses identify where the pain and anxiety lives in their bodies and then to take small "underpromising" steps to move through this discomfort and make a plan for facing the job search.

The long road back to successful employment and a fulfilling life can be walked, and new ways of dealing with stressful situations pay off for those who've had some coaching. They discover how to recognize situations that might have ethical or legal ramifications. What they learn to do so as not to repeat trouble with licensure is to take a time out—that break when faced with another ethical dilemma—that five minutes to step back and find someone to talk with to help them sort out what is the correct next step, and to trust their inner voice of wisdom.

Beth Warshaw, MA
Is Group-Coaching As Effective As Individual Coaching?

I gained newfound respect for the value of group-coaching after my first group session done by teleconference was very successful. I'd never facilitated a group-coaching session before and wasn't sure how to apply what I'd learned about coaching one-on-one. I wasn't sure if it would be as effective and was also hesitant about how the group would come together once everyone was on the phone, but there was tremendous support and acceptance from the participants. This experience taught me to trust the coaching process as well as my coaching capabilities. By facilitating the group conversation, I was able to emphasize confidentiality and non-judgment among the participants, which allowed them to open up to me and to the group.

The focus of the three group-coaching sessions was anything related to health, and having each person choose an individual health issue to address worked well. I might have had a tougher time staying with the energy of the group if we hadn't had a health theme—if instead people were concerned with a range that included work, relationship and illness. This general focus allowed participants to learn from each other's experiences and to be inspired by things they wouldn't have come up with on their own. Members felt supported by knowing that they weren't alone in their health struggles. Also, hearing about everyone's progress motivated participants, perhaps because their accountability was to the entire group.

Besides coming to appreciate the effectiveness of group-coaching I also realized the advantage of being able to empower more people than I could working one-on-one. With teleconferencing I can coach people in all different parts of the United States as a group. Because of this positive experience, I'll continue to coach groups as well as individuals.

Kate Sadowsky, MA
Avatar Association and Behavioral Change

I facilitate support groups for a weight loss program called Club One Island that takes place in virtual reality, which requires some explaining. Our participants and instructors, in our self-designed avatar bodies, share in an immersive online environment designed to support their behavior changes around weight loss and movement, together through the Island. We hold support groups in luxury tree houses, sitting underwater on giant crabs, relaxing on clouds in the sky—what better environment to test our own perceptions on what's possible!

Even in this environment, tone of voice, breathing, choice of clothing, posture of people's avatars, and where they choose to sit in the circle offer clues as to how they're doing in their process of change. Sharing this unique environment, combined with sharing the challenges of making healthy changes in our lives, is surprisingly intimate. And the playful educative qualities of a virtual world allow all of us to question more freely, to find more creative solutions, to move outside of our usual patterning. Using a virtual environment gives participants an opportunity to literally try out a new behavior through their avatars, and see if it fits. When you're flying on a magic carpet, many things seem possible that may not have before!

In the group setting, I'm aware that any questions I ask of one person will be heard and adapted by the group, so through asking powerful questions I'm modeling a process of inquiry that can be adapted to any life situation and any environment. I see the clients' fullness, strength, and potential; I hold a mirror up to them so that they can see it, too. The play of coaching is in slightly altering the angle of that mirror so that it can reflect people's true selves as clearly as possible. And since the mind behind the avatar and the mind behind the physical body are the same, these new ideas, behaviors, and tools are carried from the digital experience into our physical realities.

[1] The International Coach Federation (ICF) was created in 1995 and currently has a membership of over 19,000 in 100 countries, according to their website (www.coachfederation.org/about-icf). The IAC was created in 2003. According to its website, the IAF has over 13,000 members in 80 countries (www.certifiedcoach.org/index.php/about_iac/iac_overview).

[2] ICF Code of Ethics," International Coach Federation, accessed May 17, 2011 www.coachfederation.org/about-icf/ethics/conduct.

[3] Check the International Association of Coaching (IAC) website for the latest on certification (www.certifiedcoach.org/index.php/get_certified/learn/certification_overview).

[4] "The IAC Coaching Masteries," International Association of Coaching, accessed May 17, 2011, (www.certifiedcoach.org/index.php/get_certified/the_iac_coaching_masteries_overview).

[5] See notes 1 and 2.

[6] "Core Competencies," International Coach Federation, accessed May 17, 2011, www.coachfederation.org/icfcredentials/core-competencies.

[7] The ICF hired the Association Resource Centre Inc. and PricewaterhouseCoopers LLP to conduct a study about the coaching experiences of clients who responded between September to November, 2008. The executive summary can be obtained from ICF and covers such issues as the demographic of the 2165 client respondents from 64 countries; characteristics of coaching experiences; why and how clients seek coaches, and satisfaction levels of services; and return on investment from coaching. On page iii of the executive survey, the surveys found that clients wanted coaching because they felt they could generate an action plan rather than explore issues as they thought was done in therapy or counseling. See ICF, "International Coaching Federation Coaching Client Survey Executive Summary, April 2009," accessed May 18, 2011. www.coachfederation.org/includes/media/docs/ExecutiveSummary.pdf.

[8] Vicki Hurt and John Blattner, "Coaching Versus Therapy: A Perspective," *Consulting Psychology Journal*: Practice and Research vol. 53 (Fall, 2001): 224-237. The authors highlight six critical differences in their article. Another resource looking at the difference between therapy and coaching is a book by Patrick Williams and Deborah Davis, *Therapist as Life Coach*, (NY: W.W. Norton & Company, Inc., 2002).

Chapter 4
Helping People Navigate Change

Clients hire coaches because they want something different in their lives—like Sandra, whom we met in Sample Session 1A, they want change. Maybe they know where they want to go, but don't know how to get there. Or, like Sandra, they don't know exactly what they want; they just know they're missing something—a tempting mystery needs to be incubated, nurtured, discovered, and explored. These mysteries come into our lives at various times because change is inevitable, built into our DNA. Think of snakes. They must shed their skin to survive.

As we let go of our old skin, or things that no longer fit us, we discover that change can be exciting, adventuresome, scary, and sometimes overwhelming. At this juncture a good coach can help transform change into an effective learning process. Think of all the transitions you've made, or thought of making. Maybe you wanted to start a new career or business, go back to school, or strive for a promotion at work. Do you remember how you went from there to here? Perhaps you wanted to learn to be more assertive or proactive when relating to others, or to explore how to be more kind and easy on yourself. Whether it's discovering ways to reinvent a life or to change a smaller piece of it, coaching helps people reach their goals by bringing awareness to the path of change.

Even though change is inevitable, its impact can be on the surface or deep, and the process can be comfortable, smooth, or rough. The coaches understanding and guidance of the change process can raise the level of the clients self-knowledge. From a new level of awareness clients can integrate past conflicts, just as Sandra accomplished when working with opposing voices that called for change and resisted it.

What's a change in your life that's waiting to be uncovered? Are you itching to shed your skin and discover what's underneath? What transition would allow you to be happier, healthier, more fulfilled? What is the one question that when answered would significantly impact your life? As you read through this book, you can use the approaches and tools to transform in this area. Using the tools in your own life will help you to apply them with others.

Holistic Approaches Support Change

Like Sandra (Sample Session 1A), we're most familiar with mental, logical approaches. Sandra had been using the mental approach for months, and it alone was ineffective. She found out that the more parts of herself she included in her transition process, the faster and more easily it occurred. I like offering a holistic approach so my clients can access the wisdom of the body, mind, and spirit.

Remember my coaching questions that helped Sandra tune into her body? For one thing, I asked her to stand up and actually shift to various parts of the room, thereby moving out of using only one process—thinking. Her standing and moving facilitated access to her body. I asked questions about physical sensations, checking in with her jaw, shoulders, and stomach. She wasn't aware of these but did notice feelings in her head that increased her awareness, which led to new action.

From my questions about her spirit, Sandra realized that her career needed to be meaningful—that question took her exploration to a deeper level, bringing insight about her sense of purpose.

I'm not advocating that we drop thinking and listen only to wisdom from body and spirit. I sincerely value a mental approach since it allows for measurement and a look at behavior patterns, as well methods for planning and evaluation. I just want access to all aspects of our selves! I want this for myself and for my clients, if they're willing to experience and enjoy more of themselves.

Imagine the many windows through which you can view a situation. I've been talking about the holistic windows of body, mind, and spirit, but we can add others, for an even richer view. This book presents an additional set of windows: structures of human consciousness that have evolved through time, and that are still alive in us, just as evolutionarily older brain structures (for instance, the limbic brain stem) continue to play a role in autonomic processes such as breathing. These consciousness structures were identified by Jean Gebser, a philosopher who wrote in the 1930s. Based on meticulous research he identified five major ways of thinking since the beginning of human development, calling them Archaic, Magic, Mythical, Mental, and Integral. An integral approach is being able to come from multiple perspectives, and one way we're doing that is by tapping into these older structures, from a mental lens. Chapters 5 through 9 describe coaching tools based on each structure and chapter 9, the Integral chapter, suggests ways to expand the whole picture.

One example of a tool that comes from the Mythical structure of consciousness is imagery, which I tried out in the very first minutes of my conversation with Sandra when I described the horse at the gate, pawing the ground and unable to move forward. That she reacted so positively to my image-based summary of her situation suggested that this would be a powerful way for her to speak from her different parts. Through working with imagery, Sandra managed to transform an underlying battle between different aspects of herself. Even though she didn't mentally "understand" the process, this transformation allowed her to relax at the end of the session, resulting in being able to sleep and reducing her teeth grinding. Here's another example of tapping into older consciousness structures with mental awareness.

Teresa Corrigan, RN, MA, BCB, CLYT
A Full-Spectrum Approach to Surgery Coaching

More experienced with the expert role, I became intrigued with coaching when I realized the power of skillfully holding the moment, the inspiration, or just the space for people to do their own sorting. A coach helps provide structure and can be the catalyst to help move the client into action, or in some cases, out of action. The client comes up with the answers and the coach is able to watch the amazing revelations and transformation come forward.

After taking the BCI training course and understanding more about the integral model, I realized how to integrate teaching and coaching. Sometimes I have valuable information that my clients want to learn and I switch into consultant or education model and answer questions. At other times, I wear the hat of the coach and ask powerful questions that allow for those wonderful empowering breakthroughs.

I often find that clients have concerns that haven't been addressed and need more information or a second opinion. Using *Mental* and *Intuitive* tools, I help them define what they need before surgery, whether it's more information, talking to another patient who's had the same surgery, help with prioritizing preparation tasks, assistance with resources, and in some cases, language to temporarily postpone their surgery (if appropriate and not life-threatening) until they feel more prepared and ready.

Often surgery is pending, and we may have time for only one session. Asking powerful questions is one of the main keys to effective surgery coaching. I'll usually ask questions such as, "What is the one thing you need most right now?" "What is your worst fear?"

Once we've addressed clients' concerns and discussed the nuts-and-bolts of the hospital, anesthesia, and pain management, we explore options to help lessen their stress and anxiety. This allows me to use many skills from this coaching model, depending on what appeals to the client. I teach diaphragmatic breathing and a slow extended purse-lipped breath, body scan relaxation, and positive affirmations coupled with aromatherapy.

I love bringing magic to this work and employ many tools from both the *Mental* and the *Intuitive* consciousness structures. A recent favorite Mental tool based on the 1-10 scale described in this coaching model is having the client stand on an imaginary pain scale, moving up and down the scale as insights and shifts occur. (We also use this scale to alter anxiety and stress, and to discover how prepared clients feel.) Combining their insights with physically experiencing the changes as they move has been very revealing. In addition, working with an imaginary magic wand is sometimes the best tool when clients are really fearful or stuck. The wand helps clients relax and stop being so much "in their head" by tapping into our mutual playfulness.

During the coaching session(s) we might also do interactive guided imagery (a *Mythical* tool), in which the patient imagines the entire day of surgery and the hospital stay. We dialog about what they're seeing, sensing, hearing, touching, and sometimes tasting, and in these moments we have an opportunity to connect with their deep inner wisdom. They also image themselves healed and healthy down the road—bringing their image alive so they can keep it with them during surgery and recovery.

Creating the space for silence to be present is probably the most powerful coaching tool for a surgery coach. Holding the space with the client for the pain, grief, sadness, fear, or whatever, to be present brings palpable healing that provides a basic readiness to meet the challenges ahead.

Having a large and holistic toolkit offers so many options for reaching people's whole selves! It's as if my clients have cars, and each tire stands for a different approach. If they only use one approach, like the mental or thinking method, and ignore the other ways—represented by the other three tires being flat—they *can* move forward. However, if the other three tires also had air, the clients would arrive at their destinations more quickly and with much less struggle. The illustration here also shows us the fun we can have with a partner!

Chapter 4: Helping People Navigate Change

My clients and I use these multiple perspectives to give us insight into the wisdom of what's going on inside as well as becoming aware of the external factors that influence us. Having the option of selecting approaches from this very broad perspective facilitates faster and easier movement toward goals.

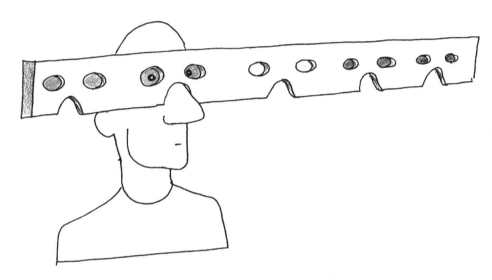

Energy is created when more parts of self are aligned. Think of the effort it would take to move your belongings by yourself across town versus moving with seven people helping you. When a variety of tools are appropriately used together, they "potentiate" each other. If you're taking one drug and add another, the first drug may actually become stronger—doctors warn about this all the time. The total effect is more than the sum of the parts, and good coaches tap into this increased efficacy. Clients often experience an "ah ha" moment as a result of the synergy of different approaches.

One instance of that potentiating for Sandra was the "ah ha" moment after a minute of silent breathing, when she said that she wanted to imagine pushing down the sides that were holding her. I encouraged her to do that. "Whew," she exclaimed, "that feels better. I don't know how this worked, but now I have a voice." As you'll read in Part Two, taking a breath is a "Intuitive" tool, in this case, effectively followed by imagery—a "Mythical" intervention—and the combination brought a shift. She felt it in her body, and she could take the next step in her change process.

I always enjoy asking clients how they experience a shift because I have found that people vary: some take a big inhalation; others exhale; some feel lighter; some feel freer; some feel calmer or more peaceful.

> *What happens for you when you have an "ah ha" shift? How do you feel? What happens in your body, mind, and spirit?*

Stretching the scope and tools of coaching to include holistic (body/mind/spirit) aspects and structures of consciousness (Archaic, Intuitive, Mythical, Mental, and Integral), as well as other integral approaches, provides clients the opportunity to be more completely aligned with their whole selves or, in other words, more congruent. The outside mirrors the inside more completely. Why is this important? False starts are often eliminated. Clients are more in tune with more of their truth. Decisions and actions are more correct and change long-lasting.

Before I present the many tools, you need an overview of ways of thinking about change so you'll be ready to use them at the best possible places in the process. As you might expect me to say, being guided by only one model or approach is not nearly as rich with possibilities as understanding and integrating insights from several of the best.

Maps for Change

I offer maps for change so my clients can understand how they actually make transitions. People differ in their pace and approach to change. Appropriately using the maps below, I help my clients develop language to talk about change as well as assisting them to become aware of how they maneuver in a change process. For example, in later sessions (at the end of this chapter), I talked with Sandra about her style of transition, and she began to realize how distasteful she found the gap period between the old situation and the new situation. I use two different maps for transitions, and both provide a basic step-by-step framework: Bill Bridges' model and a map I developed in my graduate studies.

Bridges' Map for Change

In the 70s, when I was working on my master's degree in counseling and focusing on life transition, Bill Bridges, Gail Sheehy, and Daniel Levinson were writing about transition and change. I studied with Bill Bridges, a pioneer in the field of transition management and have loved using his model because most people can quickly identify their place on this continuum, which gives them a map for transitions.[1] The change process becomes less mysterious and more user friendly. Also, using this model, we can identify a client's style for change through learning what they find helpful and what's challenging for them during transitions.

As illustrated below, Bridges' model for change has three stages—endings, the gap, and new beginnings. At the left side is the *ending* stage, when people are letting go of a relationship, job, approach, or other aspect of their lives. This stage can be accompanied by a plethora of emotions, such as grief, sadness, relief, anxiety, and/or excitement.

The middle stage is called *the gap*.[2] The old is gone but the new beginning is not yet formed. Some people avoid this stage and have the new relationship established, or the new job in place, almost before they've let go of the old form. (Of course, with career changes, financial considerations may cause people to skip the gap, even though their style may be different in other types of change.) Some people land in the gap but want to get out as soon as they can. Others enjoy this period and find it's one of the juiciest parts of life. They may find themselves engaged in activities that are a bit foreign to them, like writing poetry, painting, or dancing. One client said to me, "Before I start something new, I just want to exhale. . .to be in the gap and see what comes up rather than force new beginnings." The gap can be exhilarating but also scary. What will happen? What will the future bring? Will I find the right next thing?

Some people avoid the gap.

The last stage in this model is *new beginnings*; this is the stage where the new relationship or the new job begins. Of course, this stage also has emotional aspects, such as excitement, fear of failure, anxiety, or a sense of accomplishment and/or celebration.

Bark Coaching Institute Model of Stages of Change

During my graduate studies I learned something else about transitions: people see changes as either voluntary or involuntary. Younger people experience involuntary changes, such as their family moving, requiring them to change schools and find new friends. When people feel they're involved in an involuntary transition, they're more likely to feel angry and disempowered, and the change process might reflect these feelings. Later, as adults, clients may have decided to leave a job, start a new relationship, or go back to school and change careers. These changes would be considered voluntary changes, and thus, empowering because they come from choice.

Bill Bridges' model works with both involuntary and voluntary transitions. I created my model based on a voluntary change I observed during my master's thesis research—that of nurses leaving the hospital setting and starting private practices. In 1977, I surveyed approximately 400 nurses who were in private practice and received over 300 returns. I found that these nurses could identify with the following change model, which simply adds detail to the model Bridges created.

The first stage I found was an *Incubation Period*, which lasted about a year. A trigger event opened up the nurses' thinking about moving into private practice. Although the idea sparked a new concept, the new idea was quiet and "in the back of their minds." (The role of a private practice for nurses was quite unknown at that time.)

The second stage was an active period of *Pro and Con*. During this period, which lasted about nine months, the nurses were actively considering the change. During this stage, they rehearsed the new role in their minds. They would think, "I could keep track of my income by using a certain type of accounting system." Or, "If someone asked me what kind of services I provided, I could say such and such." As yet they were not taking concrete steps: only pondering them.

I labeled the first action stage *Surrender*. I didn't see this as passive, but as giving in to a compelling new way of being that felt like "the right thing to do." It was described as "surrendering to the correct path" and spoke to a pressure to grow, advance, and develop.

The fourth stage of my model I called the *Awkward Period*, a stage in which nurses talked about not wanting to work the old way anymore but not yet being comfortable with new ways. This stage lasted about six to nine months, and during this time they were starting their practice, learning how to set fees, handle money, schedule appointments, find clients, describe their roles, and generally manage and grow their private practices.

Integration was the stage in which the new role was fully incorporated into the nurses' professional identity. They thought of themselves as nurses in private practice and were comfortable in their new role.

In subsequent years I've added a stage, commonly experienced by those nurses and many I've coached: the *Redefining Period*. What the study pointed out was that after the nurses were comfortable in their new identity, they returned to parts of their old role that were still valuable. It fit the old adage of "Don't throw out the baby with the bathwater." I found from my investigation that this step only occurred when nurses were comfortable with the new role.

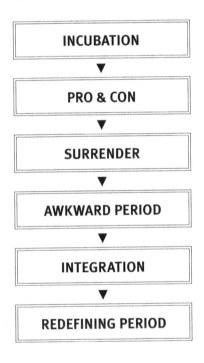

If you're going through any kind of change process, can you identify with a location on one of these maps? If so, where are you? How do you imagine coaching might be helpful in this stage?

The following Life-Line Exercise is a unique way to summarize any type of life event. I use it with my coaching clients to explore transitions. I invite you to use this to look at your life changes and investigate your process and to use the survey with your clients.

EXERCISE: The Life-Line

Turn a blank piece of paper long ways and draw your life line. At one end put zero for your age when you were born. At the other end, put your current age.

- First, mark *major* transitions during your life and label them with a word or two, as in the example below.

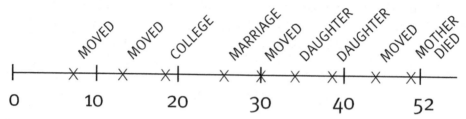

- Next, put an "I" for an involuntary change and a "V" to denote a voluntary transition.
- After completing that, see if you notice a pattern of change in three's or seven's. The old adage of the seven-year itch refers to people changing partners or having an affair after seven years of marriage. The idea that we have seven-year cycles has been borne out in my experience—many people do have major transitions more or less on this schedule, even if they don't have an affair! The second most popular cycle is the three-year cycle. At five years, there may be a period of consideration for change to see if someone wants to go forward for two more years.
- Then write a word or two to describe the kind of support you had during the transitions. Did you have support from family, from friends, from a particular person, from the spiritual aspect of your life, from an animal, or from any other source?
- Now look at the overall pattern. What else do you notice?
- Then go back as see if you left something out, which happens. Once a client put down her divorce, but forgot to record her marriage. Another time someone forgot to add that her mother died. This feedback can be useful to trigger lines of inquiry.

Models of Change Facilitate Awareness

I select one of these two models by deciding which best mirrors my client's transition. Sometimes I'm drawn to use one or the other by how my client describes change. If s/he talks about ending a job or relationship, I describe the Bridges model and aim to explore how s/he executes finishing something. Does my client seem to draw out endings, perhaps telling me that her or his friends are tired of hearing "one more time" when s/he is leaving their job or a relationship? Does my client hang on to the old relationship, pattern, or job until a new one is in hand?

Or my client may be in the time interval between life structures—the gap period marked out in the Bridges' model. I'll learn whether my clients consider the gap to be a time to enjoy, to explore, to find new parts of themselves, or just a time to endure or avoid. With reference to Sample Session 1A, in the beginning, Sandra hated the gap. (Also, she was at her job for seven years, which alerted me to a normal transition time.) Though it didn't happen with Sandra, some clients begin false starts just to get out of that place. Others are able to follow their energy to find what really fits with their life purpose or goals, rather than merely grabbing something that advances them to the next false start. Perhaps my client takes advantage of the gap with career issues but has another pattern of change when it comes to relationships. When I was working with Sandra, she found the concept of the maps of change reassuring.

Each degree of awareness can help my clients learn more about how to change and become more whole. If my client is describing a process of rehearsing new behaviors in a voluntary transition, I switch into my change model and describe that map.

Coaching Readiness

Besides learning about where clients are in a change process that may have begun before they met me, I explore possible gaps between people's stated goals and their actual readiness to change. Many people start into coaching and other self-care practices because of a doctor's diagnosis, some kind of life crisis, or because important people in their life advise them to do something. I need to know is my client actually ready to make a change now, or is change in the distant future? Also, I've found that someone comes for coaching in the middle of one shift and along the way discovers that another change is necessary, though they're less willing to change that other thing. In the beginning of our coaching sessions, Sandra was certainly ready for a change in career but not at all interested in altering her nutrition or exercise behaviors.

I find James Prochaska's readiness scale essential in this type of assessment.[3] In his groundbreaking book about change, published in 1994, he shares that his motivation to find out how people change stemmed from his personal frustration of trying to have his father stop drinking. Because his father denied that his drinking and depression were a problem, and Prochaska and his family were powerless to change that perception or motivate him to change, he ended up dying from the effects of alcoholism. Prochaska devoted his life to examining how and why people change, enrolling the help of two other acclaimed psychologists to study more than 1000 people who were able to change on their own. He created a transtheoretical approach that combined psychoanalysis, behaviorialism, cognitive therapy, existential philosophy, and humanistic psychology. He and his group concluded that change actually unfolds through a series of six stages: precontemplation, contemplation, preparation, action, maintenance, completion and they developed interventions for each stage.

96   CHAPTER 4: Helping People Navigate Change

1. Pre-contemplation—People at this stage can't see a reason for changing their behavior. They're not coaching clients yet, and they probably wouldn't hire a coach because they don't have any intention of changing. Most pre-contemplators have no insight into their own behavior, and if they do move into the next stage it's frequently because of pressure from family or friends. When this is the case, the change may be short-lived because it's not coming from an internal commitment but motivated by a need to reduce tension or stress put on them by others. Pre-contemplators resist change because they deny a problem and choose to remain ignorant despite obvious indicators to the contrary. An example would be smokers who continue to smoke despite serious health problems. Their behaviors include these:
- *Denial*—"I don't really have a problem."
- *Minimization*—"Well, I may have a little problem, but it isn't really significant."
- *Rationalization* (good excuses)—"I need a way to relax, and smoking helps me."
- *Projection, displacement, and turning outward*—"I would change but my spouse is always getting after me. Who could change with his constant criticism?"
- *Internalization and turning inward*—"I can't make any progress with this problem anyway. I just don't have the will power. I've never been able to do it before, why would I think I could do it now."

While people typically don't hire a coach in this stage, they may already be working with a coach about some other issue. For example, the client may be in coaching to create an action plan for graduate education but in the pre-contemplation stage about a major health concern that does impact going back to school.

> *Are you at the pre-contemplation stage with something in your life now? What's the most common pre-contemplation behavior you find yourself using—denial, minimizing, rationalization, projection, displacement, turning outward, internalization, or turning inward?*

How do clients move into greater readiness? Consciousness-raising is the intervention of choice for a client who's in this stage. Sometimes the pre-contemplator needs information and awareness to help them move forward. Identifying which of the defenses the client tends to use can help to target the consciousness-raising. For example, if a pre-contemplator is using internalization and feels that progress isn't an option, a coach can inquire into past successes—even if they were small—and build on those examples. If a person is projecting and raising issues about not being able to do something because of someone else, s/he may be open to inquiry into what impact others truly have and how unhelpful patterns could be changed.

An approach that's become increasingly popular in healthcare is called Motivational Interviewing (MI), which was created in 1983 to improve outcomes in problem drinking.[4] Although this method shares some basic tenets of coaching (partnership, active listening, asking powerful questions, addressing resistance), to me it feels quite different from coaching. When I'm coaching clients, they have the complete control to address any issue they want during a session, and we spend as much time as possible in that Square 2 described in chapter 1.

Granted that in many applications of MI interviewers ask if clients want to talk about the ambivalence, the method is still focused on ambivalence to change in a scripted and fairly rigid manner. In MI, the interviewer often uses a 1-10 scale to measure interest, confidence, and motivation. In some styles of MI, interviewers make a direct, simple statement of their opinion of the benefits of making the change, advise a reasonable goal, restate only the part of a client's statement that reflects wanting to make a change, or state the entire ambivalence but end the paraphrasing with the negative aspect so the client hears that statement last. However, they do also acknowledge that clients are in control of making their own decisions and validate that position if they're not ready to change. I don't want to throw the baby out with the bathwater here and feel that questions about interest, confidence, and motivation to change can be used in coaching when appropriate and in a non-scripted manner. Despite the differences from coaching, I'm encouraged and excited to see the application of MI grow because it's a great improvement over practitioners only giving advice. Now that some healthcare systems have been using MI for several years, they are taking the next step to set up a more complete partnership and educating their staff in coaching.

CHAPTER 4: Helping People Navigate Change

2. Contemplation—People are in the contemplative stage when they accept that change is needed and begin to think about doing it in the future. Coaching can be helpful in this stage, but people usually don't hire a coach when they're not committed to the change process. However, as we discussed, a coach may already be working with someone who's in the contemplation stage. A typical statement is "I want to change my job, but I'm not ready yet. I'll think about it after the holidays." The contemplator is not quite ready for action steps and may stay in this stage for a while. Consciousness-raising is as helpful here as for those in pre-contemplation.

An emotional trigger, event, or thought may quickly move the person into the next stage. For example, the death of a friend may be the catalyst for someone to change health habits or rethink their sense of purpose. Other times, people move slowly into the next step. If they really feel stuck and uncomfortable, they might hire a coach to help them move toward the next stage. For example, a coach working with a client who smokes might ask, "How would your life be changed if you didn't smoke?" Meeting clients where they are in the change process is key. In this case, it involves bringing awareness to the smoking habit and how life may be different without smoking.

> *Looking at the issue you identified in the last section, what would it take for you to do something about moving from pre-contemplation to the next step of contemplation?*

3. Preparation—When people reach the preparation stage, they're planning to take action soon. This stage is so important that if people don't take the time and energy to prepare for change, they're less likely to make a lasting change. For several reasons coaching is suited to helping people in this stage.

First, there's often a desire to cut short this stage and move quickly into action, but that's not wise. The awareness generated in the coaching process can help clients take small, steady steps in making plans that are unique and designed for them—and even to identify possible unexpected events that may interfere with the change. Developing these plans may reduce the possibility of false starts that undermine motivation and success. Second, benefits of the old pattern are still available, even though the negative parts are obvious too. If the person does not replace the benefits of the old behavior with benefits of a new behavior, lasting change is very unlikely. Finding the benefits and identifying how they'll be replaced sometimes requires practice and evaluation. Motivation is very important in this stage, and is the third reason coaching is valuable at this stage because the coach can assist the client in holding the new goal day to day, using methods such as imagery, self talk, and other tools. The fourth reason involves accountability, and coaches can help with follow through, for example if the client sets a date for change. Lastly, coaches can help clients set up the kind of support system that will be useful, which is often key, especially in the maintenance stage when the new benefits might not be flowing smoothly and effectively.

4. Action—This phase of change is the busiest and requires energy and commitment. It gets the most attention from others since people are seeing the results of the change. Again, coaching can be very useful during this stage—helping clients to evaluate and modify the plan that was conceived in the previous stage. During the preparation stage, the type and amount of support was set up. Does the person want praise, and if so, when, by whom, and in what way? How are planned rewards working? Is the person able to feel the new benefits?

Coaches can help the person set up environmental controls. It's important to avoid triggers of the old behavior. Especially in the beginning of the action phase it might be best for your clients not to have their favorite ice cream in the refrigerator when they're starting to eliminate sugar. It's maybe not a good idea to carry cigarettes in a pocket when quitting smoking. However, it is also important for the client to be exposed to cues or triggers little by little without responding with the old behavior. Using imagery is a good beginning method to do this and can also be used to practice on weaker cues and build up to the stronger ones. Coaching can help the client plan, practice, and evaluate these types of techniques so they can do them by themselves as situations arise.

During the action phase, clients are accomplishing much and often need to be reminded of their progress. Keeping a good, clear vision and continuing to build motivation is vital in this stage. Clients can become discouraged and anxious when they deal with the day-to-day elimination of an old behavior and the building of a new one. Approaches to stress management come in handy here and can be supported by coaching.

5. Maintenance—The action phase lasts for several months, and the first and second month is when relapse is most common. However, the next stage (maintenance) has some hidden dangers. Even after five or six months of successfully behaving in a new way, going back to the old behavior can still seem like an option. Social pressures, special events or situations, and internal stress are all threats to maintaining the newly developed change. The old habit still holds an attraction, and temptations to return to it can be difficult to anticipate.

As the preparation and action phases fade in clients' memories, they might think that the change was a fairly easy process, and indulging in just one pack of cigarettes or a giant hot fudge sundae won't really hurt anything. As the illustration shows, a person might have one part of them saying, "Hey, live a little!" and another part saying, "Stay the course." Coaching can help during the maintenance phase by helping clients address these issues. Perhaps there's a middle road between staying with the achieved change and sliding back to the beginning. Coaches encourage clients to use this time wisely and learn as much about the old ways as possible. When are they tempted, or when do they slip back into the old pattern? What helps get them back to the new pattern? How do they feel on body, mind, energy, and spirit levels? Is there some part of the old pattern that's still useful?

Sometimes this is the period when the client realizes that a lifestyle change is not just for six months but is really a *life*style change. This new realization calls for an increase in motivation, vision, benefits, and rewards. Again, coaching sessions during this time can help clients achieve their goals.

6. *Completion*—In this last stage the new behavior is part of the person's life, like brushing teeth at bedtime: most people just do it. Coaches participate through suggesting review and celebration. Each step needs celebration, and certainly the end does too. Often we complete something and go to the next change. We don't allow any time for a festive occasion and a thoughtful review of what could be learned from moving through this change process into completion.

Using Models of Change

A word of caution is necessary about all types of linear models of human behavior and dynamics. Linear progression from one stage to the next is often not as tidy and clear-cut as our models suggest. So, what's the best way for you to work with a client as they cycle through the change process? The answer is that you meet each person where s/he is in the change process.

For example, I was working with a client who usually completed his homework, but for several weeks, he wasn't doing it. After some exploration, we found that he was not ready for action yet, so, he began to take steps from where he actually was in the change process—in preparation. Or, let's say you have a client who stopped smoking, but then started up again. How might you work with them through this? One area you might look at is whether the need that was being fulfilled by smoking continued being met after the client quit. For instance, if smoking was helping the client to relieve stress, how did the client get stress relief when not smoking? We'll examine other ways to explore this with a client when we discuss behavior patterns in Part Two.

When we revisit Sandra's coaching (Sample Session 1A), we can see from the first few sentences that she was in the preparation stage for career transition—ready and raring to go—and just needed awareness and a plan to find her new place. However, when it came to exercise and nutrition, she was in pre-contemplation at the beginning of our work. She knew she had something to change but wasn't interested in addressing that area of her life until her career issue was resolved. We'll conclude Part One with the rest of Sandra's story.

Sally Arnold, RN, MA, AHN
From Contemplation to Preparation for Action

I needed nursing CEs and didn't want to take a "filler" class, but had no specific sense of how learning coaching might change my life. I'm halfway through the training now, and my intuition tells me that learning this is the start of something new and exciting.

It's hard to describe the experience, but one way is to think about a very large Christmas present that you unwrap to find a smaller box, and then a smaller box, and another, until you get to the last one that's very small. For me this class is just the opposite! I had a brief experience as a coaching client (in another system) and the experience was very mental and linear, though useful, so I thought I was signing up for a "small box" class that would approach coaching in a similar way.

However, as this training continues, the little box is turning into one larger, then one larger, and even though I'm only halfway through the training, the boxes are expanding almost to infinity. I'm beginning to truly understand what a holistic and integral approach to coaching can offer. It's as if the sides, top, and bottom are gone—so I guess, no more box. The gift is that I can use all of me in this coaching model.

Sample Session 1B—Change Process Interrupted!

Sometimes life's twists and turns facilitate transitions. Before Sandra's third coaching session, she completed the assessments in my "welcome to my coaching practice" packet, and from her responses, I realized that she was a kinesthetic learner, had a fiery personal constitution, often avoided change and found support from friends and family during transitions.

During the next two weeks, Sandra continued to work on moving toward her goal of finding out what she wanted to do, and then early one morning, I got a call from Sandra. She was crying. I said, "What happened?!"

Between sobs she said she'd just been notified that her son, who was stationed in Afghanistan, had fallen down a ravine, breaking his pelvis, knee, and collarbone. The officer said that her son wanted her to know that he was really okay and for them not to worry.

This shows how the focus of coaching can shift and incorporate new critical issues that arise while still addressing long-term concerns. Needless to say, Sandra and her husband were very upset, as well as somewhat relieved. Her son was flown to Washington to have surgery, so both Sandra and her husband went there to be with him. Sandra and I talked often during the next two weeks. I continued to coach her, but at her request I shifted into a consultant role. In my role as coach, I heard that it would be useful to shift to a different modality of interaction rather than force coaching on her at the time. She had questions about basic anatomy, physiology, and how hospitals work, and my many years in nursing informed my knowledge of these topics.

After she returned home, our coaching sessions refocused on her career issue. She said, "Now that things are settling down a bit with Bruce (her son), I'm feeling that push to leave my job again, but really, I'm lucky to have it. They've been great about my emergency family leave, and because I know my job so well, it's been pretty easy to keep things in order during this stressful time. I feel very fortunate. Their being so understanding makes it hard for me to even think about leaving. So much has happened these last several weeks, not only with my work situation but with my ability to listen to my inner voice and to help Bruce and Dave (her husband) because, of course, he went through a lot too. After all, he was in Vietnam, and although he doesn't talk much about those times, I know that it brought back memories for him because he was injured as well."

I commented, "Bruce's injury has impacted each of you a great deal."

"Well, more than you know," added Sandra, "It's introduced me to a whole new world, and I'm wondering if it has something to do with a new direction."

"What is the new direction?" I asked.

"Since I've spent so much time over the last weeks at hospitals, I've seen people there—not all of them, of course, but many—who are really dedicated to helping people. At Walter Reed, and also at Bruce's current rehabilitation hospital, I've befriended many families. It's like we became instantly connected since we were all in the same boat. I don't know exactly what's happening, but something is," said Sandra.

"Would you like to explore the change now?" I inquired.

Sandra was silent. Finally she asked, "I don't know where to go with this. Can you introduce one of your exercises to help me learn more about this?"

"Okay," I said. Let me take a breath and see what intuitively comes to me." I took a deep breath and the magic wand tools instantly came into my awareness. "Would you be interested in pretending that you have a magic wand and could create any kind of job you wanted?" I asked.

"That sounds strange but interesting," said Sandra. "So let me see, I have a magic wand in my hand now and am waving it around. It has lots of sparkles. It's really fun, and as I wave it in the air, it spells out the word 'meaningful' and my heart area warms up again. This is very strange, but I am learning to trust these feeling more. I want to go back to that idea of being radioactive. Somehow, this really is a clue. I see myself in communications or something like that—teaching or talking. I don't know, but something is here."

"How interesting. The word 'meaningful' comes up again, and communication seems to be key to your inquiry." I commented.

"Correct. I did take some college courses in communication. I saw the impact that communications can have on helping people change or move to a new place. Yes," she said quietly, "this is right on. Now I feel like a Geiger counter, and as I imagine walking toward the communication field, the noise is picking up. . .click, click, click." For one of her coaching homework projects, she decided to call her former communication professor for information about what was happening in this field.

Just as I thought that Sandra was honing in on her goal, she took a different turn and said that her work situation had changed. Her company was struggling financially, with many people being laid off, resulting in her continuing with her regular job as well as taking over a new division. At first she was fairly overwhelmed, but as she began to make progress, she delighted in her mastery. Bruce had almost fully recovered and was transferred to a new military base for retraining. During the next eight weeks, most of our coaching sessions dealt with challenges in her expanded job and her feelings about Bruce reenlisting, going for more training, and staying in the military.

Sandra emailed one day and asked if we could reschedule our session to an earlier time, and we picked a new day. When she began to talk, she sounded very serious. I began to wonder if something had happened to Bruce, because during our last call, he was struggling with some recurring health issues due to his injuries, and as a follow up to our last contact, I asked if Bruce had had a setback.

"No," she said, "I have. I've had a setback, or maybe a set forward, or maybe a set sideways, or a set down, or a set up, or really I guess an upset. I don't know, but now that my job is slowing down a bit and I've figured out how to manage my new three-ring circus, I'm having those old feelings about that word 'meaningful.'" She began to cry, "At first this job felt meaningful, and it was wonderful. It certainly has advantages, which we both know, and I don't want to even think about it anymore! As I look back at the last several months, in some unexpected way, the self-confidence I gained in managing my old department and my new one is actually giving me the courage to finally move. Besides that, I'm grinding my teeth again, and we know what that means—parts of me are fighting again. I know I need to listen to all of them, and I need to move!"

"Okay," I said, "what do you want to do?"

"I want to google the word 'communications' and my town and see what comes up. In fact, I want to do it right now!" she exclaimed.

"Wonderful," I responded.

"I'm on it and I will let you know what I find out!" she said jubilantly. We hung up and about an hour later, she emailed with some options she'd discovered, but she said nothing set off her Geiger counter. She said she was on a mission now. During her next coaching session, she did continue to narrow her focus and interest using her inner voice, which was often drawn to the word 'meaningful.' The next day she called, ecstatic. "I've found it!" she said, "I've already sent off my application!"

"What is it?" I exclaimed.

"Can you believe it? There's a job with a private communications network in the next town that's producing education programs for veterans who've been injured. It even has a family component to the project! It's a non-profit, and they are looking for me. I'm a match for this at every level. I love their website. I love what they say about their values and company culture. Now it remains to be seen if their company values really drive the organization, but it looks promising. My initial contact involved a person who was clear, organized, and seemed sincere about their mission and vision. If I could get this job, I would leave my current position in a heartbeat. The salary is lower, but not if I consider the real cost of staying in my job—antacid and headache medicines, doctor and dental bills, and who knows what else would have developed. Some of my work at the new company can be done from home, which would save me money and time commuting. And how much value can I put on peace of mind, feeling aligned with my purpose, and a good night's sleep? Honestly, I can do with a little less money. The tradeoff is worth it."

"Bravo!" I said, "Sounds like a great opportunity."

We continued our coaching relationship for a couple more months because having worked through this major transition she was ready to take on lifestyle issues, such as exercise and nutrition. Change is the result of life experiences and the way we react to them. In terms of her career transition, Sandra felt truly fulfilled, said she was happy, and everyone around her could see the positive change. She even went on to be part of a team that won some national awards for communication programs.

---

[1] Bill Bridges, *Transitions: Making Sense of Life's Changes*, Revised 25th Anniversary Edition (Cambridge, MA: First Da Capo Press, Perseus Books, 2004).

[2] Bill Bridges later changed the name of this middle step from the gap to the neutral zone. Having first learned the stage as the gap, I really much prefer this label because it seems to describe the stage better. When people are in the "gap," they rarely consider it a neutral zone. They relate that they're experiencing many feelings, questions, and processes.

[3] James Prochaska, John Norcross, and Carolo Diclemente, *Changing for Good: A Revolutionary Six-Stage Program for Overcoming Bad Habits and Moving Your Life Positively Forward* (New York: Harper Collins, 1994).

[4] Stephen Rollnick, William Miller, and Christopher Butler, *Motivational Interviewing in Healthcare: Helping Patients Change Behavior* (New York: Guildford Press, 2008).

Part Two

When I began teaching my method, I wanted students to benefit from my years of learning what worked and how various techniques could be integrated. I wanted to organize and succinctly impart fundamental knowledge from many disciplines, and to systematically present the many coaching tools necessary for extraordinary coaching. In partnership with Dea Daniels, a close friend and colleague, I created a framework for looking at holistic healing, which I then expanded and used for classifying coaching tools.

My coaching model, like our framework for holistic healing, is based on Jean Gebser's book *The Ever-Present Origin*.[1] Looking at philosophy, poetry, music, visual arts, architecture, work on the psyche, religion, physics, and the other natural sciences, Gebser identified the emergence and subsequent collapse of specific structures of consciousness during history. Gebser's twentieth century Western examination of consciousness is supported by writings from over a thousand years ago.[2] The structures of consciousness have also been supported more recently by the work of Anna Wise, who worked with special EEG technology by which the structures can be traced and analyzed.[3]

As a coach who comes from a whole person perspective, I found Gebser's five structures of consciousness to be a useful framework for classifying coaching tools. In essence, I've created a user-friendly, fun and easy file cabinet to contain and categorize valuable tools, based on Gebser's classification. We'll explore the different file drawers in more depth in the chapters throughout this section. Let's take a deeper look at the model and relate it to coaching tools.

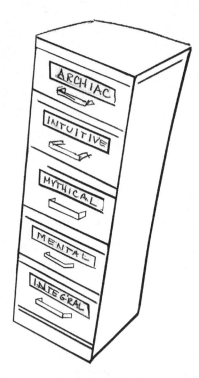

How Developmental Models Work

Since Gebser's model traces human beings from earlier times until the present, it can be used as a developmental model. Are you familiar with how developmental models work?[4]

Development proceeds from simple to complex. Someone or something starts with a basic form or idea and then grows bigger and more multifaceted. An example is my work in expanding the core coach competencies. Another example is a baby who moves from simple crawling to the more developmentally complex processes of walking. The baby starts learning language with simple sounds and words and proceeds to more complex sentences.

The developmental process is usually considered to have a driving force of its own. Ask any parent of a toddler who finds the child in front of stairs. The young child is compelled to go up and down the stairs, over and over again: driven to master this skill and to explore. The baby's also compelled to learn to speak in order to communicate.

Aspects of earlier stages of development are sometimes still available, even as more complex phases come into existence. This makes sense—as an adult we can still crawl and roll around, even though we learned to walk long ago. And we can still use the basic letters and words we learned as a baby, even though now we can read and write words and sentences.

Let's look at Gebser's model, which addresses consciousness. What do we mean by consciousness? In everyday speech, we refer to someone who is conscious as awake, aware, and responsive to the environment. Here we'll define it as a way of thinking that informs a person's actions.[5] A simple example is looking at someone who recycles plastic bags and paper, or turns off lights and a computer not in use. The person is conscious, awake, and aware that these decisions affect sustainable living and planetary wellbeing.

Archaic

Gebser investigated the fundamental awareness and actions of human beings, considered collectively, and saw broad orientations that changed over time. He called the first and earliest structure of consciousness the *Archaic* stage. The archaic represents no separation between person, environment, and creative energy. "All is well" in this stage of thinking and being.

According to Gebser, these stages of consciousness aren't only present in collective human development, but also in individual development: the Archaic has some similarities to our early experience as a fetus. At that time, baby and mother are one, and, with this connection, all is well. Although our goal is not to go back to the undifferentiated state experienced by the infant, our organism is familiar with that quality of oneness and can carry it forward as we develop beyond the mental, into the integral. Coaching tools that could be associated with this state are presented in chapter 8. They facilitate a sense of connection with a greater wholeness, taking us out of exclusive identification with our small personal selves:
- meditation, contemplation, and prayer;
- being in the now—in present time;
- sense of life purpose or meaning based on a true and deep connection to source;
- compassion;
- three faces of God.

In my work with Sandra (Sample Sessions 1A and 1B), tuning into the Archaic sense of connectedness brought inner knowing of what was purposeful. Her sense of wanting more meaning demonstrated her desire to connect more deeply with her own motivating forces.

Intuitive

In the Archaic, everything is completely merged, but in this next structure of consciousness, some separation is apparent, according to Gebser. During the historical period where this structure was dominant, people lacked a sense of individual self, acting in terms of the group or tribe, which was slightly differentiated from nature or the environment.[6] In this stage, people had no sense of time or space and a close association through using instinct and intuition. There was no recognition of linear causality but a sense of an allowing.[7]

Gebser entitles this structure of consciousness *Magic* and points out that the word "magic" is related to words such as "make," "mechanism," and "might," referring to a probable common root.[8] When we think of magic, we think of something happening for no reason. An ill person has a spontaneous remission, or some desired positive event happens unexpectedly, as if by magic. The tools in this structure of consciousness relate to subtle energy, and include drawing upon intuition and individual and group energy—all elements that cannot ordinarily be seen by the naked eye. When we access that older structure of consciousness, still alive in us, we are able to imagine and associate, recognizing how things intertwine and are interchangeable. For us moderns, the magic structure of consciousness is a capacity we can draw upon rather than our dominant worldview.

When some people today hear the word *magic*, they react negatively— they quickly dismiss it, along with all that's connected to it. However, the Magic structure of consciousness is rich and offers much to our lives and to coaching. To avoid the unfortunate rejection of valuable ways of thinking and being, I've renamed this structure of consciousness, *Intuitive*, underscoring the root of the magic when people of that time acted from intuition and instinct. This repositioning acknowledges the underpinning of this structure and may allow more people to appreciate its inherent gifts.

We can look at this stage in terms of individual development—a time when the young child believes in such things as Santa Claus, magic wands and the tooth fairy. A young child doesn't have a clear sense of time or a clear sense of self as separate from other people or the environment and often acts instinctively. Chapter 7 will give you more information about coaching tools that tap into that intertwined and magic sense of possibility:
- walking the talk;
- intuition;
- silence;
- magic wand;
- accessing energy in the body—centers (chakras), pathways and flows;

- tapping into group energy among people—species learning, classroom energy, family and group constellation, Law of Attraction;
- spending time in nature;
- food, mood, and nourishment log;
- ritual.

Looking again at my first session with Sandra, remember that she used the magic wand that comes from the Magic—or Intuitive—part of coaching. It helped her break through her usual boundaries and analyze her situation from a completely new vantage point.

Mythical

The third structure of consciousness in Gebser's model is the *Mythical*, pointing to a time when people discovered a new perspective. Nature was now seen as separate from people and could be observed. Cave paintings began to portray mouths on figures, and language became more developed during this time. Myths or stories were created to explain nature. Gods and mysteries were not symbols but alive as realities that impacted people's lives.

In individual development, this is the time when the child develops greater language skills. Every parent knows this stage as the land of "why"—children frequently ask questions in an effort to understand themselves and the world around them. The child is beginning to see the distinction between self and other and is also interested in learning how to navigate in that relationship. As they develop a sense of time, children may ask questions like "How long will you be gone?" They live in a pre-rational and pre-causal world but want to move to greater understanding of the next level. We bring the Mythical forward in our quest to see ourselves in terms of interdependence, relationship, and context, using Mythical tools presented in chapter 6:
- understanding personal constitution;
- learning empowerment language;
- story;
- imagery;
- dialogue;
- affirmations.

Most of the first session with Sandra (Sample Session 1A) applied a dialogue tool—imagining warring parts of herself talking to one another. This tool helped by giving her more objectivity, clearer insight into the phenomenon, and more acceptance of what was going on. I took that basic tool a bit further by asking her to incorporate a holistic perspective and bring in body and spirit. Even though from a logical mental viewpoint she didn't understand how this imagined dialog worked, it brought insight and catalyzed physical changes. The dialog was also the basis for her homework.

Mental

The fourth developmental stage in humankind—the *Mental* structure—is going to sound familiar. People living indiscriminately in this "reality" operate from a very clear, separate sense of self. Nature is distinct from people, and they may think they can control nature. Things can be clearly defined, divided, classified, and observed. The key elements of this stage are logical, sequential, and mechanistic thinking. The whole is broken down into the sum of its parts, and how they might relate to each other is ignored. The scientific method is an exemplar.

As we look again at the growing child, this is the stage when abstract thought develops. Concepts can be created and understood. Self is at the center in a more complex way. The late childhood years are an especially ripe time for coming to see how cause and effect work, for individuation, and ego development. In teen years the young person ponders this: "It's all about me, but wait a minute—who am I?" Needless to say, these developmental tasks continue as people enter adulthood and later, and they become more refined. With a sense of self comes the possibility of discernment and accountability, and in chapter 5, you can learn about some mental coaching tools:
- assessing learning types;
- critical thinking and decision-making;
- 1-10 scale;
- choosing between options;
- pie chart;
- prioritizing;
- To Do and Ta Da lists;
- examining behavior patterns;
- plans and timelines.

Most people with a Western cultural background view the world through a Mental lens. Sandra was aware of her mental perspective, and together we noticed how uncomfortable she was outside of that orientation in the beginning of our coaching sessions.

Integral

Gebser and others think we're currently moving into the fifth structure of consciousness—the Integral. When we look at Gebser's description of the Integral structure, we see that it's a combination of all of the above. Because the other stages intertwine, interact, and amplify each other, the sum of the whole is *greater* than the sum of the parts. One structure is not seen as more important; rather, they're all important, and accessing the gifts from each of them allows for a more fulfilling experience. Time, space, and causality are not constrained.[9] An Integral perspective allows skillful integration of the coaching tools presented here, and chapter 9 gives examples and possibilities. An Integral perspective helps brings clients to those "ah ha" moments of holistic knowing.

Remember what we've said about developmental models, and how earlier stages can still be accessed? This is the basis of the Integral structure of consciousness.

Accessing the Gifts of Earlier Structures

In contemporary culture we can see a resurgence of interest in aspects of ourselves that arose during earlier stages of consciousness, though we don't go backward and lose the selves we've grown into but rather enrich them by this awareness. Remembering the Archaic we bring forward the possibility of self as something larger than the personal. Seeking this, many turn to meditation practices from India, China, and other traditional religious systems. More people than ever are using prayer and meditation to deal with their hectic and stressful lives.

Certainly the popularity of the Harry Potter books and movies attest that people are fascinated with the Intuitive or Magic structure of consciousness, seen through modern Mental eyes. The first novel was released in 1997 and the seven-book series in 2008 had sold more than 400 million copies and had been translated into 67 languages.[10] The books have spawned movies, video games, and a plethora of merchandise, making one writer call Harry Potter the "15 billion dollar man."[11]

The Mythical structure of consciousness is being tapped into by a return to oral history and storytelling and interest in myths and archetypes—again, understood and used from Mental/Integral perspectives. The National Institute of Adult Continuing Education published an article describing the effectiveness of a narrative approach to learning and change, even in the workplace.[12]

Each structure of consciousness begins in a pure form, or, as Gebser refers to it, the *efficient form* of the structure. Over time, the structure begins to degenerate and becomes *deficient*, calling for a mutation to another form. Currently we're experiencing the deficient form of the Mental structure of consciousness, setting the stage for the emergence of the Integral structure.

Examples of the deficient Mental abound and point to the lack of understanding of the connection among parts of a situation and too great a focus on personal point of view. For instance, many people deny or ignore the link between personal health and the health of the planet. In another example, using police or military resources to contain or diminish resistance or terrorism without addressing their root causes—poverty, lack of education, hunger, and joblessness—does little to provide lasting change. Taking a pill to mask a message from the body about some growing malfunction or pathology is not useful in the long run. Looking for and addressing the core cause is bound to restore health and healing.

You can probably recognize many other examples of the deficient Mental and feel the shift to the Integral structure of consciousness. Perhaps you can observe how you operate from a more multi-level way of thinking and being. There might be a moment when you are in a meditative or prayerful state, do not feel much separation from others and our environment, and could say that all is well (Archaic). Using your intuition, you might start seeing synchronicities and wonder if things are happening magically. The Mythical might be part of your thinking as you hold stories about yourself and events of the day. The Mental may be functioning as you identify the next step of a plan or describe your progress toward an objective on a scale from 1 to 10.

A Note about Coaching Tools and the Structures of Consciousness

Coaching from an Integral perspective is so very effective, but without a structure or system for categorizing the tools it's daunting to figure out how to cover them in trainings and how to use them in practice. That's why I've structured the BCI model around the structures of consciousness. Even though I've listed many coaching tools for each, the list isn't definitive. However, I like this theoretical framework because as you and I discover new modalities or tools, the model seems to have a place for them, and there's plenty of room for coaches to choose tools they most relate to.

Whole books could be written about many of the tools. Some, such as Ayurveda (the East Indian healing system that lays out a way to think about and use personal constitution or fields of energy), take lifetimes to master, and yet we can draw from them when appropriate, acknowledging our level of expertise. I've included tools that I'm not an authority on, but know enough to find useful in my coaching practice. My goal is to include enough information about each tool so you can see how it could benefit the coaching partnership.

Some approaches, such as family constellation work, are covered in greater detail, not because they're more important to coaching but because they may be less well known and yet inspirational. Some areas are very important but so much has been written about them that I'll refer you to other resources so you can learn more if you're interested.

All models have their shortcomings, and this one is no exception. Sometimes it seems that originators try to fit square pegs into round holes to fit the theory. As you read the chapters ahead you may think that a certain tool belongs in a different structure of consciousness than

I have listed. Believe me, over the years, I have moved a few of them around. For example, people who are working professionally with flower essences, energy, Ayurveda, or Chinese Traditional Medicine might be offended that these tools are listed in the Intuitive chapter. They might argue that there's increasing research in quantum physics and other areas of science to support the energetic principles, and that these modalities should really be considered Mental tools. However, no tool relates to one aspect of consciousness only. I've looked for the dominant or key characteristic of each tool to access where it belongs, paying special attention to when they originated.

The more we become Integral—thinking and acting from all of the structures of consciousness—the more we can see how most of the tools could have an aspect related to each structure of consciousness. However, my main goal in practice, in teaching coaching, and in this book, is to make things user-friendly—simple but substantive. Students have found that classifying the tools this way allows them to come from a very broad base and to work with all kinds of clients who operate from various ways of thinking and being. I hope that the placement of tools and how the model accommodates others you might know will serve you well.

Because we're more familiar with the Mental model, we'll start with the present and go backwards in time. Chapter 5 is about the Mental aspect of coaching, chapter 6 the Mythical aspect, chapter 7 the Intuitive aspect, and chapter 8 the Archaic aspect. We bring them together in chapter 9—the Integral aspect of coaching. The sample session in that chapter is set in a different format, presenting what we talked about on the right, with my thoughts, intuitions, and sensations as I work with my clients given on the left. I hope this helps you better understand the coaching process as she or he considers options. Throughout all of Part Two you'll find questions for you to consider, set apart in boxes. You can skip them, but participating as we go brings this material to life for you and enacts our learning partnership.

PART TWO: The Toolkit

---

[1] His work has formed the basis of a number of works, in particular Ken Wilber's *Up from Eden*, Rudolf Bahro's *Logik der Rettung* (translated into English as *Avoiding Social and Ecological Disaster*), Hugo Enomiya-Lassalle's *Living in the New Consciousness*, Daniel Kealey's *Revisioning Environmental Ethics*, Georg Feuerstein's *Wholeness or Transcendence*, William Irwin Thompson's *Coming into Being*, and Eric Mark Kramer's *Modern/Postmodern: Off the Beaten Path of Antimodernism*.

[2] Rudolph Ballentine, *Kali Rising:Foundational Principles of Tantra for a Transforming Planet*. (Ballentine, NC: Tantrikster Press, 2010), 206. The author is referring here to the Manduka Upanishad, which lays out realms of consciousness that parallel Jean Gebser's Structure of Consciousness.

[3] Anna Wise, *The High Performance Mind: Mastering Brainwaves for Insight, Healing, and Creativity* (NY: Jeremy P. Tarcher/Penguin, 1997).

[4] Although Gebser says his model is not developmental, it appears to operate that way. He used the concept of mutations for more complex development.

[5] Of course, there are different realms of consciousness, as addressed in the Mandukya Upanishad and many other texts, but for describing a coaching model, looking at the waking state of consciousness in this manner seems to be the most useful.

[6] Jean Gebser, *The Ever Present Origin,* trans. Noel Barstad with Algis Mickunas (Athens, OH: Ohio University Press, 1985), 9.

[7] Ballentine. *Kali Rising*, 206.

[8] Gebser, *Ever Present Origin*, 46.

[9] Ballentine, *Kali Rising*, 207.

[10] Alison Flood, "Potter Tops 400 Million Sales," *theBookseller.com*, June 17, 2008, www.thebookseller.com/news/potter-tops-400-million-sales.html.

[11] Beth Snyder Bulik, "Harry Potter, the $15 billion man," *Advertizing Age*, July 16, 2007, www.adage.com/article/news/harry-potter-15-billion-man/119212.

[12] Stefanie Constanze Reissner, "Learning by Story-telling? Narratives in the Study of Work-based Learning," *Journal of Adult and Continuing Education* 10, no. 2, (Autumn 2004): 99-113.

Chapter 5
The Mental Structure of Consciousness in Coaching

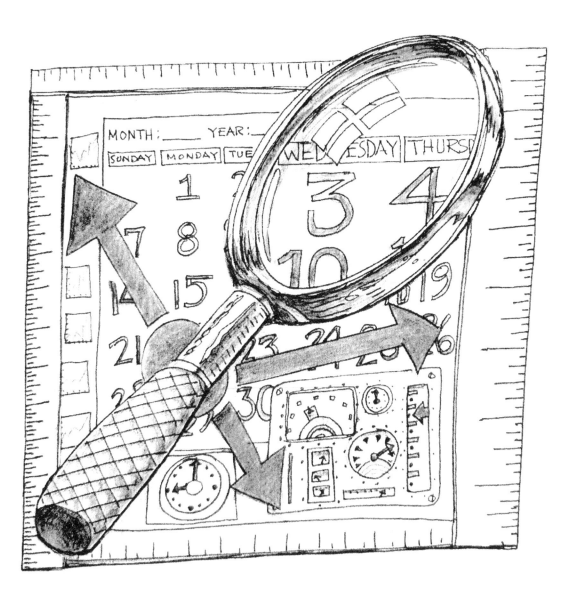

Sample Session 2A—"Help, I'm Falling Apart!"

"My doctor handed me a whole bunch of papers and told me I needed to change everything. I can't eat what I've been eating for years, and I have to start exercising. I don't think she heard that I have a desk job and a long commute, and I don't have time to exercise. My wife does all the cooking and I looooove her cooking. It's just like my mother's, and it's the food I grew up eating. She said I'm pre-diabetic, and if I don't change my ways, I'll get diabetes and have to give myself a shot of insulin every day. I guess I could have my wife give me the shot, but that sounds awful. My grandmother had diabetes, and she had a terrible time with it and lost her foot in the last years of her life. I don't know what to do," says Frank in a pressured pace and tone.

"Hummmm. All of that sounds overwhelming and frightening," I say slowly, empathetically, and seriously.

"Yes, and that's not all," he continues. "My blood sugar numbers are high, but it's hard for me to believe that I'm really on the edge of diabetes. I think they made a mistake because I feel okay. I mean I'm not as young as I used to be, but everyone gets older, and I think of myself as still young. After all, I just turned sixty, and these days that's not really old. I hope I don't start falling apart now that I'm in this new decade," states Frank, quickly and with conviction.

"Okay, what I'm hearing is that you've been told that you're pre-diabetic, but you really wonder if they're right. You feel good, and in fact, feel on the young side of the equation, and wonder if that will change now that you're 60," I summarize.

"Yes, and I'm not motivated to work on this stuff. It really doesn't seem right." A half-minute of silence occurs, and then he continues, "Well, mostly I guess it really doesn't seem fair. I guess I could be pre-diabetic since diabetes is in my family. Some years ago they told me my sugar was a bit high, but I think I just tried to ignore it. Mostly it just doesn't seem fair," he says with a deep sigh.

"So now, as you think back, you see that perhaps you were on the path toward becoming pre-diabetic, and you ignored it, so maybe now it is true. I am curious about your comment about it seeming unfair. Would you explain that more to me?" I inquire.

"Well, even though I tried to ignore it a couple of years ago, I did change some things. I park my car at the edge of my bank's parking lot, and I don't eat as many desserts. I really cut down. That should have done something!" he says in an angry tone.

"Oh, so a couple of years ago you did make some changes, and now it just doesn't seem fair that you've been diagnosed as having pre-diabetes," I paraphrase.

"Yes, but I guess I didn't do that much. Maybe I did slow the progress and I guess I could think that I bought myself a couple of years," he says thoughtfully.

"Okay, so what you're considering now is that you may have had some success in dealing with blood sugar levels," I summarize.

"I never thought about it that way, but yes, I guess I could hear that perspective. And honestly," he says cautiously, "that sounds a lot better to me. But all that said, here I am now so what I did before wasn't enough to turn it around. My question is how can I really change things and not continue down this path, and really change things. I'm overwhelmed. I don't know where to start. Do you have any ideas?"

"One option would be to use a 1-10 scale to get clearer about your goal and how you might accomplish it. Are you willing to experiment with the scale?" I query.

"Yes. I like numbers, and at this moment I feel motivated to focus on this. I hear now that I have another warning, and I want to get it right this time. I used to see my grandmother give shots to herself, and it seemed terrible. I guess I was looking at it through little kid eyes, but even at this point, it doesn't seem like something I want to do. Tell me how this scale works?" he asks.

"You sound motivated now, so what would you like to accomplish?" I ask.

"My doctor said I could beat this if I really worked at it, and that's what I want to do. That's why I signed up with my insurance company to go to some pre-diabetic classes and the reason I'm also paying to work with you. I know we have about eight sessions over three months, so I guess I'd like a miracle—to get that blood sugar down," he answers.

"Okay, let's talk about that miracle. What's your blood sugar now, and what would you like it to be in about three months," I ask.

"She said this one test that measures blood sugar over a period of three months is now at six, or a blood sugar of about one hundred and twenty. She said if I can get it down to five, then I have a chance of really changing my health now and in my later years. As much as I loved my grandmother, I don't want to follow in her footsteps." Frank explains.

"Great, so your goal is for your A1C, which is the name for that blood test, to be at five, which is where you want to be in three months, so let's call that the 10 on a scale of 1-10. What would your life look like?" I inquire.

"Well," he says thoughtfully, "I guess I would be eating better but not denying myself everything I like. I would still have some favorites, and I would have figured out some way to get more exercise although I have no idea how that could happen," he says emphatically.

"Right, you don't know how this could happen yet; however, I do hear good motivation, and that does make a difference. Okay, you've described your goal of 10, and let's say that 1 is the opposite of 10, so how would you describe 1 on that scale?" I question.

"One would be no exercise, eating whatever I want—yummm—and having a high blood sugar. I would probably be giving myself shots," he concludes.

"You're clear about the two ends of this scale. This next step may seem a little strange, but what I invite you to do is rather than think about this in your head, I'd actually like you to imagine a line from 1-10 on your floor and then stand on the number where you are today. There's no way to do it wrong. Using this exercise, I will be setting up some structure and directing you a bit. Willing to experiment and continue with this exercise?' I ask.

"You're right; this is weird. Okay, I'll do it, and I'm glad my office door is closed so no one can hear me as we talk on the phone. I guess I'm at a 1, and I have a long way to go," he says in a discouraged tone.

I start to talk, but he interrupts me and says, "No, I'm not at 1 because I have been making some changes, so I guess I'm more like 2.44. You know I'm a banker, so I'm good with numbers. But as I think about it, really I'm a 2.75. There, that's the right number," he says with pride.

"Okay, great that you know where you are now. Standing on 2.75, are you willing to look backwards and tell me the key to why you're at 2.75 and not at 1?" I question.

"Yes, I can look back but let me think about that," he replies and takes a minute before he speaks next. "Even though I acted like I ignored my other doctor's warnings about my blood sugar climbing, I did hear him, and I kept thinking about my family history and decided that I'd better do something or else I would end up like my grandmother. I didn't talk about it with anyone. I didn't even tell my wife. I just did some things on my own."

"So your motivation came from learning from your family pattern and you quietly made some changes," I paraphrase.

"Yes, that's it. I didn't realize until now how much impact my grandmother's struggle with diabetes had on me. I think I can learn from her mistakes. She didn't change anything when she was told she had diabetes," he reports.

"How could you learn from her approach?" I inquire.

"Well, that's a good question. Let me think again about that for a minute." After some silence, Frank continues, "I have learned to make changes in other parts of my life. At my work, I'm successful. I don't want to mislead you: I'm not the president but I'm up there. My office does have a door that I can close, and these days that says something! To get this office, I've had to change with the times and keep up with new technology and new management styles. I used to keep to myself and work by myself, but due to some training, I've learned to work more with a team. I find this not only seems a bit easier, I think our results are more impressive," he says slowly and thoughtfully.

"I hear that you have been successful in making changes in your work life regarding technology and leadership styles. Is there anything more to glean from looking backwards?" I ask.

"No, I'm ready to go forwards!" he says emphatically.

"Okay, then how about moving to a 4 on that scale even though you might not know how you would get there?" I ask.

"Alright. Guess you don't want me to go to 3.75," he laughingly comments.

I laugh too and say, "I made a mistake—3.75 is exactly the next step."

"Okay good. I am on 3.75. Now what?" he asks but suddenly says, "I don't know how I got here, but now that I say that, I guess I do have some ideas, and they have to do with that last comment I made about working with a team. I guess, even though it would be hard, I could tell my wife about the lab results and see if we could talk about working on this together. Now that I think about it, she might benefit as well. And really, if I start refusing to eat some things, she would feel hurt and think I didn't like something when that really wouldn't be the case at all," he explains.

"Great idea. Anything more on 3.75?" I ask.

"No, I'm already on 4.75. Somehow this feels easy. It isn't all on me. Somehow I think by this time, I could even have figured out some way to get more exercise. Maybe there's something my wife and I can do together. It would be good for her too," he says with some enthusiasm.

He continues up the scale, but at 6.75 he starts sounding discouraged. I ask, "You sound heavy, and I don't hear as much energy about this change. What's going on for you?"

Chapter 5: The Mental Structure of Consciousness in Coaching

"Well, something is becoming clear to me at this point, and I don't like it. I'm hearing a little voice saying to me that these are not just some changes that I need to make for a few months. This sounds like a really big change that I do for the rest of my life. Suddenly this doesn't seem as much fun. I can give up things for a while, but this seems serious," he laments.

"Where do you want to go with this awareness?" I inquire.

"I feel stuck and depressed. I don't know what to do about 6.75." Frank says.

I ask, "What happens when you feel stuck?"

"Another good question so give me time to think about this." Shortly after that request he continues, "Well, I say to myself, 'Frank, you are stuck. What are you going to do about it? You know that sitting around and sulking won't help. *Do Something*!' and then I try to think about it in a new way and take action. That sounds good but I can't think of a new way to deal with this diagnosis. Do you have any ideas?"

"One option comes to mind. You could pretend it was three years from now and then look back at this current time and finish this sentence: 'That pre-diabetic diagnosis was hard to hear but it was the time when. . . . Does that sound useful?" I ask.

He's silent for a minute and then comments, "You ask hard questions sometimes, but they really get me thinking. The honest answer to that question would be that this sounds like the time in my life that I started taking my health seriously. And it was also a time when I got help from some other people and the road wasn't so lonely. Thanks, this is important. I thought I would just sail to my goal, but this is a significant step. I am glad that I stumbled here so I can see what to do in the future. I'm sure this will come up and probably stopped my changing after the first warning."

"I'm moved. I agree. This is a noteworthy awareness," I say slowly. "Congratulations on learning more about how to make this change in a deeper and more compelling manner."

"Gee, I never thought these things would be discussed. I got more than I bargained for—and I mean that in a good way—at least so far," he adds laughingly.

"What do you want to do now?" I inquire.

"I want to go step by step to 10!" he says with enthusiasm.

"Okay, what happens at 7.75" I ask.

Frank explains, "This is still a little bumpy with new things to learn but I can do it. I am moving to 8.75 now. This place has some wobbles too but I'm motivated since I am close to my goal now."

"So both places have some rough places but you are able to keep moving." I summarize.

"Yes, I feel I can really do this, and I hear what my grandmother would be saying if she were still alive. She would really want me to do it differently than she did. Now my only question is should I go to 9.75 and then 10 or just go to 10 next?" he asks.

"Up to you," I say. He decides to take one step to 10 and really enjoys the feeling of reaching his goal. Next, I request that he go back to his chair where he started the call. After he sits down I say, "At the end of each session, it's helpful if you select some fun and easy homework that you want to do between now and next week."

"Oh," he says, "this sounds like where the rubber meets the road. No more imaginary lines. This is the hard part. I'm stumped. All I feel is resistance," he says.

"This might be completely off, but I have this intuitive feeling that you might want to think about this next step from standing on the line again?" I cautiously inquire.

"Your hunch is right—as silly as it sounds to me, somehow I do feel better on that line. This is very odd, but I feel like I can do it when I'm on that line. Again, I'm glad no one's hearing me. Here I go back to the line, but surprisingly I'm no longer at 2.75. I have already made some progress just in this little time. Now I feel like I am at 3.10, and when I stand here I do have an idea. And I actually want to do it! Somehow, standing up, I feel like I can make progress. I wonder if I should have all my meetings standing up. Who knows what would happen! Anyway, a sidetrack there, but what I want to do is tell my wife about this and not deal with the food thing right now, but she's been hounding me—yes hounding me for months—for us to take dance lessons. I used to be pretty good at dancing, and I think it would be fun. Yes, that's it. That's my homework. I know as soon as she hears the sound of my voice saying yes about this dance thing, she'll have us at a class in a matter of one week. It could really be fun. Strange. I see what you mean. I really do want to do this. Now I'm very motivated. Thanks," he adds.

"It is my pleasure—really. Thanks for trying out some new things. You did a great job," I say with conviction.

In the middle of Frank's coaching sessions with me, his grown daughter had a routine physical, and her nurse practitioner found that her blood sugar was elevated—not to the point of labeling her as pre-diabetic, but she felt it was a lab value to monitor closely. That impacted Frank deeply. He and his daughter became a team, determined to change this pattern in their family, and they both moved into a healthier lifestyle. By the end of the three months, Frank was not at 9.75 on the imaginary scale, but he did get to 8.75 on that line on the floor, and he reminded me of something I say to clients often—the turtle does win the race. He was happy with his progress, and his doctor said he was headed in the right direction. His A1C after the three months of our working together was 5.4, and he was satisfied with the change and planned on lowering it even more in the next three months. In our last session, he amended the way he finished that sentence in our first conversation by saying, "That diagnosis of pre-diabetic was the time when. . .I realized that working together is far superior to working alone, and it gets better results."

Overview of the Mental Part of Coaching

I want to begin presenting tools based on Gebser's structures of consciousness, starting with what's familiar to the majority of us—the Mental structure, with its numbers, measurements, logic, and sequential approach. In Frank's first coaching session, he experienced the 1-10 scale coaching tool, but I added the body approach, so instead of asking him to tell me his goals and his progress to date to establish a baseline for our beginning work, I invited him to stand on an imaginary line. This is an example of taking a Mental tool and expanding it holistically—to a body and spirit level.

The Mental structure has much to offer coaching, even without expanding it. The illustration at the beginning of this chapter depicts the essence of this stage. Here we see examples of ways to measure and sequence, such as a magnifying glass to see smaller and smaller parts of a conceptual framework or a pattern, clocks, and a calendar for planning and setting timelines.

Coaching tools in this chapter and in subsequent chapters will be presented according to when they are usually used in a coaching session. Of course, this is just a guideline. As your experience with this model grows, you'll probably find that tools can be used in different places in sessions. In each of the chapters, a table identifying application principles and powerful questions based on the tools are listed for easy reference.

Mental tools are frequently brought into coaching sessions. Often used for initial client analysis—and hence the first tool described in this chapter—is *assessing learning types*, a system for analyzing at the way people communicate and learn. Some people are more visual, while others favor an auditory or kinesthetic approach. As with other tools, *critical thinking* and *decision making* are skills that can be learned and evaluated. The *1-10 scale* and the *pie chart* may be used for measurement during a session. *Listing, prioritizing, weighing options*, and *analyzing behavior patterns* are often used in the middle part of a coaching session. Setting *plans and timelines* is essential in the last part of a coaching session, leading to creating homework that helps the client move forward toward their goal.

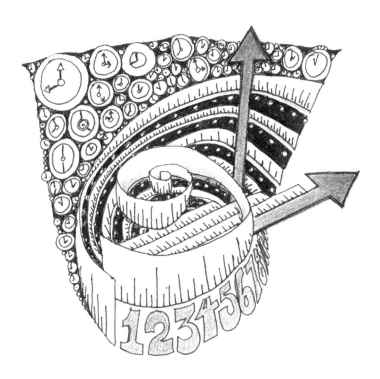

Assessment (beginning of session):
- Learning Types

Middle:
- Critical Thinking and Decision-Making
- 1-10 Scale
- Choosing Between Options
- Pie Chart
- Setting Priorities
- Lists and Prioritizing (To Do and Ta Da Lists)
- Working with Behavior Patterns

Homework (end of session):
- Plans and Timelines

Mental Tools for Assessment at the Beginning of Coaching Sessions

Before I become involved in what kind of change my client wants to make, I first want to know "Who is this person?" and "How do they learn?" We can use a Mental approach to classify and organize the ways people learn. Over the years I've found the following system very useful.

Assessing Learning Types

Some theorists feel that people are hardwired in preference for taking in and communicating information. Some of us are very visual. You can hear it in our language as we say, "See you later," or "I can't picture that." Others of us come from an auditory perspective. We might say, "talk to you later," or "I've never heard of that." Still others of us have a kinesthetic way of perceiving. We'd say, "catch you later," or "that really grabbed me." It's important for you to know your own personal learning style and the *learning type* of your clients. If you mostly communicate visually, for example, and your client kinesthetically, you might have trouble reaching each other. On the other hand, if you can match your client's style, communication and understanding can be improved.

The following Exercise was created by Marcia L. Conner as a quick way to assess an individual's learning style.

EXERCISE: Learning Assessment[1]

Learning style is the way(s) you prefer to approach new information. Each of us learns and processes information in our own special ways, though we share some learning patterns, preferences, and approaches. Knowing your own style also can help you to realize that other people may approach the same situation differently.

Take a few minutes to complete the following questionnaire to assess your preferred learning style. Begin by reading the words in the left-hand column. Of the three responses to the right, circle the one that best characterizes you, answering as honestly as possible with the description that applies to you right now. Count the number of circled items and write your total at the bottom of each column, giving you insight into how you learn.

1. When I try to concentrate...	I grow distracted by clutter or movement, and I notice things around me other people don't notice.	I get distracted by sounds, and I attempt to control the amount and type of noise around me.	I become distracted by commotion, and I tend to retreat inside myself.
2. When I visualize...	I see vivid, detailed pictures in my thoughts.	I think in voices and sounds.	I see images in my thoughts that involve movement.
3. When I talk with others...	I find it difficult to listen for very long.	I enjoy listening, or I get impatient to talk myself.	I gesture and communicate with my hands
4. When I contact people...	I prefer face-to-face meetings.	I prefer speaking by telephone for serious conversations.	I prefer to interact while walking or participating in some activity.
5. When I see an acquaintance...	I forget names but remember faces, and I tend to replay where we met for the first time.	I know people's names and I can usually quote what we discussed.	I remember what we did together and I may almost "feel" our time together.
6. When I relax...	I watch TV, see a play, visit an exhibit, or go to a movie.	I listen to the radio, play music, read, or talk with a friend.	I play sports, make crafts, or build something with my hands.
7. When I read...	I like descriptive examples and I may pause to imagine the scene.	I enjoy the narrative most and I can almost "hear" the characters talk.	I prefer action-oriented stories, but I do not often read for pleasure.

Chapter 5: The Mental Structure of Consciousness in Coaching

8. When I spell...	I envision the word in my mind or imagine what the word looks like when written.	I sound out the word, sometimes aloud, and tend to recall rules about letter order.	I get a feel for the word by writing it out or pretending to type it.
9. When I do something new...	I seek out demonstrations, pictures, or diagrams.	I want verbal and written instructions, and to talk it over with someone else. ○	I jump right in to try it, keep trying, and try different approaches.
10. When I assemble an object...	I look at the picture first and then, maybe, read the directions.	I read the directions, or I talk aloud as I work.	I usually ignore the directions and figure it out as I go along. ○
11. When I interpret someone's mood...	I examine facial expressions.	I rely on listening to tone of voice.	I focus on body language.
12. When I teach other people...	I show them.	I tell them, write it out, or I ask them a series of questions.	I demonstrate how it is done and then ask them to try. ○
TOTAL	Visual: ④	Auditory: 1	Tactile/Kinesthetic: ④

Your primary learning type: _____
Your secondary learning type: _____
The column with the highest total represents your primary processing type. The column with the second-most choices is your secondary type.

Now that you know which learning style you rely on, you can boost your learning potential when working to learn more. For instance, the following suggestions can help you get more from reading a book.

If your primary learning type is visual, draw pictures in the margins, look at the graphics, and read the text that explains the graphics. Envision the topic or play a movie in your thoughts of how you'll act out the subject matter.

If your primary learning type is auditory, listen to the words you read. Try to develop an internal conversation between you and the text. Don't be embarrassed to read aloud or talk through the information.

If your primary learning type is tactile/kinesthetic, use a pencil or highlighter pen to mark passages that are meaningful to you. Take notes, transferring the information you learn to the margins of the book, into your journal, or onto a computer. Doodle whatever comes to mind as you read. Hold the book in your hands instead of placing it on a table. Walk around as you read. Feel the words and ideas. Get busy—both mentally and physically.

What is your learning type?
What is the learning type of the three to four people closest to you?
What similarities do you see in those with a similar learning type and style of communication?
If someone has a different learning type than you, does matching their style make a difference in your communication?

Chapter 5: The Mental Structure of Consciousness in Coaching

When we look back at Frank (Sample Session 2A), we see that he had an auditory preference. Here are some sentences that cued me:
- "The honest answer would be that this sounds like the time in my life that I started taking my health seriously."
- "This is weird. You're right. Okay, I'll do it, and I'm glad my office door is closed so no one can hear me as we talk on the phone."
- "I know as soon as she hears the sound of my voice saying yes about this dance thing, she'll have us at a class in a matter of one week."

I responded in the auditory style too. Here are some examples:
- "Hummmm. All of that sounds overwhelming and frightening."
- "Okay, what I am hearing is that you've been told that you're pre-diabetic but you really wonder if they're right."
- "You sound motivated now, so what would you like to accomplish?"

Considering learning style is effective at early stages of working with clients. Sometimes you'll want to ask a powerful question relating to this or have clients fill out the exercise sheet on this topic.

Mental Tool #1	When to Use	Steps in Using	How to Gauge Effectiveness
Learning Types	In working with a client, direct your interactions to their learning style.	Visual—drawing & imagery & symbols Auditory—verbal conversation Kinesthetic—physical movement.	Client feels heard and communication seems easy, as if you and the client are speaking the same language. Client owns a new concept or behavior with increased awareness and more effective action.

Powerful Questions about Learning Types:
- How do you learn best?
- How could you use your unique learning style to clarify, understand, or see new options about this situation?

Mental Tools for Clarification and Awareness throughout Coaching Sessions

As a coach, it's useful for me to attend to how my clients analyze issues that come up for them. Analyzing situations, making reasonable inferences, skillfully discriminating, and accurately evaluating options and results, represent the best of the Mental mind at work.

Critical Thinking and Decision-Making

Critical thinking can help my clients examine how beliefs, judgments, and previous experieces influence analysis, opinions, and actions. It's an invaluable skill, allowing people to make more effective decisions and consequently lead more successful lives. However, people are seldom taught how to use analysis effectively to produce the best results.

Unknown elements are a factor in most decisions; however, people often make faulty inferences about these based on what they've come to know by analyzing known factors. They overgeneralize and adopt similar mindsets for all situations. For example, if someone likes to take on responsibility, the person may feel overly burdened by failures and infer culpability even in situations where s/he had limited control. On the other hand, if someone is more comfortable not taking responsibility, the person may choose to blame others, overlooking what they don't or can't know about the circumstances.

Making reasonable inferences is a skill and an art—one that many people struggle with throughout their lives. Becoming more competent in this helps clients become more powerful in making choices and acting upon them. The ability to operate effectively is largely a measure of the ability to accurately apprehend the situation in which someone finds themselves. Throughout sessions coaches model this aspect of critical thinking, especially by asking powerful questions. Clients learn from this the importance of coming at any situation from as many angles as possible so as to have enough information for successful decision-making and they learn the habit of questioning assumptions they and others might be making.

Skillful discrimination is another essential aspect of functioning effectively and depends on analysis and inference. In this age of information overload we're barraged with information from multiple sources—some much more reliable than others. We get advice from friends and relatives and the internet; we have to continually choose between different streams of information with conflicting points of view.

The complexity of contemporary life also requires the ability to distinguish between various elements that may appear to be similar. For example, being told something repeatedly on a news channel may make it believable. Yet evidence now demonstrates that myths are often created by the echo chamber effect of news—if a statement is repeated often enough, it's seen as true, whether or not it is. Likewise, if we're repeatedly told by a parent that we're a certain way, we might need much evidence to the contrary before we can let go of this "fact." Discriminating between appearances and truths is a prerequisite for evaluating how to respond to situations.

Our capacity to evaluate the validity of a statement is dependent on our ability to assess it. People who have trouble making decisions often lack confidence in their analysis of situations. Often they have trouble aligning their decisions with their values and aspirations because they're not enough in touch with these parts of themselves. A holistic inquiry process can bring all the relevant data to light. Clients who become overwhelmed by indecisiveness often need to go back and analyze their decision-making process: have they considered all the variables? Are obstacles really what they seem?

Critical thinking skills help people to become better decision-makers, and clients can learn a great deal about this subject in their coaching sessions.

Mental Tool #2	When to Use	Steps in Using	How to Gauge Effectiveness
Critical thinking and decision-making	When client needs to make a decision.	Model analysis, inference, discrimination, and evaluation and ask powerful questions that take clients through the process so they can learn it.	Client makes decisions that are effective and successful.

Powerful Questions about Critical Thinking and Decision-Making:
- How would you define, name, label, list, write, or state that situation? (Pick one verb for your question.)
- How would you explain, summarize, paraphrase, describe, or illustrate the event or goal? (Pick one verb for your question.)
- How can you define and differentiate the cognitive (thinking) and affective (emotional) objectives of the plan?

- How can you compare and contrast the situations, events, or plans. (Pick one.)
- How could past successes be applied to the situation you're exploring?
- How could you recommend, critique, or justify the plan or action? (Pick one verb.)

1-10 Scale for Measurement

Clients hire coaches because they want to make changes, so when I first work with them I want to find out what are my client's goals. Like Sandra (Sample Session 1A and 1B), clients might not know specifically where they want to go, but they usually have some general ideas—a job that's meaningful and aligned with their sense of purpose, work in a values-driven organization, a lifestyle that allows a person to wake up in the morning excited about getting out of bed, a relationship that brings out the best in each partner, a way to live with a health challenge that allows for the most vitality possible, given the situation, or a work/life balance that supports personal and professional priorities or the completion of a project. As we saw with Frank (Sample Session 2A), using a 1-10 scale is a Mental measurement tool that has several advantages: it defines the goal; it offers a snapshot of current progress; and it can highlight key factors in progress toward the goal to date.

Here's how I use it, in greater detail. I ask my client to describe the future goal in as much detail as they can, which would be represented by the number 10. For example, if the client wants to write a book, I would ask, "Tell me about how things will be when you finish the book." The client might say that s/he goes to the mailbox and receives the first copy of the book. After reading the book the client finds it's even better than she originally thought, and immediately call friends for a celebration party.

The client might be able to describe 10 right away, or might need some time to develop the picture over one or more sessions. After the client is clear about the precise target, the next question to ask is what's the opposite of the goal, and that's labeled as 1. For instance, 1 could be the act of deciding to write a book.

Of course, this exercise can be done in my clients' minds, but I find having them actually imagine an imaginary 1-10 line on their floor to be much more powerful. I ask them to actually stand on the imaginary line designating where they are right now. Are they at 5—feeling they're halfway to the goal? Should the clients stand on 2, since the project or goal is in the early stages? Maybe they're at 8 and almost to the end of the process of achieving their goal?

Once they've selected a number that represents their current progress, I ask them to look back, unless, of course, they're at one. I invite them to identify what was key in helping them arrive at their current number. Sometimes clients say support from others, listening to their in-

ner voice, or being persistent was the essential element. The answer to the question can shed light on future planning.

Next, I ask clients how their current situation feels. I invite them to describe thoughts, feelings, body sensations, energy, and their sense of spirit. Let's say that the author in our example feels the current level of progress is a 3 and portrays this level of completion in the following way:
- feeling overwhelmed with what is left to do;
- feeling pressured by wanting to make progress;
- feeling the weight of the book on their shoulders;
- seeing an image of walking up a large mountain;
- feeling a knot in their stomach;
- sensing low energy;
- wondering if the book is really a worthwhile project;
- feeling vague about this project and the connection with their life purpose.

I ask them if they're willing to move to the next larger number and simply imagine how they might think, feel, and experience that stage. Sometimes clients move forward immediately and start explaining how being at that number seems, and other times, clients need a bit more cueing about how to be there. I've found it helpful to explain that they don't need to know how they got there—that this is just an experiment and can't be done incorrectly.

I continue to invite clients to move forward, and I never know how it will proceed. We're in that second square on the coaching grid—neither of us knows this territory. Some clients get to a certain number and don't want to continue to the 10; others are excited to reach their goal. The progress can lead to a gradual shift toward increasingly positive body, mind, energy, and spirit experiences. However, I often find that the movement forward doesn't proceed that way. My client might find 6 to be a wonderful place: over halfway, goal in clearer sight, feeling more in the flow of making progress—and then boom—something happens at 7, and progress feels very difficult. Questions might come up about what impact accomplishing this goal might have on their life or do they have the energy to continue to proceed. The pathway forward is always a mystery, and a great deal of awareness can result. I don't push people forward or have an idea about the right way this should go.

After clients have gone as far as they want to go, I ask them to return to their original seat by the phone and ask them for significant insights. Often they report action steps that they know will help them move forward, a compelling embodied sense that they can really achieve their goal, or a realigning of purpose or energy.

Even if clients only take one step forward, the real power of this tool comes from greater awareness, not only in their thinking but in their learning to listen as much as they can to body, energy, and spirit signs—an integration of their whole being. Calling this a *Mental* tool reflects using discernment, no matter what aspect of ourselves is being considered. Layering of investigations produces a rich knowing and can lead to potent actions.

This tool can be used with any goal, and if clients are not skilled or interested in checking in with body, energy, or spirit parts of themselves, they might become more interested as time goes on and can usually learn to increase their skill in exploring more aspects of themselves. Once clients see the benefits of having more inner guidance in their progress toward a goal, they often want to expand this ability. The 1-10 scale is usually fun and easy and helps people progress more quickly toward their goals. Besides being used when goals are set, the scale can be used as an ongoing feedback system for the client to measure success and learning.

I didn't ask Frank (Sample Session 2A) to tune into his body or his sense of purpose in that first session. It seemed like a big enough step for him to stand on an imaginary line in his office at the bank. As our work continued, I invited him to explore these other aspects, but he wasn't very interested, so I stayed with what was working. If we'd continued longer than three months, he might have taken me up on the request and examined other areas of his life. His process worked to help him change his health habits, and it also helped him uncover some very meaningful aspects of his life. He got there on his own without my specific questions about life purpose and values.

Besides using this tool with coaching clients when I work one-on one, I've introduced it to small and large groups. I ask the kinds of questions presented above, based on the goal, interest in whole person approaches, and skill levels, and the participants answer the questions quietly to themselves. Then I either ask them to talk in twos or threes to discuss insights, or I just ask people in the group to comment on their awareness.

Staying with a coaching orientation, I encourage group members to identify a next action step. If it's an ongoing group I repeat the exercise at various times, which allows for many types of learning. For instance, if this is a project group moving toward the launch of a product, members who are moving faster may want to share practices that seem especially effective. Or if someone is moving very slowly and feeling challenged, the group can use a systems perspective and identify some dysfunction in their process—perhaps a bottleneck that's caused by a member not having the right equipment or supplies. Maybe that person is seeing something that others are ignoring. The opportunity for insight is enormous.

EXERCISE: 1-10 Scale

You can try the 1-10 scale exercise with one of your goals. Think of a project or goal that you want to achieve. Get very clear about the outcome, which will be at 10: the paper is finished, and you're turning it in; the desk is clean, and you feel more relaxed as you work at your desk; you've completed a talk with your boss, and it went very well; you're putting on new clothes that are a size smaller; you're finishing four weeks of daily meditation, and you notice that you're more relaxed, and those weeks went much more smoothly; or you feel more closely aligned with your life purpose, and things seem to be falling into place with grace and ease. Think of the opposite situation and name that 1.

Find an imaginary line on your floor. Decide your current number. Take a deep breath and tune into your whole self. What thoughts arise? What feelings are present about this stage of your movement toward your goal? What do you feel in your body? How are you breathing? What does your stomach feel like? What other body sensations are you experiencing? What is your life purpose? How does this path toward your goal match or detract from your life purpose? If you'd like to add a spiritual or religious support for this change, how could that happen? Who can help you with that aspect? Experiment with any of these steps and see what you can learn and what helps you along the path of change in your life.

Mental Tool #3	When to Use	Steps in Using	How to Gauge Effectiveness
1-10 Scale	When client has made some progress on a goal and wants to become clearer about the goal or the steps required to obtain the goal.	Have the person place themselves on an imaginary 1-10 scale: ask them to look back and see what helped them get to their current number; ask them to move forward on it, identifying body/spirit/mind experiences (if they are interested in all three) at each step.	Client has insights, identifies what helps them move forward, or learns how to tune into body, mind, spirit information that helps them achieve their goal.

Powerful Questions about the 1-10 Scale:
- What is your goal? How will it look and feel when you complete your objective?
- Are you interested in using an imaginary 1-10 scale that you could actually stand on and explore your steps forward and see what helped you get as far as you have along the line?
- What do your body and spirit tell you about the change and how to accomplish it?

Choosing between Options: An Orienting Tool

The 1-10 Scale is one of several Mental tools for helping clients explore seemingly complex situations. It cuts through overwhelming feelings that can result from having to take into account various factors that seem "all over the place."

Another orienting tool is looking at options in a systematic way. This is a tool that Sandra used (Sample Session 1A) in addition to the 1-10 scale, and it served her well. Again, I never know what will come up. Sometimes, as with Sandra, conflicting parts of the self are identified and explored. Other times, my clients uncover new aspects of an option. Drawing upon the Mental using these tools, and inviting body, energy, and spirit to impart wisdom, helps clients develop a new composite, a more full-spectrum picture.

Very simply, the coach asks the client who is choosing among options to pick a place in the room for each one, and to go to them in turn, and see/feel what comes up. This kind of tool is especially effective with kinesthetic learners.

I used this orienting tool with a client named Bob when he wanted to explore options related to a possible move from California to the East Coast, near New York City. He'd lived in many places in the country and even overseas. I invited him to explore his present California location by standing in a place in the room. I asked questions about his feelings, his thoughts, his energy, his body sensations, and his spirit, or sense of purpose. He was surprised to discover a tension in his body about all the open space where he lived in California.

Then Bob moved to a new place in the room to explore the New York locality. He again was amazed to feel his body relax as he spoke about the trees and the lack of vista. The New York spot seemed like a cozy nest. He also felt his energy change positively as he thought of trips to some of his favorite haunts in Manhattan.

I asked him to go to a new place in the room and see if there was an option he hadn't yet considered. He stood in the new location in silence, tuning into his "gut" (he said), the place he could access his deeper sense of knowing. He was quiet for a couple of minutes, and I wondered if I should cue him with questions or just remain quiet. My deeper knowing encouraged the latter.

He started to cry softly. I was shocked. I gently asked what was going on. He said that this idea of moving was really based on being lonely. He said that he wanted not so much a change of scene but a change in connection. His wife had died several years earlier, and although he'd dated, he hadn't found a significant partner. He spoke slowly and often sighed deeply. He said he wanted to sit down again and continued talking about how he felt that he was still in mourning.

He realized that while he'd explored some relationships, he hadn't really been open to starting a serious one. He was afraid of losing his next partner as he had his wife. A wall had been up between himself and others, and he hadn't been ready to let someone new into his life, and more specifically, into his heart. He said that he really needed to think seriously about a woman he'd been dating who wanted to become closer. He realized now that the idea of moving to the East Coast was motivated by wanting to escape this opportunity to move into a more serious relationship with her.

Bob concluded that he was on the precipice of a significant move all right, but it wasn't between one coast or the other—it was away or toward connection. He decided that his homework for the following week would be to take a day and go to the ocean by himself and look honestly at his needs and feelings. In his follow up session, I found that he'd decided to stay in California and to move forward slowly—and he emphasized slowly— toward a committed relationship. Most of his subsequent coaching was devoted to the relationship issue.

The real power of this tool is the layering of exploration in a body, mind, energy, and spirit sense, with the additional impact of breaking out of an either/or scenario. The mindset for this is represented by a figure looking at three options and deciding the next step.

EXERCISE: Reader Question or Exercise

Want to try this one? Think of a decision between two things that you've been considering.

Go to a place in the room and explore one option as much as possible from a whole person perspective (body, mind, energy, spirit). Go to another place and explore a second option. Then see what a third option could be. Here you're going to step outside the box and imagine an option you haven't yet considered. You might even want to consider a fourth option. Play with the opportunities. See what you can learn and how this might help you develop a next step toward a goal.

Mental Tool #4	When to Use	Steps in Using	How to Gauge Effectiveness
Choosing between Options	When client is deciding between or among various alternatives.	Invite client to experience each option in an assortment of physical places in a location. If there are two points of decision, ask client to move to a new place in the area to consider a third scenario. Ask body, mind, spirit, and energy questions.	Client sees new aspects of options, creates a new option, or becomes clear on which option to select— or becomes more skilled in accessing body, mind, spirit, and energy knowing that leads to action toward a goal.

Powerful Questions about Choosing Between Options:
- Sink into the experience of the first option—what do you experience from a body, mind, energy, and spirit perspective?
- In terms of your body, what do you notice? Check out your breathing, your shoulders, your jaw, your stomach, and notice any other body feedback.
- Energetically how do you feel here: heavy, light, big, small, etcetera?
- In terms of your spirit, how does this link to your sense of purpose or life meaning?
- Move to the second option—what is happening at a body, mind, energy, and spirit level?
- Besides the two things you are considering, what other options are possible?
- How can your body wisdom, energetic awareness, or sense of purpose inform these alternatives?

The Pie Chart

Another way of measuring and evaluating a complex situation is to use a pie chart exercise. Let's say I'm working with clients who want to have more work/life balance. I could use the 1-10 scale and ask my clients to describe the desired life as the 10 and then ask where they are in relation to accomplishing that goal. However, I like to use a pie chart for situations that have limiting aspects—meaning, in this case, that my clients only have so many hours in the day, and something needs to be let go in order to add other things.

For example, one of my clients, Paul, wanted to have more time with his wife and children. I asked him to draw a circle and divide it into quarters and said that each quarter contained 6 hours. Then he figured out how much time he spent on a weekday getting ready for work, commuting, and working. I asked him to draw the big piece of pie that comprised work, which he suddenly realized was 13 hours. Then I asked him to draw the piece of pie that was sleep (8 hours). He recognized that he had only 3 hours left for eating dinner, doing professional reading, answering emails, catching up with the news, and checking investments. Seeing how he was spending his time, he felt discouraged. He asked, "Where will I find more hours in the day? No wonder I don't have time for my family." I asked him to move into a very creative space and see what would come up as he drew another circle with different sized pieces of pie. He played around with it for some minutes and realized that the hours for family time needed to come out of his work time. No other way around it. He decided his homework for the upcoming week would be to come home 30 minutes earlier 2 times that week. As he talked, he became clearer that he could work more efficiently by delegating more and not taking on a new project. Over time, he was often able to cut his work time down to 12 hours a day, and although that seemed like a small change, it allowed him some quality time to help his children with homework. He and his wife hired a babysitter and had a Saturday night date every couple of weeks. These changes made him feel like he was doing a better job as a husband and father.

Clients can do this on a piece of paper or imagine the circle on the floor (for kinesthetic learners) and experience the different parts of the pie, noting how they think, feel, and experience various activities in their lives. The pie chart shows people where they commit most of their time and where they may be able to make changes to bring about more balance in their lives. It helps make changes very concrete and realistic.

Clients can react to pie diagrams from a whole person perspective, checking into their body, mind, energy, and spirit. The power of this tool is to help clients realistically prioritize their time based on their values.

24 Hour Old Pattern

- Prof. Reading — 1
- Eat, News, Relax — 2
- Sleep — 8
- Work — 13

24 Hour New Pattern

- Kids — 1
- Prof. Reading — 1
- Eat, News, Relax — 2
- Sleep — 8
- Work — 12

Mental Tool #5	When to Use	Steps in Using	How to Gauge Effectiveness
Pie Chart	When working with limitations such as 24 hours in a day.	Have the client portray the current way time is used in a pie diagram and then see what's expanded or added and what's reduced or taken out.	Client puts together a realistic plan for change that satisfies current needs.

Powerful Questions about the Pie Chart:
- What is your goal?
- How will it look and feel when you complete your objective?
- Would you be interested in using a pie chart to help with this situation where you have a limited amount of hours in a day?
- What do your body, mind, energy, and spirit tell you about the change and how to accomplish it?

Lists and Prioritizing

It's easy in these days of constant rushing for people to feel overwhelmed. A great recipe for relief in this situation is to set priorities, another helpful Mental coaching tool I use with most clients. An essential part of setting priorities is to be clear about how you're setting those priorities—what is the organizing principle or goal? Often people don't consider this and arrange things without a conscious direction.

The tool is explained in the exercise box. Its power is that it can be done in ten minutes—even within the session—and it can completely change the mood, frustration level, and stress that a client is experiencing and move them into action. Clients can continue to use this tool to keep them on track and moving forward on the things that matter most because they've taken time to be conscious of the values that guide their prioritization.

EXERCISE: ABC Prioritizing [2]

Here are the instructions for *ABC prioritizing* so you can do this process yourself and suggest it to clients.

Make a list of the things you need to do to reach a particular goal—perhaps about twenty items.

Before you rank them, don't forget that the key step is to decide how you want to sort them. In other words, what are your decision-making criteria? If you're trying to better use your time, do you want to prioritize the things that bring in money, that are the most fun, that will help you relax, that will clear your desk, or some other criterion?

Now that you have your key to ranking, pick the five most important things, according to your criterion for prioritizing, and put an "A" by them. Next prioritize the five items by putting 'A1" by the one that will most effectively move you toward your goal, "A2" by the one that will next most effectively move you toward your goal, and so on.

Look at the remaining items. Select the next five most important items and put a "B" by each one. Then again decide on which is "B1," "B2," and so forth.

Make all the rest "C's." Often people don't do A1 or A2 because they are more difficult. They go for the "C's," but those "C's" really won't help people get to their goal. Realize that you may want to cross off some of the "C's" because doing them may not be useful and may distract you from ultimately reaching your goal.

148 **Chapter 5: The Mental Structure of Consciousness in Coaching**

I keep an ongoing prioritized list at my desk so that even if I sit down for just fifteen minutes, I'm quickly able to focus on what needs to be done first. My list is computerized, so I cut my accomplished items out of my "To Do" list and paste them into my "Ta Da" list[3]. This second list helps me realize and celebrate what I've accomplished. So often we finish one thing and move directly into the next without giving ourselves that pat on the back, that "great job" comment, or some other reward for meeting our goals. The power of this tool is that it not only helps us prioritize what we do but also helps us rest and renew and celebrate between steps. The list acts as a balance and builds our self-esteem because we see things that we've actually accomplished.

What's a familiar theme in setting your priorities for work? Is it bringing in income, responding to your organization's or other people's priorities, or moving a favorite project forward? What about your personal "To Do" list? If you wanted to experiment with a new focus or direction, what would it be? Do you want to set your priorities based on fun, adventure, what would bring in money the fastest, what sets up life balance, what gives you the most energy, what helps you make a difference in the world, what directly fits into your sense of purpose, or adds to your life meaning? Try creating a list of your priorities based on a new key to rank them and see what develops.

Mental Tool #6	When to Use	Steps in Using	How to Gauge Effectiveness
Lists and Prioritizing (To Do Lists and Ta Da Lists)	When client can't figure out which steps to take toward a goal, in which order, or when client doesn't notice or take time for celebrating accomplishments.	Have client use an ABC system to decide which items need most attention, based on guiding values. (Examples: Most fun; quickest money-making; pleasing boss; establishing work/life balance.) Ask client to list all the things accomplished on a Ta Da list to celebrate the things that have been done.	Things get prioritized correctly, the important things get done first, and more things get celebrated.

Powerful Questions about Prioritizing, To Do and Ta Da Lists
- What are the things you want to accomplish?
- What is the best theme or value for ranking your priorities?
- How can you let go of any of the "Cs" in the ABC exercise to prioritize your tasks?
- How can you celebrate what you have accomplished? How could you use a "Ta Da" list?

Observing and Working with Behavior Patterns

The Mental structure of consciousness offers an indispensable coaching perspective for helping to change behaviors. Remember that the Mental part of coaching includes measurements, as well as being able to look at pieces—and more importantly in this instance, pieces in a sequence.

In order to change a behavior, your clients need to be able to observe it. The more your clients can see it, feel it, and sense it, the better they will be able to change it. This awareness can be developed, and you can help your clients become proficient. *Observing behavior patterns* helps your clients witness their actions so they can choose how they behave rather than unknowingly reacting.

150 CHAPTER 5: The Mental Structure of Consciousness in Coaching

One way to help clients learn how to change a behavior is to help them distinguish among four steps on the way to change:

1. Seeing an opportunity for change after the behavior happens.
2. Seeing an opportunity for change while the behavior is happening.
3. Seeing an opportunity for change before the behavior happens and sometimes doing it anyway.
4. Seeing opportunity for change before the behavior happens and not continuing the pattern.

If you've ever been involved in potty training a toddler, you've experienced this process. The child comes and tells you that the diaper is wet. Unless you understand this learning process, you might not be too excited about that news, but this is really the first step—for the toddler to recognize that the behavior has occurred. Next, the child tells you that s/he is wetting. Again, if these stages are not familiar to you, you'll miss this opportunity for celebration and not praise her or him at this significant step. Lastly, the child tells you before wetting that it's time to go to the bathroom—albeit, not always, at first. Of course, this is the time that most people recognize progress, but they may have missed the other noteworthy milestones.

Remember when we were examining Prochaska's change model (in chapter 4) I mentioned that looking at behavior patterns can be helpful in working with someone at the various stages of change, such as when someone had quit smoking but restarts? Knowing about this learning sequence gives you "stations" to investigate when someone wants to change a behavior but isn't succeeding. It's extremely beneficial to study what steps actually come before a behavior and what happens after the behavior. Here's a common pattern for smokers—the cigarette at break time:
1. Break starts at 10:30 am.
2. Smoker leaves the building with coworkers.
3. The group shares a social time discussing the morning.
4. Person smokes the cigarette.
5. Person experiences a sense of relaxation and connection.

Let's look at the beginning sequence—what happens before and during the behavior, as it currently happens—to see what can change the pattern. It's initiated by a time. Can the time be changed? Could the person schedule an earlier break? Does leaving the building help with the result of relaxation? Could a different destination be relaxing? Can the sense of connection with the smoking group be replaced by connection with an alternative group? How can the rewards be modified? The new behavior pattern might be suggested based on the answers:
1. Break starts at 10am.
2. Ex-smoker leaves the building with a friend who doesn't smoke.
3. They take a short walk.
4. Ex-smoker does some deep, relaxing breathing.
5. Ex-smoker gives herself one dollar for not smoking on the break.
6. Ex-smoker realizes sense of relaxation, accomplishment, and connection.

Someone may want to change the pattern of TV watching and overeating. A client might observe the behavior pattern and writing down the steps. The pattern might look like this:
1. Eat dinner in front of the TV.
2. Put the dishes in the kitchen and go back to watching another show.
3. Enjoy the feeling of being entertained, "zoned out," and relaxed.

Eating while doing other things decreases the attention paid to food, and sometimes people eat more than they want or need due to lack of attention. The client is used to eating while watching TV. If there's a need for something going on while eating, would music work? Together coach and clients can consider questions about the behavior pattern and alternatives. The new steps might go like this:
1. Eat dinner with a candle burning on the table and be aware of eating the food—taste, texture, satisfaction, and so on.

2. Listen to relaxing music during dinner.
3. Take a short walk after dinner, which may help with "zoning out" and increase relaxation. Reading could be substituted here as well.
4. Select one program on TV that's watched after the walk.

In this plan, TV watching is used as a reward to build a new pattern. It may also work to put TV first and the new behaviors after the TV. The basic idea here is that the new behaviors start to become relaxing and will be seen as benefits so that little by little the TV watching can be reduced or eliminated.

When considering changing behaviors, we tend to focus on behaviors that are to be limited or stopped. Creating new behaviors is equally important. *If the building of a new behavior does not accomplish the same benefit, then lasting change is less likely to be achieved.* Talk to any smoker who's quit and started again and ask why they re-started. Often it's that the person could not produce the benefits of smoking in another way. In my earlier years as a therapist, especially when dealing with serious addictions such as drugs or alcohol, without the reward—such as relaxation, a sense of wellbeing or a feeling of confidence—changing for good is unlikely.

> *What is the hardest pattern you ever changed? What was essential for arriving at success? Do you want to change a behavior now? What will help you most in arriving at your goal?*

A way to bring body and spirit wisdom into the Mental tool of working with behavior patterns is physically acting out the behavior pattern. You and your client can practice the current pattern and then actually practice walking a new pattern. For example, if you're working with a client on smoking, you and your client (even if you are working over the phone) can act out the situation of leaving for a break and finding a work friend to walk with during break, and then practice the entire new sequence. Your client can do this where they are, and you can do it in your workspace, so it's a combination of imaged scene and actual movement. Powerful questions about how your client feels, including body and energetic sensations, thoughts, and insights from spirit, will increase awareness that can lead to new actions.

Mental Tool #7	When to Use	Steps in Using	How to Gauge Effectiveness
Observing and Working with Behavior Patterns	When a client wants to replace or change a behavior.	Help your client learn the triggers that initiate a behavior and all the steps in the pattern, including the reward or benefit from the behavior. Then create a new behavior to satisfy the benefit. If this step is not accomplished, lasting change is unlikely.	Reduction or elimination of the unwanted behavior and increase of the new behavior.

Powerful Questions about Behavior Patterns
- What behaviors need to be eliminated?
- What are the steps in this pattern? How can the steps be changed before or after to alter the behavior?
- What behaviors need to be added? How and when?
- What is the benefit from the behavior you want to change and how can it be met in another way?

Laurel Wachtel, BS
Changing One Aspect Changes the Behavior Pattern

I train horses and people, making them a team. We practice at home and at the horse shows to have success in the show ring. Horses are very sensitive to my clients' feelings and directions, and often my clients are nervous and tense. Riding is a complex skill, but when you add the stress of competition, the task becomes even more multifaceted and challenging.

I use my coaching skills almost every minute when working with my team of rider and horse. I'm committed to having that team on the same page. The first part of this adventure is to help my riders know what kind of thoughts, movements, and feelings they're experiencing in a behavior pattern and to know how those affect their partner—their horse. The second part is for them is to see how changing just one aspect of the behavior pattern affects the whole riding picture. The good news about this is that the horses give immediate feedback when riders can listen and take it in.

Helping riders become aware of their behavior patterns can facilitate deep learning. For example, one of my clients, Sandy, has a habit of leaning forward, but she's unaware of it until I let her know that she's too far forward. Her horse is also telling her, but she needs to learn what the horse is signaling. When she's sitting correctly—providing a secure sense felt by horse and the rider—then both can more easily focus and succeed in the riding pattern of the event. Needless to say, this is not a lesson learned in one trip around my indoor arena. It takes time, as well as repeated somatic or body experience, for the rider to know "Oh. . .too far forward. . .I experience how this feels in my body and how that affects my horse. . .oh, okay. . .sitting straight now and I experience how that feels in my body and how that affects my horse."

Mental Tools for Homework at the End of Sessions

Let's say that you and your client have used one of the Mental tools and have explored the 1-10 scale, looked at changing life balance by using the pie chart, listed and prioritized "To Do" tasks, or investigated a behavior pattern. The next coaching step is for your client to select some type of homework—some small step that will cause movement toward the goal.

Plans and Timelines

Creating action steps is a vital part of sessions as well as being the hallmark of coaching. "Out of the ether and onto the street," I say sometimes. The homework needs to be observable, measurable, and clear. Your client who uses the 1-10 scale to move toward a less stressful life may decide to take a walk for ten minutes on Wednesday during the next week just to "smell the roses." As a result of using the pie chart exercise, your client may decide to take his wife out on a "date" on the following weekend as a way to bring more balance into family life. Your client who uses listing and prioritizing, may want to pay herself or himself $1 for each item moved from the "To Do" list to the "Ta Da" list. For your client who wants to stop smoking, the homework may be to talk to the boss about changing the break time. With this type of homework commitment, you and your client have a clear idea what will happen, with whom, and when, so your client can report in the following session how things went with the plan. The power of the *plans and timelines* tool is that it helps clients create traction in moving toward their goals.

Remember that homework with plans and timelines is about learning. It really is fine if the client accomplishes the homework and fine if the client doesn't. Important patterns, values, and insights can be identified from looking at homework that wasn't completed. We simply gain feedback, with no need for blame or sense of failure. The power of plans and timelines is bringing the learning aspect of coaching home to clients in an impactful and meaningful way.

In setting plans and timelines, I encourage my clients to *underpromise*, or to set goals just a little lower than they expect they could achieve. This is often hard for clients because they think that they won't make progress. However, clients tend to overpromise and put together plans that are too ambitious and that they can't accomplish. This leaves them feeling that they're not able to accomplish their goals and they end up feeling bad about themselves.

The power of underpromising when planning is that it sets up steps clients can accomplish. Don't underestimate the power of clients completing a small step week after week and feeling successful. It adds up to a level of empowerment that can flow into all aspects of their lives. They're more confident, may try new things, may feel happier, and may feel more successful at work and at home. Remember: the turtle won the race.

Rachael Friedman, MD
Baby Steps to Create Health

I took the BCI training with Linda Bark at the beginning of my Residency in Family Medicine. I use the tools every day in my practice and find my patients most responsive. They especially respond to taking "baby steps." Rather than focusing on health problems, I ask my patients to consider what they can do and what's the smallest step towards better health they could easily take. These baby steps grow to bigger steps, and my patient's lives change—without struggle. When I ask patients for their own goals and wishes for their health, I find they're more likely to take self-supporting steps rather than self-sabotaging steps. Linda's course helped me to ask the right questions and to be a co-creator of well-being with my patients. I support my patients to expect health. One of my patients who has multiple health issues, including kidney failure, has made significant gains in her self-designated wellness program—taking baby steps. Having sustained recovery from a drug addiction, she found quitting smoking a bigger challenge. Unable to quit, she worked with me to create a program in which she could gradually decrease the number of daily cigarettes. A two-pack-a-day smoker, she committed to decreasing by one cigarette every four days. She then began to be able to stop each time she was going to smoke a cigarette and tune in to herself, asking her body and mind if she "needed" the cigarette. She was able to begin to distinguish when the answer was "yes" or "no" and to follow this choice. Currently she smokes 14 cigarettes per day. A significant decrease from 40! This patient is also morbidly obese. We did a supermarket visit together and found a TV-dinner brand she would easily change to that had significantly less sodium than the brand she'd been eating. At her last visit with me she'd lost the first 2 pounds she'd ever lost by taking a simple step that she could do.

A married couple has begun a cooperative weight loss program together, initially by changing from regular Coke to diet, then to no soda. Inspired by their success, the wife began cooking soup (rather than buying readymade less healthy versions), with the husband's step being to eat it. After less than a year, taking baby steps, they've collectively lost almost 60 pounds.

The success stories could go on and on! When patients choose their own health goals and identify the baby steps they're willing to take toward them, they're rewarded by change, which in turn inspires them to take further steps. Coaching and medicine are a perfect complement.

CHAPTER 5: The Mental Structure of Consciousness in Coaching

Mental Tool #9	When to Use	Steps in Using	How to Gauge Effectiveness
Plans and Timelines	When clients are trying to achieve a goal. Use for setting up homework.	Have clients create small, steady, reasonable, and fun steps toward their goal.	Clients meet their goals and feel empowered. They have learned about patterns, values, or perceptions about meeting goals or not meeting goals.

Powerful Questions about Plans and Timelines
- How can you make your homework observable and measureable?
- How can you use underpromising in setting your homework?
- How will you know that you have accomplished your homework?

---

[1] Marcia L. Conner, *"What's Your Learning Style?"* www.marciaconner.com/assess/learningstyle.html. Accessed on May 19, 2011. Used with permission.

[2] Nancy Loving Tubesing and Donald Tubesing, Editors, *Structured Exercises in Wellness Promotion* (PO Box 3151, Duluth MN 55803: Whole Person Press, 1984). Used with permission. These editors have compiled many handbooks and even though they were printed years ago they still have vast applications to individual and group work.

[3] Susan Drouilhet, a colleague and coach, created this wonderful concept and shared it with me. You can read more about it in her blog at livingasifourlivesdependonit.com/2011/05/10/to-do-ta-da.

CHAPTER 6
The Mythical Part of Coaching

Sample Session 2B—"I Want to Get Things Done!"

"I feel overwhelmed. I can't seem to get my life in order and make any headway. Things are going so fast, and I just can't keep up with them. I have so many good ideas, but it's hard for me to get any of them going. This has always been a problem, but I'm tired of living like this. Things have to change. My desk is full of lists, but they don't help. I lose them or never finish them. I feel discouraged. I just had a birthday, and I thought I would be further along with my life by now. I thought I would have a better job, be making more money—just be more successful. I have lots of friends, but that isn't my concern. *I want to get things done*," exclaims April.

"So you don't lack vision. The challenge seems to be about follow through, focus, and getting enough traction so you can complete projects, and the trigger for addressing this issue now is your recent birthday?" I question.

"Exactly. I change from one thing to another, and I don't get to step four or five with some things," April says in a state of frustration.

"So you said that this is a familiar pattern, right?" I ask.

"Well, this is pretty much how I get sometimes—well, maybe about 60% of the time," she adds.

"It sounds like you have times when you're able to move one thing forward to the end, so I'm curious about what's different in those situations," I ask.

"Silly as it seems, I've never considered it, and here I am thinking myself to be such a good contemplator. I guess when I can accomplish things, I have fewer things on my plate, but right now I just have all these good ideas and my plate is overflowing," she says thoughtfully.

"Would it be correct to say that these seductive ideas are spilling over your plate and floating around your head, and each one wants your attention, so it's hard to stay focused on one over another?" I question.

"Correct. I like them all. Like having lots of boyfriends who are all very handsome, and it's hard for me to pick just one. I just don't know where to go from here," she states.

"Would you like me to take my coaching hat off here and put my consulting hat on and describe a system that identifies how people operate differently?" I ask.

"Sure, I am open to hearing some new information if it helps me get traction," says April.

"Let's see if this helps. People have different styles. Some are slower but steady, very loveable, and stable. It takes time for them to get ideas, and they may stick with an idea even when it no longer works for them—they're kind of earth types. Others have an idea and run straight ahead with it like wildfire, although they may be impatient if others don't keep pace. Still others have lots of ideas and have the ability to be flexible and change with the times; however, they may lose focus. Each type has advantages and challenges. Does this make sense?" I question.

"Absolutely and I'm the one you described last, and you're right about that flexibility. I'm the one at work who can react the best to new management approaches—and we've had many! We're on Plan M—long past Plan A, B, C, D, E, etc, and then we almost learn how to operate in new ways, and bingo—onto Plan N. It drives my coworkers crazy, but I just say, 'Let's see what this Plan N will do for us.' Coworkers tell me that my attitude really helps them, so I guess that's the positive part of being this type of person. But in my personal life, all those plans are flying around, and I don't even pick one and stick to it," she explains.

"What's the difference between work and your own life in regard to how things get done?" I ask.

"That's easy. At work, we have a cast of thousands. Well, not really, but we have a large team, and everyone has a piece of the action. Certain things have to be done certain ways, and that moves us forward. Even though we get new directions, we don't have to reinvent the wheel every time, and we do make our deadlines," she explains.

"Where do you want to go from here?" I inquire.

"I want to see if I could bring my team home," she laughs but then adds, "That's not a bad idea. I could hire someone for a little help, but I don't know if I could really afford that. Now that I'm thinking about it, I especially need one person on our team—Dan. He's the one that keeps us focused and on track. He's great at it and even does it in a way that's not pushy. I could do that for myself. We also use project management software, but as I think about it, I could just see myself with twenty projects, and it would take forever to keep track of them all. I guess what I need is to stay focused on one, or at least limit it to a couple."

"The most helpful team member is Dan, and you would like to take on his role with your work projects and focus on a couple of projects. What do you want to do now?" I ask.

"Well if I keep pretending I'm Dan, he would say it's simple—make a list!" she laughs again, and says, "I'm feeling more relaxed as though something can be done. My ability to change quickly is an asset, but sometimes I overdo it. If we go back to thinking of these ideas as boyfriends, I can only date a couple at a time!"

"What is next?" I ask.

"I need a minute on that question. Maybe it would help if I could write all my projects down," she replies.

"Great idea. We have time for you to do that now," I respond.

"Right now?" she asks.

"Yes," I state.

"This is continuing to sound kind of easy. I thought I had this big problem, but as we talk, it's getting smaller. Okay, I'll try it. I might not remember all of them," she says slowly.

"Okay, I'll keep track of the time. Are you ready?" I ask.

"Ready! This is even fun," she says with delight!

She lists all her projects and then says, "Okay, I'm done. I have fifteen, and I am sure there are a few more hiding out that I can't remember right now."

"Wonderful," I say, "What is next?"

"You know, I want to say that I really like your appreciating my ability to think well. It's one of my best attributes, and as you said earlier, it's like a double-edged sword but it is helping me now. What I've found is very interesting. I notice some patterns and themes. Many of them are art projects. Some are ways to help other people. Some involve my family, especially my niece and nephew, whom I really love deeply. Some I love to do because they relax me," says April.

"Terrific. So what would the Dan part of you say about these projects?" I inquire.

"He would say pick one from two to three categories if I want to make progress on them," she says with confidence, but then adds that he really wouldn't understand. "He's always focused on getting us to the finish line, which is good but not relevant in all circumstances. I realize now that some of these ideas are ways for me to relax, be creative, have alone time—and they don't necessarily have a finish line. They're ongoing. However, since my living space is pretty small, leaving projects all out doesn't really work. It just clutters up my apartment and makes me a bit crazy. When I was a kid, my mother used to insist that I had to put one toy away before I could get the next one out. As I think about it, that was a good rule, even though I hated it at the time. But this is confusing because some of my projects inform others and help me be creative. I guess it's not an all-or-nothing thing. Some things could stay out on the wall or on an easel to keep my imagination inspired, and other things could be put away. Okay, got it."

"So one category of projects is about expressing your creativity, and you want to have a limited number of examples of those projects around you for continued inspiration but not have all the projects ongoing at once," I paraphrase.

"Exactly," she says.

"So what about the other themes or categories and how you want to prioritize your activities?" I query.

"One track is for making a little extra money, and that overlaps with my ongoing creative projects. Dan would come in handy here. He would say pick one, not two or three, but only one, and move forward with it," she says with some hesitation.

"I notice you slowed down when you said that. What's going on for you now?" I ask.

"This part feels hard. The idea of doing only one seems really out of character, but I think he'd be right that if I want to bring in some extra money, I really have to focus," she states.

"What helps you focus?" I ask.

"Good question, Dan!" she says laughingly and then adds. "Maybe you could be my Dan, or oh, I just got another idea. If I can see something that pictures a pathway, that really helps. I could use our project software for this kind of project. That would help keep me on track. That's it. I could print out the project process path and put it on my wall. That would really help. I could add colors. Gee, this might even be fun. Okay, check. One money-making project," she says excitedly.

"Next?" I ask.

She's silent for a couple of minutes. "I just ran through all of the ones left, and what's important to me is time with my niece and nephew. And as I think about it, there can be overlap between this one and my creative work. One of the ways we love to spend time is using my art supplies, going to museums, and exploring some old ghost towns. We love having adventures together. Okay, that's it. I want to put a cap on this for now. Dan is right. These will be good focuses for me," she says emphatically and with certainty.

Chapter 6: The Mythical Part of Coaching

"What will you do when some of those other ideas start pounding on the door to be let into your life or even new ones come along? We know that thinking of new ideas is one of your talents," I inquire.

"That's a very good question. I don't know the answer. What do you think I should or could do?" she asks.

"You have such good ideas, could we just take a breath together and see if something comes up for you," I suggest.

"Okay, got it. I could put them in a beautiful colored folder entitled 'Wonderful Ideas,' and then at some point I could look at them. They'd be like a new toy, so I'd have to put the old idea away before I could bring the new one out," she states.

"Would some kind of schedule help with looking at this folder?" I inquire.

"You know me well. Yes, that's a good idea because I would want to do it every week, and then I would lose focus. Humm...I guess I could look at the new idea folder quarterly, and that would give me some time to make progress on current projects, and if I wanted to stay with those I could, but I'd have an opportunity to explore new ideas at some point," she explains.

"You want to have three focuses: one, to keep art projects going, one at a time—with some on the wall for inspiration; two, to spend time with your niece and nephew; and three, to pick one money-making project and use the project management software to help keep you focused. If new ideas come up in the meantime, you'll put them in a decorative file folder," I summarize.

"Yes, that really sounds Dan-like. This is great. I have the best of Dan, but yet I feel that I have freedom too," she says enthusiastically.

"In coaching, the client usually comes up with a plan for a next step between now and next week. What would you like for your homework?" I ask.

"The first thing is to write my plan down. Sometimes I come up with great ideas and then lose them. I don't want to misplace my plan, so I'll put it on my home office wall. I might even take a picture of Dan and have it on the list. He'll get a kick out of my appreciating his organizational skills. By next week I will use our project management tool to map out my money-aking idea," she says excitedly.

"Does that feel realistic?" I ask.

"Not really. I guess too many boyfriends again. Let's see. I will write down the plan, select one money-making project and take Dan's picture. Yes, that feels doable. It's so interesting. When I don't overpromise or over extend myself, I feel more relaxed. I would like to continue coaching and learn more about how that works.

We ended our session and April continued to work with me to fine-tune her skills at crafting the balance between creating a structure that helps her move forward with her ideas and allowing room for her fast mind and creativity. When she had that balance right, she was able to move toward her goals and felt that now she could make the progress she desired. Her birthday was a turning point for her future.

Tools Based Upon the Mythical Structure of Consciousness

The Mythical way of thinking came before the Mental structure, which is the more scientific method of thinking described in the last chapter. In the Mythic era, people used storytelling, imagination, and contemplation to discover and describe natural phenomenon, and the myths, rites, and practices became part of cultural knowledge. Myths represent universal images and understandings. Our creation myths were fashioned during this period. People spoke of gods, goddesses, ancestors, and archetypes. It was a period in which people could feel disempowered or find power by contact with the gods.

Examples of the Mythical in our current day include stories and rituals at the heart of religious practice, great contemporary stories and dramas, "old wives tales" passed down through generations, and many common cultural beliefs accepted as true and adhered to despite their lack of "proof." Our individual and cultural myths tell us who we are and what we should do, how our lives should be shaped, and how we should relate to each other. Sometimes our stories become a straightjacket, limiting us, but when we become aware of them we can learn to use them skillfully to help us see possibilities.

In this chapter we'll be working with tools based on the Mythical structure of consciousness: personal constitution, the language of empowerment, working with personal story, dialog, and imagery. Affirmations are another powerful tool from the Mythic.

What helped me work with April was my knowledge of *personal constitution*, based on traditional healing systems in Chinese Traditional Medicine and Ayurveda, from India. These systems originated in an era where people saw themselves not so much as individuals but as embedded, the way characters are in stories. "As above, so below" meant personal characteristics would be seen in mythical terms rather than based on specific scientific measurements (which would be the Mental structure of consciousness).

The constitution types describe physical characteristics, inner processes, thinking tendencies, and a multitude of other personal aspects. One size does not fit all, and basing how we work with people on personal constitutions ensures that we address their unique needs and qualities. In the pages to come, I'll go into more detail about several personal constitutions, and you'll see how April is a classic example of one type.

I'll also introduce tools that assess and increase personal empowerment, since that's such a strong focus in coaching. I want to evaluate my clients' level of empowerment, which can be indicated by how they speak. Are they speaking from their own position—using "I" instead of speaking in generalities? Do they take responsibility for their actions? Are they able to identify needs? Do they use *empowerment language* that mirrors their own sense of realistic authority? In this chapter, you'll read about approaches that support personal power and responsibility, such as "I messages" and non-violent communication.

After assessing personal constitution and the degree to which a client uses empowerment language, I'm curious about how my clients think about their lives or a particular goal. A Mythical tool that can be extremely powerful is identifying and perhaps helping clients revaluate and/or recreate their *personal stories*. The illustration that starts this chapter pictures a client with a notebook doing just that. The perceptions or stories of past times or versions of current life lie on the shelf as versions of "my book 1.0" and "my book 2.0." Notice that in the rows of information, there are many, many sections, such as adventure, balance, health, legacy, and others. Also on the shelf you can see a face on a book that has several different sets of glasses built in, to remind us that we have the choice of looking at things from varied perspectives. Each adds a unique dimension.

The Mythical tools of story, imagery, and dialog are tools often used in the middle of coaching sessions, and these are described in more detail later in this chapter. *Imagery* is usually a visualization of stories or situations and another Mythical tool that can create meaningful shifts of consciousness and spur action. We saw the benefits of imagery with Sandra in Part One. *Dialog* is a two-way conversation about an event, a situation, or even a part of someone, such as a pain or body part. A focus on the *critical voice* is included in the section on dialogues since so many people experience an overactive blaming and demoralizing inner voice.

Discussion of *affirmations* (positive statements about having already attained a goal) concludes the Mythical chapter. This is a tool that can be used at the homework stage of a coaching session. Finding unconscious negative "affirmations" is helpful during this phase.

> **Assessment** *(beginning of session)*:
> - *Personal Constitution*
> - *Empowerment Language*
>
> **Middle**:
> - *Story*
> - *Imagery*
> - *Dialog*
>
> **Homework** *(end of session)*:
> - *Affirmations*

Mythical Assessment Tools

A coach doesn't need to quickly or rigidly draw conclusions about who people are, but having a framework of characteristics can facilitate the coach's ability to tailor the work to clients' needs. Considering the extent to which clients feel a sense of empowerment is also important at the beginning of working with them.

Personal Constitution

A key aspect of traditional, long-standing healing systems such as Traditional Chinese Medicine (TMC) and Ayurveda is focusing on the uniqueness of each individual. The first question a doctor in these systems would ask is not, "What's wrong with my patient?" but rather, "Who is my patient?" If we consider, for example, that the same cultured bacteria can affect people differently, this approach makes perfect sense.

Assessing personal constitution is especially useful for addressing health promotion and wellness. For instance, among other things one's diet needs to account for specific bodily needs, geographic locale, and seasonal changes. In other words, one diet does not fit all people or occasions. Similarly, one exercise program doesn't meet everyone's needs or even one particular person's needs at all times.

CHAPTER 6: The Mythical Part of Coaching

> *When you think about your own life, how have your nutritional and exercise needs changed over time—for instance, when you moved to a different climate, as you aged, as a result of illness or an increased demand of intense physical training?*

In TCM and Ayurveda assessments help identify an individual's personal constitution. Each system employs a model based on a five-element theory—in Ayurveda, those five elements are Ether, Air, Fire, Water, and Earth, condensed into three elements, and in Traditional Chinese Medicine they are Water, Wood, Fire, Earth, and Metal. You might think these concepts seem mythological, especially as the terminology used doesn't match our current scientific model and understanding of the body. Nevertheless, Western science is beginning to research and corroborate the beneficial effects of these treatment modalities, even as the theoretical foundations upon which they are based remain foreign or "mythic" to the Western mind.

I find the Ayurvedic system of personal constitution to be the easiest to use in my coaching practice. Even the basic application of this ancient healing system can facilitate profound shifts in my clients. Therefore, I include information about Ayurveda here, with the understanding that what I'm sharing is the very tip of a rich and powerful iceberg.

EXERCISE: What's Your Constitutional Type?

To help determine your Ayurvedic constitution you can fill out this short questionnaire. You may find that you are a combination of constitutions (and many of us are). In that case, knowing that there are multiple ways to get out of balance and many ways to return to equilibrium is very helpful.

Constitution Markers[1]

Marker	Earth/Water Kapha	Fire Pitta	Air/Ether Vata
Body type	Solid, sturdy	Medium, muscular	Extremes (tall, short, thin)
Hair	Thick, lustrous	Fine, thinning	Course, dry, wild, unruly
Hands	Wide, strong, cool	Medium, red, warm	Dry, cold, pallid
Activity	Prefer to relax	Assertive and to the point	Fits of excitation followed by fatigue
Mind	Slow, but good memory	Quick, certain	Drifts off
Temperament	Calm, difficult to ruffle	Easily irritable	Changeable, erratic
Common symptoms	Heaviness, congestion	Irritability, acidity	Nervousness, exhaustion, jumpiness and gas

To use for self-assessment, circle the markers that apply to you, then go back and write in each circle a number: 1 if it is mildly true; 2 if markedly accurate; 3 if extremely descriptive of you.

Then add the numbers for each vertical column. If two columns have high numbers that are close, you're a mixed type.

There are three major classifications of personal constitution in Ayurveda—Kapha, Pitta, and Vata. A person is usually dominant in one or two types, even though we experience all of them, to varying degrees. Each constitution is described below: first the essence of the type in balance or when in equilibrium, stable, and steady. Next the out-of-balance constitution state is described, followed by coaching approaches that can help rebalance the constitution. Notice the difference between *dominated*, or out of balance, and *dominant*, or natural tendency, in the descriptions below.

You and your clients might like to use the constitution marker exercise to help determine basic constitution. As you become more experienced, you'll become better able to recognize signs of the constitutions in balance and out of balance. Note that life-stage is a factor in constitution. As children, we are more Kapha-like as we continually add to our substance by gaining weight, growing taller, and maturing our bodies. In our middle years, we move toward action and accomplishment, engaging our Pitta natures in this process. And in our elder years, as our attention turns toward spirituality and sharing our wisdom, we enter a Vata phase when even our bodies may become less substantial and more Air-like.

1. Vata, or Air-Like (Air + Ether)
Balanced

Think of air or wind. Air-dominant people move quickly, especially in their thinking. They see ahead of others and are often described as visionaries. Just as wind shifts easily, Vata types can change quickly. They may also speak rapidly and change their tones in conversation. Albert Einstein was a classic example of an Air-dominant individual, as demonstrated by his visionary inventions, and even his hair, which was frizzy and all over the place! Vatas may be very spiritually focused. They also make good entrepreneurs, with their quick minds, hosts of great ideas, and natural enthusiasm for sharing them. Vata-dominated people may not be the best suited for the long haul or for attending to details, but rather make good start-up consultants. They enjoy a degree of structure, but only as long as it doesn't impede their freedom.

I imagine that you can identify April, the client in the sample session that begins this chapter, as a classic illustration of this type of personal constitution. She had a fantastic ability to think fast and to be flexible, but as she said, her abilities were a double-edged sword. She found herself out of balance, as described in the following section.

Out of Balance

Too much "Air" can lead to excessive movement, such as tremors or heart palpitations. Ever notice someone tapping their pen or shaking their leg during a meeting? Out-of-balance Vatas feel fatigued, weak, and cold. Alternatively, they can become so excited and overly enthusiastic that others may keep their distance from them in order to avoid being pulled into the whirlwind. Moving into action too quickly and without adequate preparation, they can then have difficulty staying focused on the long-term goal. Anxiety and fear are two of the most obvious symptoms of air-dominant folks out of balance.

Coaching Approaches

Given Vata's creativity and visionary ideas, an individual with an Air constitution makes an inspirational coaching client. Imagine coaching Einstein, who changed the world! Like the wind, the person can change easily. Vatas may come up with wonderful ideas, but their enthusiasm can wane quickly, and with the smallest barrier they can leave one idea and start moving enthusiastically in a completely different direction. It's the curse and blessing of "changing easily."

If you're coaching an Air-dominant person and s/he becomes out of balance, you can suspect certain possible issues. For instance, fear and anxiety may come up for your client, which people usually want to extinguish. However, a normal degree of anxiety and fear is an opportunity for being curious. What's underneath the feelings? Is there a message that needs to be heeded? Are these emotions allies warning the client of a realistic concern, or are they simply old patterns that are not appropriate to a current movement forward?

Another possible difficulty when a person with a Vata-dominant constitution is off balance is forgetting quickly. In this case, using lists and helping to set priorities will usually be helpful. You might want to ask powerful question about ways your client can stay focused, build just the right kind of structure, and take steady steps toward the long- term aim.

Additional ways to facilitate a return to balance may involve the skin and ears. For instance, you can suggest increasing body awareness through exercise or massage, walking in nature, or even walking barefoot on the lawn. Also helpful are chanting, playing comforting music, and identifying sounds and touch that may be disturbing. Creating structure can help, but remember, it's key that your client desires it—and that it's not too confining. For instance, your client may like to organize a desk but keep current projects right in front so that s/he can jot down the continual flow of new ideas. In terms of co-creating homework, your client may enjoy commitment to a particular action but then want to change the assignment after a few weeks to maintain interest. Diet may help—"grounding" warm, cooked foods, such as potatoes, beets, and carrots can assist the "return to earth." In terms of eating, it's helpful to pay attention to time, eating regular, scheduled meals and warm foods and drinks. Remember that these diet options do not work for all Vatas, just as no diet works for everyone. Re-creating or changing the environment and surroundings can also help—less stimulation usually means less distraction and a greater sense of calm.

2. Pitta, or Fire-Like
Balanced

Fire-dominant people are decisive; in conversation, they cut to the chase, and in action, they get things done. Enthusiastically pursuing long-term goals, they often want feedback to check if they are on track; if not, they quickly readjust and realign their sights on the target. They are dedicated, and thus make excellent project directors and office managers. They want to be organized, are fantastic with details, and love lists. Clarity is a defining feature of a Pitta-dominant person. They communicate well, although their voices may be a bit loud and sometimes shrill. They tend toward sharper facial features and directionality in their movements, their gaze, and even their words. With very quick intellects, Pittas can be very optimistic and positive. Brightness and luminescence are defining characteristics. They are cheerful as long as things progress at a pace deemed fast enough and in their chosen direction.

Out of Balance

Too much fire burns. And this is what can happen for Fire-dominated individuals. The sharpness of their minds can be advantageous and cut directly to a point, but it can also slice through others with blame and anger. Unbalanced Pittas are very critical of others and also of themselves, especially with their desire for things to be perfect. Their intensity and obsession often lead to extremely heated conversations.

Coaching Approaches

A Fire-dominant client brings great joy to the coaching relationship—and also specific opportunities for growth and transformation. Once your client is clear on aim and has the tools needed, watch this Pitta client go. Pitta's tag line is like Nike's—"just do it." They move toward a goal enduring the long haul with a positive attitude, although they'll want to know why and need information. They'll benefit from time on the internet and will want to explore other resources. Information organized in charts will stimulate a Pitta's quick and sharp mind. Your curiosity as coach will also feed your client's hunger for knowledge. Together you'll learn a great deal on this very exciting and informative journey.

When off balance, a Pitta-dominant client often becomes angry and blaming. This frustration will be aimed at others but even more so internally. At these times, your client may need extra external approval. If your client doesn't complete homework, s/he may not admit it, feeling a sense of shame about the homework behavior. Overly focused on perfection and success, your client may miss the forest for the trees as her or his work/life balance begins to decay.

A coaching strategy is to model giving permission for performing less-than-perfectly. As your client learns to surrender the need to be in control (and therefore "perfect") at all times and redefines success such that "failure" becomes just feedback, your client's excessive heat will begin to cool and your client will feel the calming effects.

Pitta-dominated people can be fiercely devoted to others but often don't connect with their own nurturing. Powerful questions about self-care may be just the thing to help with this tendency.

Certain foods may also facilitate re-balancing for Fire-dominant clients. While Pitta may love spicy foods (and the hot climates they grow in), fermented, and very oily foods, when they are out of balance these foods will usually contribute to a lack of peace. Again, remembering that diet is very individualized, not only to constitution but season and individual needs, out of balance Pitta may benefit from cooling foods, such as salads and other cuisine that people enjoy in the summer.

3. Kapha, or Earth-Like (Earth + Water)
Balanced

When people have this constitution as dominant, and are in balance, they're content, pleasant, loving, warm, stable, and nurturing—in other words, they embody the mother earth type. Being so strong, they don't need to say anything quickly. They might live in the same location for years and have stayed in touch with their kindergarten teacher. In contrast to their air-dominant friends, whose fast minds catch on quickly, Kaphas may appear to grasp things more slowly, but once they get the picture, they really get it. People love to be around the melodic voices and calming energy of this type. As they don't jump to conclusions, others trust them, knowing they've been thoughtful and thorough in their decision-making processes. Earth-dominant folks are less concerned than their fiery associates with moving up professional ladders; rather, they focus more on the quality of relationships at work. Very loyal and dependable, they treasure their commitments to family and friends. They enjoy surrounding themselves with nice things, not to show off but as a way to enhance comfort, an important factor for them.

Out of Balance

Think of the earth—slow, steady, and solid. When kaphas get too "earthed," they stop. They may become stuck and stagnated and would rather lie down than do anything else. "Why move?" they ask. Snoring is the Earth-dominated person's mantra. With a tendency toward laziness, depression, or darkness, they gain weight easily and find letting go of emotional or personal attachments difficult. In an attempt to comfort themselves, they may over-collect and slip into hoarding. They also tend to help others before they help themselves.

Coaching Approaches

There are special treats and some particular challenges to embrace when working with an Earth-dominant client. On the treat side, you'll develop a solid, enduring partnership, and when you see her or his name on your calendar, no doubt you'll smile and have a warm sensation in your heart.

When your client becomes overly "earthed," s/he may need tough love or a kick-in-the-pants—figuratively speaking. They may need a push because they have trouble getting started on their own. They might request more frequent check-ins to keep moving. Setting up a reward system and clarifying benefits will help in this situation. Exploring the question, "Why move?" may also prove fruitful. Your client may find the motivation to change behavior based on some family need rather than a self-need.

The Earth-dominated client may rest in *pre-contemplation* (denial of a need to make a change) or *contemplation* (interested in making a change in the future but not in the present). Helping your clients raise their consciousness will help in both instances. Is your client denying (not recognizing the problem), rationalizing (making excuses for the current situation), or projecting (by displacing responsibility from self to others)? Knowing which type of pre-contemplative thinking your client employs can be helpful. Would examining the facts and solid information concerning the situation help to shift motivation and the engagement level? How about recognizing the history of successful changes?

In terms of eating and taking care of health, pay attention to quantity. Smaller portions of warm food may be helpful. Focusing on just the right incentive or reward that may be based in relationship or comfort can help Kapha get moving. Self-care is another path to help Kapha balance loyalty and focus on the other with focus on the self.

OTHER APPLICATIONS OF PERSONAL CONSTITUTION

Knowing about personal constitutions can be helpful when working with groups. In the 1980s, I coauthored a book on menopause, and as part of the process I worked with many women around the signs and symptoms they experienced. As I grew to know each of the participants better, patterns based on constitution became clear. The women who were Air/Vata-dominant would complain of feeling "fuzzy headed" and experienced serious short-term memory loss. Those who were clearly Fiery/Pitta were more likely to become stressed and frustrated from severe hot flashes. The Earth-like or Kapha women suffered from edema and lethargy. In our comprehensive approach, we found the use of constitutional interventions helpful.

Mythical Tool #1	When to Use	Steps in Using	How to Gauge Effectiveness
Personal Constitution Types (Vata, Pitta and Kapha) **Vata (Air)**—mental; quick learner; good at concepts and abstract thinking; can become spacey and disorganized, so needs structure, embodiment, reduced stimulation. **Pitta (Fire)**—sharp; a doer; organized; effective; can become easily frustrated; hot-tempered, so needs cooling, calming. **Kapha (Earth)**—stable; loyal; great memory; has comforting energy; can stagnate, so needs movement and action.	When listening to a client, the coach may hear words or issues that relate to personal constitution, such as: the client is spacey and unorganized (Vata), or the client is too busy and easily frustrated (Pitta), or the client is stagnating (Kapha). Coach may also want to support constitutional strenghts.	Ask client who has unbalanced personal constitution if specific interventions might be helpful. Coach uses knowledge of personal constitution to inform choice of powerful questions.	The client experiences more balance and experiences the positive characteristics of personal constitution.

Knowledge of constitutions can be utilized in organizational settings as well. When I worked as a health consultant in a .com company, I realized that many of the employees were Vata-dominant. To counter organizational stress, we minimized stimulation and used structure. During a software launch, we applied several constitutional interventions: brought food to share that was made of root vegetables to help with grounding; hired a body worker for chair massage to assist employees in finding balance and feeling more embodied and less in their heads; and set up a quiet room with less stimulation for breaks. The staff discovered that these inputs reduced their stress levels and improved their work efficiency.

Powerful Questions about Personal Constitution:
- If your clients are interested, or may profit by this learning system, ask if they would like to take the constitutional assessment.
- How does your constitutional dominance express itself in your life?
- How does your constitutional dominance influence this situation or issue?
- How can you become more in balance from a constitutional perspective?
- What helps you stay in balance, and what moves you out of balance, from a constitutional viewpoint?

Empowerment Language

The Mythical is alive in us in how we relate to ourselves, each other, and what's happening in our lives. Our style of relating arises from personal constitution and also shows itself in the degree to which we feel ourselves to be empowered agents. Attention to empowerment is an extremely important element of the coaching process, and working with language is one powerful way to engage.

EMPOWERMENT SOUNDS LIKE HAVING A CHOICE

In addition to considering constitution and other factors in who my clients are and how that influences what they bring to sessions, I'm also listening to see if they speak from their own position using the pronoun "I," for instance, "I like to have control." Or do they speak in a more general mode, commenting that "people like to have control." Using "I" demonstrates clarity about their preferences, needs, awareness, or values and shows a willingness to take responsibility for their statements. There are times when speaking about people in general is appropriate, but often clients project their feelings or values onto others when it's not really true that all people value one thing or feel a certain way. If I hear my clients speaking in generalities, I'll ask if they could speak from their own position and see if that feels different. I can't think of a time when someone didn't feel the difference. If it's all right with my clients, I continue to point out when they're not speaking from their position, which helps them take responsibility for their feelings, values, and perspectives.

Another style of speaking that I may notice is words suggesting a "victim consciousness." When we use phrases such as "have to," "makes me," "got to," and "don't have a choice," we speak with little power, and in effect, resign ourselves to not having options. Coaching your clients toward empowerment is essential for healthy change. This shift could be as simple—and profound—as using different language. "Have to" becomes "want to" or "choose to."

EXERCISE: Becoming Empowered through Changing Our Language

Think of the last time you felt like you didn't have a choice in a decision. Describe your role or action, saying a sentence out loud that includes one of the following:
- had to;
- made me.

For example, let's say that you decided to volunteer to work on a Saturday instead of taking the day off. You might say, "I had to work on Saturday instead of going to the beach." Sense how you feel in your body. What happens in your jaw? In your muscles? In your stomach? With your breathing? What kind of sensations and energy do you experience?

Now say the same sentence using empowerment language, with one of the following phrases:
- chose to;
- wanted to.

Rewording that sentence would yield, "I chose to work last Saturday instead of going to the beach." How does that feel? What's different?

The issue of choice can be complex. We may feel that we have choices in certain matters but not in others. For instance, people might question whether someone living in a country at war or subject to famine chose that existence. However, even in these situations, while participants may not be able to change the larger circumstances, they can choose how to feel on the inside. An example of this kind of situation would be Nelson Mandela's demonstration of dignity and acceptance of his situation during the years he was jailed. I've found that the more people experience making choices and taking responsibility for those choices, the more empowered they feel, with the result that change comes more easily. If clients see themselves as choosing, they can often choose something different.

This applies to organizations as well. I taught several coaching courses at a hospital on the East Coast. Managers, line staff, nurses, physical and occupational therapists all attended. After I'd taught the course three times, I began to notice something odd: during each course, following the fifth class, about three people would drop out. When I went back over my notes, I realized that in the fifth class we addressed victim language. Those who had dropped out were those who had significant problems with that concept. When I reworked the presentation to move more gradually into this subject, allowing for more discussion and work with any resistance that arose, people stopped dropping out. What a wonderful lesson for me in just how powerful the victim issue can be, and I wondered what effect that kind of thinking and feeling has on an organizational level.

A subtle expression of this victim mentality is expressed by an inability to notice the support and fulfillment that are already available. Sometimes my clients will complain that no one appreciates them or supports them, but in reality the care and assistance is there. The missing action may include accepting the feeling of support. What's getting in the way? Does the client have an inner critical voice that says, "You shouldn't need help?" Does the client feel that people don't really care about others and miss examples of kindness? When this is the case, my client and I explore what's stopping the client from perceiving ways their needs *are* being met.

CHAPTER 6: The Mythical Part of Coaching

THE LANGUAGE FOR GETTING NEEDS MET

Moving out of victimhood and into empowerment requires becoming proactive by taking responsibility for one's needs and for ensuring that they get met. While almost every aspect of coaching helps with bringing clarity about needs, here we're focusing on the empowerment that results from stating them in clear language. Clients may need to learn this skill, which coaches can provide directly through modeling the skills themselves or by changing hats and stepping into the consulting role.

One great way to communicate needs is via "I" messages. I learned this technique in the seventies when I taught Parent Effectiveness Training, and since that time the technique has become a standard part of many therapeutic approaches. An "I" message is an effective way to ask for what you want and to let others know how their behavior—positive or negative—affects you—now, and/or in the future.

"I" messages are made up of three parts:
- a non-blaming description of the behavior of the other person;
- the effect on you now or in the future;
- the feelings you have about the situation.

For instance, if you feel appreciated in a situation, you could send this type of "I" message:

Non-Blaming Description	Effect Now or in the Future	Feeling
When you let me know when I'm doing a good job,	I'm more effective,	and it boosts my morale.

In work settings, you may choose to stick with the effects and leave out the feeling part. This will depend on the type of culture in your company and how emotions are handled. For example, if someone on your team isn't pulling their weight, you could say the following:

Non-Blaming Description	Effect Now or in the Future	Feeling
When you don't follow through on something you said you'd do,	I'm not able to get my part of the project done.	

In a family or more personal relationship, however, you may find including feelings to be very useful and important. For instance this:

Non-Blaming Description	Effect Now or in the Future	Feeling
When you put your dishes in the dishwasher,	I can make the next meal more easily and quickly,	and I feel very appreciative.

"I" messages also provide a constructive way for communicating between coach and client. For example, if your client is late for an appointment, you could say something like this:

Non-Blaming Description	Effect Now or in the Future	Feeling
When you don't call on time,	I feel a time crunch in helping you achieve your goals,	and I feel frustrated and sad.

Your client may also give you feedback via this format, like this:

Non-Blaming Description	Effect Now or in the Future	Feeling
When you don't answer my email within a day or two,	I'm not able to move forward in the way we had discussed,	and I feel lost, confused, and angry.

At first, "I" messages may seem a bit contrived or unnatural. However, the more we use them for directly communicating our needs and for giving clear feedback, the more we'll naturally integrate them into our own communication style. Alternative, and perhaps more relaxed ways to word the above examples include these:

Client to coach: "I wasn't able to move forward as we discussed last week, when you didn't answer my email about that resume question. I felt lost, confused, and angry."

Coach to client: "I don't feel we make as much progress when we start late, and I feel frustrated."

Parent to child: "Great, I see you put your dishes away, and I can start dinner with a clean kitchen. Thanks so much."

Communicating Needs and Wants

Another area for exploration is discriminating between needs and wants. Identifying a request as a want might make a difference to the client and to the person they're addressing. Wants may be a little less important than needs. Identifying and getting our needs met is a frequent focus in coaching and of life in general.

Several movements and organizations have developed to address this issue. Because I feel this is such a vital and central subject, I want to mention two of these groups. To me these examples are taking coaching principles and communication methods to a larger arena, and if you want to become expert at working with these processes, these are wonderful organizations to learn from and join.

The Center for Nonviolent Communication was founded by Marshall Rosenberg in 1984 and grew out of his interest and work as a civil rights activist in the 1960s.[2] This worldwide organization provides skills training that's anchored in identifying and expressing universal human needs (sustenance, trust, and understanding) and operates from a platform of nonjudgment. His model goes a step further than "I" messages by teaching people how to make a request to fulfill unmet needs. This process underscores personal responsibility and builds relationships founded on cooperation and collaboration. You and your clients can find abundant information about this process on the internet, potentially including local resources.[3]

Another model, Restorative Justice, was developed by Dominic Barter, a colleague of Marshall Rosenberg. Restorative Justice applies nonviolent communication within a structure that facilitates group healing. Working with people separated by conflict situations, Barter facilitates their reconnection through a group method in which harms, needs, and obligations are brought to light so that healing may occur. To facilitate this process participants are asked questions such as these: "What do you want to happen next?" "What would you like to offer and to whom?" "What would you like to request and from whom?" In some Restorative Justice circles, the words victim and persecutor are avoided, thus allowing different perspectives and reducing the tendency toward blame and judgment. This method is used globally, and in the United States is being employed in school systems such as Oakland, CA to address bullying and harassment.[4] One of the best-known examples of restorative justice worldwide is the Truth and Reconciliation Commission of South Africa.[5]

Mythical Tool #2	When to Use	Steps in Using	How to Gauge Effectiveness
Empowerment Language	When a client uses any language that indicates lack of personal power.	The client reframes language of powerlessness to language that expresses a sense of choice and promotes empowerment.	The client sees more choices and feels empowered.

Powerful Questions about Empowerment
- What would be different if you came from a position of choice in this situation?
- How could you feel more empowered?
- What are your needs?
- How can you get them met?
- How can you express your needs?
- How do you distinguish between needs and wants?
- Is this a need or a want?
- What helps you meet your needs?
- How will you know when your needs are met?
- Are there ways that your needs could be met but you're not able to accept or let in the support?

Susan Friedman, BSN
Empowerment for Patients

A registered nurse for over 30 years, I'd learned to create care plans for people. In medicine, there are standard plans of care, and there's always the issue of getting the patient to comply. One of the challenges is the "noncompliant" patient, though we seldom stop to consider that by acting as experts we prevent patients from acting as effectively as they might if they were seen as partners.

My most recent nursing position, from which I recently retired, was as a night nursing manager for a home care hospice agency. Patients and families called during the night expecting my expertise and answers for their concerns. I was "the expert." I sometimes wondered if there was a better way.

What I love about the Bark Coaching Institute Model is the partnership between coach and client and honoring the *client* as the expert about his or her life and body. As a coach in training I learned to invite intuition, presence, and trust. The role of the coach is not to tell patients what to do. I've come to appreciate how this new role empowers patients.

Coaching encourages me to listen with all my senses and to all that is present in the field of the moment, body, mind, feeling, sensation, vision—all that shows up. It invites an unconditional positive regard for person, place, and being, and creates a space for an alchemy that transforms what might be considered a "problem" to an opportunity for personal exploration, growth, transformation, and connections with self and other.

Feeling listened to, respected, and empowered, patients who receive coaching can learn to take responsibility for their condition and choices, and also to ask for what they need.

Susan Spoelma, MBA, MSN, RN, NEA-BC, DNP (student)
Organizational Leadership

In my position as chief nurse executive of a hospital I need to directly manage my employees. I say, "The policy in this situation does not allow for that action." or "If you do X, then the results will be Y, and that's not acceptable." This stance is extremely valuable and lets employees know what's expected and what's not allowed. But if I just say don't do X, that's only half of the equation. What *can* they do? How can they accomplish their goal differently? The BCI training provided a safe place to practice ways to help my subordinates take the next step, for their growth and development.

For example, I supervised an employee who was very passionate about his job, and often became so upset in meetings that he started yelling. Others in the organization advised keeping him under control or firing him, but I didn't want to handle the situation in either way because he was also playing a valuable role. This employee often made constructive points; it was just that due to the way he made them, few people could really hear what he was saying. Some would comment under their breath, tune out, roll their eyes, or think, "There he goes again." But others were really glad he was speaking out because he often said what others were really feeling, so if I'd asked him to leave or stopped him from sharing his perspective, those opinions would have gone underground and come up in unhealthy ways.

Because of my coach training, I was better able to help this man reach his goal of expressing himself differently. At first, after I said he could no longer continue to explode, he wasn't happy and said, "That's who I am. I can't do it differently. I don't even know when I'm going overboard. Well, really I want to change but I don't know how!" Realizing that his comment was a doorway into change I asked, "How could you be a little more aware of when you were getting too wild?" It took some time but he suggested a secret code between us. If he started moving toward the explode mode, I'd touch my left ear. When he spoke, he would look at me to check for our signal. We had regular conferences about him reaching his goal, and in the beginning, he said that I looked as if I were going to pull my ear off before he finally got it and cooled down. Over time, he became better able to present his position in a way that others could hear. Our meetings were more productive because all the issues could be put on the table in a way that most could heed and respond to.

Mythical Tools That Facilitate Clarity and Awareness in the Middle of Sessions

As meaning-making beings we seek to understand who we are, what we can do, and how we should relate. Drawing from Mythical structure of consciousness gives us powerful tools for tapping into the richness of our lives: working with stories, imagery, and creative dialog.

Working with Story

My clients all have "stories" that they tell themselves (and others) about their lives, their origins, their relationships, their goals, etc. They not only have stories but they live the stories. Working with these stories and finding new viewpoints can be fascinating, creative, and fruitful. For example, what if clients thought about their lives in terms of a Hero's Journey? How would that change their ambivalence about moving forward, their reactions to periods of doubt, trials and tribulations, obtaining the goal, integrating the journey lessons into their lives, and sharing the wisdom of the journey with others?

> *Have you ever considered the power of the stories you tell yourself? Think about yesterday. How would you describe it? You might discover that in fact there are many versions or stories of yesterday, depending on your mood and attitude at the time of inquiry. For example, yesterday was Friday the 13th, and I spent my day working with clients, receiving an acupuncture treatment, checking email, and writing. If you were to stop by my office right now and ask me about yesterday, I would say that it was an extremely productive day and that I had had an extraordinary breakthrough during my acupuncture session, which led me to make a commitment to proceed with a future project. My story would depict Friday the 13th as a really lucky day. Alternatively, if I were tired yesterday and/or upset about something, I might convey a different story and describe a Friday the 13th that was unlucky or just ho-hum. My story can change from second to second based on my perspective!*

Our viewpoints color our language and our stories, and helping clients become clear about their perspectives is vital for transformation and change. For instance, my client Max realized he had a negative story about exercise—that it was boring and uncomfortable. But through our coaching, Max discovered that exercise could be fun and revitalizing, like boxing, which he loved but surprisingly never considered as exercise—it was boxing—so he shifted his perspective, redefining exercise and his relationship to it. He then began to take steps toward a healthier lifestyle.

Another client, Martha, had a hidden story about herself that was impacting her life. It wasn't until I asked her to tell me a story of her future that it surfaced. She described a struggle to find a meaningful romantic relationship, with the story ending in despair. I asked if she could tell a different story, and she lit up, suddenly realizing that something different could happen. I don't want to infer that by changing the story of the future a different ending will magically appear, but I've learned that sometimes it does, and a positive ending is more likely to happen when my client envisions fulfilling a goal.

In 1930, Joseph Campbell, a famous American scholar and author, popularized working with myth and archetype. An archetype is a model that acts as a pattern. He wrote about how archetypes are often hidden in stories. Since that time others have introduced many different archetypes such as Hero, Mentor, King, and Trickster, along with very common archetypes such as Mother and Father. Sometimes clients are not aware that they are following an archetype or pattern of how to perceive and act. When asked if they want to think in these terms, they are able to modify roles and patterns they'd like to change.

I'm interested in the stories that my clients have about themselves as well as the story I hold about myself and my coaching. One way for me to explore the unexamined stories that are the scripts for my life is to take some quiet time and ask myself to finish this statement: "Once upon a time, there was a coach named Linda Bark, and this is her story. . . ." I can continue the story in my mind but I've found my experience to be more potent if I write it out in my journal. I also ask students in the last part of their training to complete this exercise, and usually their stories point to wonderful areas for growth and/or celebration. Sometimes students see a rosy future, but it can go the other way too. They might not be able to see themselves as successful, and if that's the case, they probably won't develop a thriving practice if that is the direction they choose. If they want to join a company that provides clients, their story about finding that position and functioning effectively in it is equally important to discover. Do they think the road will be challenging and hard? How could the script describe an easier process that portrays a course of things unfolding and gracefully coming together?

I'm also interested in how to use story in paraphrasing as I listen to clients. My first feedback with Sandra (Sample Session 1A) described her energy with a short story: "It feels like a thoroughbred racehorse at the starting gate, nostrils flared, right front hoof pawing the ground, ready to go but not able to move forward. The horse really wants to run, but the gate hasn't opened yet, and the horse can't even see the finish line." She was easily able to identify with that, and that story about the racehorse stayed with her as she continued her coaching sessions.

190 CHAPTER 6: The Mythical Part of Coaching

> *What is your story about a goal that you want to achieve? Does it entail hard work and struggle or fun and ease, with things aligning for success? Does your story need changing, and if so, in what ways?*

> *Think of a time when someone listened to you and replied in a metaphor or story. What was the impact? Was it helpful? Is there also a memory of using metaphor or story as ways to give feedback to someone you were listening to? Was it successful?*

Mythical Tool #3	When to Use	Steps in Using	How to Gauge Effectiveness
Story	To help stimulate a clearer vision of the present and the future.	Ask clients to make up a story in a situation where more information is desired when they need to imagine how they would like something to happen, or describe how things are happening now.	The client begins to see more options and feels more powerful.

Powerful Questions for Working with Stories
- Can you tell me a story about that?
- How can you describe the storyline here?
- How can you change your story?
- If you gave up this story or way of looking at this issue, what would change in your life?
- If you could be a movie star or someone in a fairy tale, how would that character fit into your story?
- Who else might enter the story?
- In your story, who supports you and how?

Mike Harris, Certified Coach
The Power of Stories

In my work as a coach, I've found myths, legends, stories, and poetry to be effective at awakening the imagination and opening doors to new or different awareness. The key in working with myths and stories is that clients must be given the opportunity to see themselves within the focus of the story.

I spend most of my time working with men and men's groups, focusing on the theme of "separation, initiation, and return," which arises in many popular myths written by authors such as Joseph Campbell and Robert Bly. By integrating and enhancing myths and stories clients can shift confused or negative perceptions into a sense of curiosity and adventure, inspiring exploration and the quest for change or newness. A client can visualize himself in a story that's not about him directly, but speaks to his personal situation, allowing freedom from feeling judged about it. That person can then effectively portray or associate with what's stuck, caged up, or imprisoned in his life experience. People can begin to shed their feelings of isolation, powerlessness, or victimhood and open up to new possibilities.

An example involves a man I'll call David. This man felt unfulfilled and trapped in the cage of his occupation as an executive in a large film production company. Artistically inclined but fully exasperated, he quit his six-figure job and returned to his home in northern California. He began a quest to discover what was waiting for him to do next, and separated himself from the bondage of his previous work.

Over eighteen months, David flailed about on what seemed to him an impossible quest, spending time on the road, reading, writing, hiking, biking in the mountains and the desert, listening to what his inner voices were vaguely calling him to do. He attended a men's retreat and joined a men's group. While on the road on what he called a "walkabout," he found himself in a small artistic community in the South. His inner voice said, "This is the place!" He was initiated into this community through the offerings of his artwork, and through teaching art classes. David felt that he'd returned to who he'd always wanted to be, which was completely different from the imprisoned life he had abandoned.

As David's coach, my task was to listen and hold the space while he was on his journey. Together, we explored myths and stories, curious about how they might provide insight so he could examine the way his life had unfolded, the cumulative effects, and learn what he wanted to do differently. I enthusiastically affirmed his inner vision and the actions he was taking to fulfill it. Joyfulness was the focal point for David. Joy for him as he shared insight after insight, and joy for me as I listened in awe as he told his stories and described the experiences.

Harnessing the Power of Imagery

A positive story can be made even more concrete by using imagery, a superb technique for change and transformation. One of my clients mentioned earlier in this chapter, Martha, had been unknowingly telling herself a romantic story with an unhappy ending. I knew that if she spent time visualizing what she'd like to happen, she'd be more likely to succeed. Using imagery that evokes as many senses as possible adds richness, depth, and concrete reality to the stories we tell. A coach might ask Martha powerful questions that would flesh out what she really means by "a happy ending," imagining herself actually experiencing it.

Imagery is often used by sport coaches, from football to golf, and involves players vividly imagining themselves hitting the ball or making the shot. I've observed Olympic contestants before their run, dive, or match standing on the sidelines in quiet contemplation, and I've often heard the announcer explain that the contestants are seeing the perfect performance in their mind's eye. We're told that imagery works in sports, so why can't it be a powerful tool in life or in health coaching?

How does it work? Susan Ezra and Terry Reed, two nurses who've been teaching guided imagery for numerous years, to thousands of people, describe the process in their book about healing and transformation. They say that "imagery is a natural part of our thought process: it is simply how the right brain 'thinks'."[6] With that part of our brain, we think in images and metaphor, whereas the left part of the brain mirrors the Mental structure of consciousness that was described in the last chapter—logical, sequential, analytic thought. These authors continue by saying that "the body's response is the same whether the event is actual or imagined."[7] So when that skier is standing at the top of the slope imagining a perfect run, they're creating a practice run that tunes and informs the body, mind, spirit about their goal. It's setting up a pattern as if the person were actually going down the hill. The same thing happens when we imagine our goal and how we're achieving it. We're really practicing it.

Almost all of my clients use imagery at one point or another in our work together. For example, Ben had trouble imagining his business really succeeding, and he realized that until he could picture his goal in detail and the steps to move forward, he wasn't likely to make his target. Ben is planning his retirement and told me yesterday that he's finally starting to envision life without his 40-hour week. He's practicing his retirement. What a breakthrough!

I often use imagery for moving forward on my goals. For instance, I'm in the final editing phase of this book and I want it published by July 5th which is a special holiday I have celebrated for years and named Interdependence Day—the day after Independence Day. I'm practicing an image (a short movie so to speak) that I feel will increase the likelihood of me meeting my goal. I see myself opening a box of books on Interdependence Day, calling family and friends, and beginning to plan a big party.

194　CHAPTER 6: The Mythical Part of Coaching

> *I've just been asked if people who are visual learners are more inclined to use imagery and those who are auditory learners gravitate toward storytelling. That is an interesting question, and I don't know the answer, but now that I am curious about it, I'll collect data. What do you think?*

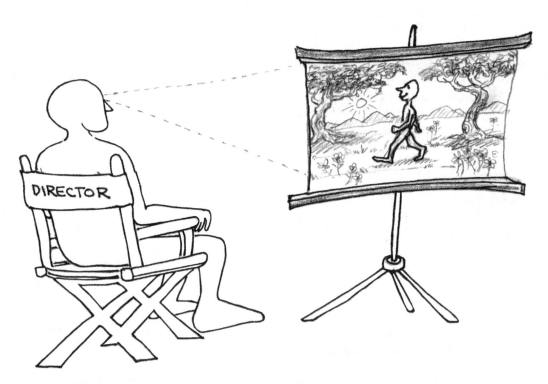

Client who wants to increase his exercise and reduce his stress by taking walks in nature, uses vivid imagery to help him attain his aim.

Not all imagery is visual. Some people don't actually see form-based images, but they may hear sounds, see colors, or sense something energetically. We can invite all kinds of imagery experiences. In fact, it's often helpful to draw from all of our senses to enrich our experience. Imagery can be used to practice a goal, and if your goal is relaxation, it can help move you to a calmer state. Luke Seaward, a stress management expert, shares a great exercise for experiencing the effects of imagery incorporating our senses.

EXERCISE: Using the Five Senses to Help You Relax[8]

Notice your current sense of relaxation and joy on a 1-10 scale, with 10 being very joyous and relaxed and 1 being very tense and unhappy. What's your number right now? Then do the following:

Make a list of 5 of the most stunning things you've ever seen.
Make a list of 5 smells that brought you great delight.
Make a list of 5 sounds that make you smile.
Make a list of 5 things you adore touching.
Make a list of 5 favorite meals/foods that make your mouth water.
Make a list of 5 times when you had a sense of oneness with a higher source or a spiritual/religious experience.

Next, become aware of your feeling as you review this list. Share them with someone else, and who knows, maybe that person might also want to create a list. After you've spent some time focusing on your lists, notice your sense of relaxation and joy.

Mythical Tool #4	When to Use	Steps in Using	How to Gauge Effectiveness
Imagery	To help a client to see goals or next steps or to change mood or stress level.	Provide space for the client to create an image that represents the client attaining the goal.	The client deepens her or his understanding and finds the imagery useful.

Powerful Questions Involving Imagery
- How do you experience imagery? Do you actually see a movie in your mind's eye? Do you hear words, see colors or have some other sense about the situation?
- How could you use imagery to practice getting to your goal?
- What kind of images would help you deal with this situation?
- How could you use more of your senses in this imagery?
- What types of images would help you relax?

Linda Chiofar, RN, MSN, HN-BC
Imagery in Coaching

As a holistic nurse in a mental health day-treatment program, I frequently use brief imagery interventions in coaching my clients. Unlike traditional psychotherapy, which is often problem focused, coaching in mental health day-treatment emphasizes client's strengths and potential. Imagery can be done with a group or with individuals to help them connect with core strengths in a more compassionate, relaxed way. I regularly provide a guided-imagery progressive-relaxation experience in stress management groups, and after several weeks clients report an increased capacity for accessing their known coping skills just by remembering to "breathe." (Script attached in footnote.)[9] This is just one example of empowering clients with a simple, holistic imagery tool they can use anywhere, anytime.

Weekly counseling sessions with clients offer many opportunities for coaching interventions. All treatment plans are goal-focused, with evolving objectives as clients move towards their goals. Monthly "focus meetings" keep clients aligned with their goals and offer a time to review progress with our multidisciplinary treatment team. Often during these meetings I'll have clients imagine where their life is heading as they move toward their goal, reflect back on where they began, and then quantify their progress on a 1 to 10 scale.

Our recently developed diabetes-prevention program provides ongoing opportunities for integrating imagery and coaching skills for managing weight, implementing behavior changes, and imagining a healthier self. Clients self-select to enroll in this six-month educational support program and identify their preliminary goals after an initial assessment. Imagery is used to help them connect with how they would like to look and feel at the completion of the program, how they can modify their diet, and what a successful experience will be for them. The implementation of a strength-training component in the program has allowed several clients to imagine a stronger, leaner self and helped to maintain continued motivation and commitment to the program.

Mental health day-treatment lends itself to brief (two to five-minute) coaching interventions using imagery with individuals and groups to access strengths, employ coping skills, and achieve goals in a whole person way that moves beyond talking about problems and towards reclaiming wholeness.

Creative Dialog

Another coaching tool aligned with the Mythical structure of consciousness incorporates dialog. I first learned about this process reading *At a Journal Workshop: The Basic Text and Guide for Using the Intensive Journal Process,* by Ira Progoff.[10] It was 1975, and I was spending much of the summer in a wilderness area. I found this journaling process fascinating. I especially liked the process of having a written conversation with parts of myself, with an event, or with a particular situation. I was amazed at what I discovered, and even after that summer I continued working with dialog, for self-care. Eventually I brought this tool into my work with others. Over the years it's become one of my favorite methods for increasing awareness that then leads to action.

The following brief example demonstrates how I used this tool with a client named Pat. She was having a problem with one knee and had been to several doctors, but they couldn't find a reason for her discomfort. In one of our coaching sessions she asked if we could explore the sensation. She agreed to talk to her knee, and here's the imaginary dialog.

Pat: Hi left knee. Why are you hurting?
Knee: I'm trying to get your attention!
Pat: Believe me, you have it, but I don't know what you're trying to tell me.
Knee: It's fairly simple. I'm hurting because you're walking on the wrong path.
Pat: What do you mean?
Knee: This is a time for you to be quieter and go inside and listen to your inner guidance. Instead you're running here and there and taking on too much. There are things you're ignoring.
Pat: Like what?!
Knee: See there you go—defensive and angry. I'm on your side. We're in this together. Really. Remember I'm a part of you.
Pat: I don't feel like you're on my side. I feel you're here to stop me from having fun, and I don't like it.
Knee: This is not about having fun or not having fun; it's about living at a deeper level. This is about balance—inner and outer—so there's time and energy to go out because there's strength and energy from staying in. That's all. I'm truly not against fun. In fact, I love fun. I just want the fun to come in ways that don't deplete you.
Pat: That feels nice, really. I can feel your support, and all this time I thought you were against me. As I listen to what you want to say to me, I think you're right. I've been pushing it, and I need some down time. I get the message. Will you stop hurting now?
Knee: I don't know if I believe that you will move closer to balance. You've tried that before. Let's keep talking about this.
Pat: You're right again. I do need some help with this, but can't you do it differently?

Knee: Let's keep on talking, and you could look at me as a helper to let you know when you're overdoing.
Pat: I want you to find another way.
Knee: Let's keep on talking.
Pat: Okay, I want that too.

After the dialog Pat put together a plan for the next week to take some time off and also to notice when her knee hurt. She wanted to see what she could learn from that discomfort rather than simply trying to get rid of it.

> *What part of your body would like to have a conversation with you? Want to find out? Following the example above—although your dialog may go on much longer, and that's fine—write out a conversation with some part(s) of your body. Allow your body to talk and your mind to listen. When finished, ask yourself, "What was my major takeaway or learning from this conversation?"*

Creating dialog is very useful for working with health symptoms, and another common application is for addressing clients' inner critic—the voice that tells us that we can't do something, we aren't good enough, or good things happen to others but not to us. Some people have loud critical voices; others' voices are not so intense. Whatever the status or magnitude of our inner critic, few of us are exempt from its disruptive and often destructive messages. Some clients try to drown it out, but I've found that approach to be the least helpful. If something shows up for me or for a client, I find it's best to explore it. Usually there's some important message or lesson to be learned.

Whatever the dialog method used to explore this critical voice (and I present a couple below), I've found it helpful to name the voice and address it directly. I want to learn more about it, so I ask lots of questions. When does it come? When does it leave? If it gets the "mic," will it say what it wants and then listen, or is it like a broken record regardless of the reception it receives? What are its purpose and intentions? Can it be helpful, for instance warning me of danger? Must it remain "critical" and bossy, or can its tone change to one of helpful collaboration?

By using some sort of dialogical approach, a deal can be struck with the critical voice, and it becomes an ally as opposed to an enemy. In the few cases I've seen in which the critical voice continues to be disruptive and loud, its owner needs to reduce contact and attention. In this type of scenario, one can say, "I hear you; thanks for stopping by; now it's time for you to leave."

> *What kind of critical voice do you have—friend, foe, or a combination of the two? Is there a critical voice that's always putting you down? Is there a more mature critical voice that helps you differentiate situations so that you don't overstep your bounds or rush into things without having a good foundation for success? How can you access your critical voice in a way that will facilitate it serving you?*

Catherine Osterbye, BS, MS
Archetypes and Sub-Personalities in Dialog

I love noticing what I call sub-personalities or human archetypes. It helps me understand my clients, accept them, and have compassion for them. I like to combine the knowledge of archetypes with dialog. Often talking with these mythical figures can be complex, since usually more than one archetype is involved. For example, when I was teaching a course on wellness, I asked my students to keep journals and identify current archetypes, health goals, and barriers to those goals. One class participant saw how her Princess archetype didn't want to get all sweaty to do the exercise that she needed to meet her goal. She was helped by dialoging with her Amazon archetype that wanted to be fit and strong. The Princess part of her was able to endure the sweating by realizing that when she was fit, she looked good in her clothes and was even more beautiful and attractive. The Princess and the Amazon became colleagues and worked toward the same goal, getting both their needs met.

Often the archetypes are stuck in an immature stage and do not align with the adult higher good. Another client example involved money. Alice had trouble with money and ignored it since she hadn't been taught to take charge of her financial life. She began to dialog with a sub-personality that was a Little Girl who didn't want to deal with money; she just wanted to play and didn't like math. There was another part of her that was a Nun who had no use for money or the material plane. The third sub-personality was a Businessman who kept telling her to track her expenditures. In her mind, he walked around with a calculator trailing a long white paper saying over and over again "Track your money." The fourth and last archetype was the Madam of a house of prostitution (her name was Belle) who continued to show her a bag of money that she should keep hidden from everyone. Alice translated this into her need for a savings account. After dialogs with all these parts, Alice took the advice of the Businessman, creating a budget, and at the urgings of Belle, started a savings account. The Little Girl and the Nun realized that having money provided them the safety that they needed to continue to play and to pursue a spiritual path.

Dialogue methods vary. Part of the Prokoff approach is to have a self-dialog—to have clients speak as their basic sense of "I" to the various parts of themselves. Another way I work with dialog is to ask my clients to speak from a particular part of themselves and for me to take the role of an interviewer.

Recently I've attended some workshops run by Zen Master Dennis Genpo Merzel, the author of Big Mind-Big Heart,[11] who suggests that we're the CEO of a company of thousands of employees or different inner voices. He says that each employee or voice has a distinct job, and it's our task as the CEO to find out who is doing what in our company. In his book, he describes the employees or voices of Protector, Skeptic, Fear, Anger, Damaged Self, Victim, and Vulnerable and Innocent Child. Genpo states that all these voices exist within us; some are acknowledged and owned, but often others lurk in the shadows—actively operating from behind the stage.

According to the Big Mind-Big Heart method, our internal voices may have an immature form and a mature form. For example, I was working with Elizabeth last week on her startup business, and she was feeling stopped by fear. She asked if we could work with that feeling, and I described Genpo Roshi's method. She was game to try it, so I asked her to talk as the Voice of Fear and refer to herself in the third person. Here's part of our conversation:

Linda: "Who are you?"

Elizabeth, talking as the Voice of Fear: "I'm the Voice of Fear."

Linda: "What's your job in Elizabeth's company?"

Elizabeth, talking as Fear: "My job is to keep her safe. I don't want her to get into trouble."

Linda: "How does she feel about you?"

Elizabeth, talking as Fear: "She tries to get rid of me. She hates me. She wishes I were not in her life."

Linda: "Oh, she wants to keep you hidden, like down in the basement?"

Elizabeth, talking as Fear: "Yes. She doesn't want me to talk at all, and that makes me so nervous. Imagine how bad it is! How can I do my job if she doesn't talk or listen to me?"

Linda: "That's a good question. How do you do your job?"

Elizabeth, talking as Fear: "Well, I try to talk to her all the time. I sometimes scream at her. I should get overtime pay! I just know things will never work out. This idea of her starting a new business is just stupid. She'll never be able to do it. Think about the economy. How could this ever work?"

Linda: "Hmm. . .I wonder if there are two different Voices of Fear. Could I talk first with the immature Voice of Fear and then the mature Voice of Fear?"

Elizabeth, talking as Immature Fear: "Okay. I'm the voice of Immature Fear."

Linda: "What's your job?"

Elizabeth, talking as Immature Fear: "To tell her how dangerous things really are."

Linda: "And does she listen to you?"

Elizabeth, talking as Immature Fear: "Well, she acts like she doesn't, but I can really get to her because I want her to know how scary things are out there."

Linda: "Thanks for talking with me, and now can I talk to the voice of Mature Fear?"

Elizabeth, talking as Mature Fear: "I'm the voice of Mature Fear."

Linda: "What's your job, and how are you different from Immature Fear?"

Elizabeth, talking as Mature Fear: "My job is to keep her safe, and I take that very seriously, but I don't see the world as a frightening place. I see it as a place to be careful—full of care—but not a scary place."

Linda: "What do you think about her new business idea?"

Elizabeth, talking as Mature Fear: "I think it's possible if she really has a good business plan and thinks things through carefully."

Linda: "Is there anything you'd like to say to her?"

Elizabeth, talking as Mature Fear: "Yes, I'd like to tell her to listen to me, to get me out of the basement, to start seeing me as one of her consultants, and not to let Immature Fear get to her so much. It makes her freeze."

Linda: "Okay, thanks. I want to talk to Elizabeth now."

Elizabeth: "Okay, I'm me now. I'm Elizabeth. That was really interesting. I didn't know about those parts of me. I actually spoke from different parts. Amazing."

Linda: "So how does this awareness impact you?"

Elizabeth: "Well, I learned that I need to listen to the Mature Voice of Fear and that (groping for words) somehow I think the immature voice is little—how strange—anyway, I want to do away with it and just listen to the mature voice."

Linda: "In this method, it's important to keep even this Immature Voice of Fear up out of the basement. All these voices are parts of us, and if we try and do away with any of them, they just go into sneak mode and come out in some way that's not usually helpful. Could you think of it this way? Imagine a triangle, and at one side of the bottom is Immature Fear, and at the other end is Mature Fear. You are at the apex or top of the triangle and can see both parts of Fear and choose which to listen to. Perhaps sometimes Immature Fear needs a bit of reassurance."

Elizabeth: "Well, that sounds more likely. I think Immature Fear is here to stay, but I just don't want it to rule my life. I really think my business idea is good, and I want to get started. Now that I can talk with Mature Fear, I don't feel stuck. What a relief!"

These dialog methods, and others you may be familiar with, might sound superficial or contrived. However, they're just the opposite. I invite you to learn them, try them yourself, and then use them with your clients. The potential of these methods is allowing clients to connect deeply with inner dynamics and gain insight that will inform major transitions.

Mythical Tool #5	When to Use	Steps in Using	How to Gauge Effectiveness
Dialogue	When the client needs more awareness and there's an identified situation or part of the person who is resistant or helpful in movement toward the goal.	To identify a part of the body or element of a situation and establish a conversation with it.	The client's awareness is broadened to include new approaches or parts of a situation. Internal conflicts are resolved/ softened.

Powerful Questions for Using Dialog
- What part of yourself is hidden in this situation?
- Would you be interested in having a conversation with that part of yourself just to see what you could learn about the situation?
- What part of you needs to speak to you?
- What parts of this situation could support you and how could that happen?
- What kind of a voice or role do you want from me as your coach now: empathy, love, encouragement, being a questioner, etc.?

Mythical Tools As Homework

Drawing upon the power of story, imagery, and dialog clients can gain insight and inspiration, moving closer to being ready and able to take concrete steps. Drawing upon the Mythical structure of consciousness also gives us some tools for homework.

Affirmations

Elizabeth worked with the Voice of Fear, is ready to identify some homework, and chooses to create an affirmation. Positive affirmations are another type of storytelling. To develop an affirmation, she'll make a statement of her goal as if it's already happened. Elizabeth can repeat the affirmation when she's awaking up, falling asleep, and/or throughout the day. To remind her about the goal, she might want to draw a picture of it or post words or phrases that she will often see. Elizabeth created the following affirmation: My substantial business plan directs my successful business start up.

Besides suggesting that clients affirm what they want, they can become aware of thoughts, feelings, and body signals that indicate resistance to having what they want or achieving their goals, as sometimes these become more evident the more we affirm the positive. For example, Elizabeth's Voice of Immature Fear may have negative feelings and thoughts of failure. Once these "negative affirmations" are recognized, as well as any triggers for them, it's more possible to decrease their hidden power.

Exercise: Creating an Affirmation

Create an affirmation about something in your life you want to change. Write a short positive affirmation as if you've already reached your goal. Some examples include these:

- I'm in a loving marriage
- I wear a size 12.
- My body is strong and flexible.
- My boss praises me for my completed projects.

Say your affirmation several times a day. What arises as you say it? Work with and learn from any negative thoughts or feelings. Explore the effects of the positive affirmation on your movement toward your goal.

Mythical Tool #6	When to Use	Steps in Using	How to Gauge Effectiveness
Affirmations	To help a client accomplish a goal in which they have self-talk that negates accomplishing it. For example, the client may want a better paying job, and part of the client doesn't think that's possible.	Jointly design a statement that claims a new perception or goal. Next, look at the obstacles to accomplishing the goal that come up as the client says the affirmation. Then, identify the truth of the assumptions.	The client moves towards the new goal, overcoming newly uncovered obstacles.

Powerful Questions for Bringing in Affirmations
- How could you put that in the form of an affirmation—a positive statement as if your goal has already been reached?
- What negative thoughts, feelings or sensations do you experience as you say that affirmation?
- Evaluate the truth of what arises. Is the statement based in fact? Is part of it true? Which part is not true?

[1] Rudolph Ballentine, *Radical Healing: Integrating the World's Great Therapeutic Traditions to Create a New Transformative Medicine* (Honesdale, PA: Himalayan Institute, 2011), 209—figure 52. Used with author permission. Another excellent reference for personal constitution is Robert Svodoba, Prakriti: *Your Ayurvedic Constitution* (Bellingham, WA: Sadhana Publications, 1998). I consulted with Kate Sadowski, an Ayurvedic practitioner, for assistance in writing this section.

[2] www.cnvc.org/about/marshall-rosenberg.html accessed on May 18, 2011.

[3] www.cnvc.org and www.cnvc.org/Training/NVC-Concepts accessed on May 18, 2011.

[4] The process can include a number of smaller pre-meetings to examine what happened in order to clarify the unmet needs or concerns that triggered the conflict. A larger meeting is then convened with all the people involved: the one/s that acted in the conflict, those that were impacted by the action, support team members, and any others involved with the situation. As part of the process, people take responsibility for their actions by addressing such questions as "What do you want the person to know about what you were looking for when you chose to act?" Out of this dialog, participants create an action plan for moving forward to meet their needs and promote healing and restoration for the group or community. Restorative Justice is being used in many locations globally: in Brazil in their RestoJ pilot projects, as part of the UN Development Program, and in UNESCO.

[5] Begun in 1995, the commission addressed crime during the Apartheid era. For a thorough book on Restorative Justice, see *Restorative Justice: The Empowerment Model* by Charles Barton. Another international resource for training, resources, mediation, conferencing and restoration circles based on RJ is the Victim Offender Mediation Association (VOMA). In the forward to the report, Archbishop Desmond Tutu said: "We are also deeply grateful to the thousands of South Africans who came to the Commission to tell us their stories. They have won our country the admiration of the world: wherever one goes, South Africa's peaceful transition to democracy, culminating in the Truth and Reconciliation process, is spoken of almost in reverent tones, as a phenomenon that is unique in the annals of history, one to be commended as a new way of living for humankind. Other countries have had truth commissions, and many more are following our example, but ours is regarded as the most ambitious, a kind of benchmark against which the rest are measured."

[6] Susan Ezra and Terry Reed, *Guided Imagery and Beyond* (Denver, CO: Outskirts Press, Inc., 2008).

[7] Ibid., 11.

8 Here are several books by Brian Luke Seaward: *The Art of Calm: Relaxation Through the 5 Senses* (Deerfield Beach, FL: Health Communications, Inc, 1999); *Managing Stress: Principles and Strategies for Health and Wellbeing with Art of Peace Workbook* (Sudbury, MA: Jones and Bartlett, 2009). Also this: Brian Luke Seaward and Joan Lunden, *Stressed is Desserts Spelled Backwards: Rising Above Life's Challenges with Humor, Hope and Courage* (Berkeley, CA: Conari Press, 1999).

9 Introduction: Let's take a few minutes to breathe so we can settle in more fully. Go ahead and set your things aside for now, uncross your arms and legs, feel your feet on the floor and the support of the chair beneath you, and then turn your attention inward. You may close your eyes, soften your gaze or just look out the window, but let the focus be on your experience.

Now take a few slow, deep breaths and allow yourself to shift into a place of relaxation. Become aware as you inhale of bringing fresh oxygen into your body, of nourishing all of your tissues and cells with fresh oxygen-rich blood. And as you exhale, let go of any tension or discomfort that you're feeling in your body right now. . .as best you can. Continue this process of breathing in relaxation. . .and exhaling tension as you scan your body. You might like to imagine that this relaxation begins at the top of your head and flows down through your face as it softens your forehead and your eyes, your cheeks and your jaw, your throat and your neck. Then feel this relaxation spread across your shoulders and down your arms through your elbows and forearms, your wrists and hands and fingers. On the next inhale take a nice deep breath into your chest, creating a little more space around your heart. . .a little more breathing room within you. Then imagine this relaxation spreads across the muscles of your back and ripples all the way down your spine to the base of your tailbone. Let yourself sink a little deeper into the chair. Now imagine this relaxation wraps around your belly. Let your belly be soft and round. And on the next inhale, think about bringing your breath all the way down to your abdomen, again, with an awareness of creating space, creating a little more room for your vital organs to do their work easily and effortlessly. Feel this relaxation spread into your pelvis and your buttocks and flow down into your legs through your thighs and knees, shins, and calves and all the way into your ankles and feet and toes. As you feel this wave of relaxation wash over you, you might imagine it washes away any last bits of stress or tension that you're holding in your body right now. (Sigh)

Now that your body is feeling more relaxed, you might notice the thoughts and feelings you have with you today. Without needing to do anything about them, just notice what's up for you right now as you breathe in and let go. No judgment or expectation—just a moment to notice your thoughts and feelings. Then gently let go of an awareness of your thoughts and feelings and turn your palms up in your lap in a posture of receptivity and open yourself to spirit, to possibilities, to all that exists for you in your world right now. Open yourself to discovering whatever you need today as the next step in your own growth and healing. Then take a moment to affirm to yourself that you already have everything you need for your own growth and healing and we are just here to rediscover that, to reclaim your wholeness. Then take one more slow deep breath, and as you exhale, gently open your eyes and return to this time and place.

10 Ira Progoff, *At a Journal Workshop: The Basic Text and Guide for Using the Intensive Journal Process* (NY: Dialogue House Library, 1975).

11 Dennis Genpo Merzel, *Big Mind-Big Heart: Finding Your Way* (Salt Lake City: Big Mind Publishing, 2007).

Chapter 7
The Intuitive Part of Coaching

Sample Session 2C—Up Against a Brick Wall

"I work in a dog-eat-dog world and I know how to survive there. In fact, I've done well. Unfortunately, enduring that kind of life has repercussions for my family and causes me some health problems. It's costing me, but I don't know how to change. My wife is talking about a divorce. This is not my first wife—I don't want to say how many times I've been married—so I've heard the complaints before. She's saying I'm never home, I don't care about her and my children, I'm too tough and rule the house like I do my office. And there are some other problems. I have this burning in my belly, and the doctor says that acid comes up from my stomach and burns my food tube. I have some heart problems too. I have two stints in my heart now, and they say that I'm due for more heart surgery if things don't change. I take enough pills to choke a horse, but instead of solving the problem, I just keep getting more and different kinds of pills. My usual way of pushing harder to solve things just isn't working. *I feel I'm up against a brick wall*," says Arny in a pressured tone during an introductory session.

"You see the benefits that your approach to life has produced, but now the deficits are accruing at a fast rate. Your regular strategies and tactics aren't helping you with these particular issues and you wonder what to do next?" I paraphrase.

"You got it. It's out of character to be stumped like this. It's embarrassing. I feel like something's wrong with me or something's wrong with what I'm doing," he says loudly.

"What do you want to accomplish by the end of our session?" I ask.

"I need to do things differently but I don't know where to begin," he roars.

"What is a completely different way of operating?" I query.

After a couple minutes of silence Arny says in a thoughtful manner, "You know, that's an interesting question that makes me think. And it brings back a method an old friend explained. He and his managers had a special way to access managers. They had a scale that went 10-9-8-7-6-5-4-3-2-1 and 1-2-3-4-5-6-7-8-9-10. The 1s were in the middle. The left side measured the ability to function in the role of 'I am the boss and do what I say!' and the other end measured the skill level to act in a manner of 'Let's work together and collaborate'. They described and evaluated managers with this continuum. For example, someone who couldn't take charge of the department and set standards, was pretty low on the 'I am the boss' side but might be high on the 'Let's work together' side, so they called him an 2-8. Are you with me?" Arny inquires.

I say, "Yes, I get it. What would your numbers be?"

"I would be a 10-1," he replies quickly.

"Do you feel you have no skills in the 'Let's work together side'?" I ask.

"Yup. My honest evaluation is that I don't. I was raised to take charge, and that's what I know to do. And it's worked—well to some extent. Interesting. Now, my friend said his company used to look for the 10-10s to hire because they valued being able to change management styles when needed. Years ago when I heard about this approach, I thought it was. . .well, let me think of a nice way to say this—it was rubbish—but now I'm rethinking it. I have some things to learn about that and it could help me at work," Arny explains.

"When you first heard about the company looking for 10-10s, people who could use 'power over' methods as well as 'power with' approaches, it didn't sound right, but now you wonder if it has some value and you want to learn something about it," I paraphrase.

Arny states, "Yes, and I can see how my wife would like me to have a higher score in the 'Let's work things out together' category."

"Where would you like to go next in this session?" I ask.

"This has me thinking in a new way, but even if I could be a 10-10 by some magical event, I don't know if it would help me with my illnesses. They keep taking things out of me and putting other things in me, and the results are not that satisfying," says Arny in a stress out tone.

"I can hear your concern and I'm curious about a connection with these messages from your body. Do you..." I say, and then Arny interrupts, "These are not little messages. This burning stuff really hurts and is very real. This is not in my mind. This stuff is real. I mean I can't eat some things, and sometimes I can't sleep," he says angrily.

"I completely get it. I didn't mean to imply that this stuff isn't real. I know it's real. I know it's painful. I know your doctor has given you a diagnosis. I know you have lab reports and x-rays. What I was trying to say is that these physical symptoms might have some connection with the issues you've been talking about. Do you see any connection?" I ask.

"Nope! Tell me what you're thinking. I want you to answer that question," he requests.

"Okay, I can switch to a consulting role and share some information about links between certain diseases and various parts of the body. Some people feel that the stomach area is about power, and if you're having trouble in that part of your body, working with different power approaches could help," I answer.

"What? Stomach and power? I don't know about that. I guess you do punch a guy in the stomach to take him down. I don't know," he replies.

"Okay, I can see where that might be a stretch but how about the heart problems? Do you see any connection between the heart and some of the things you mentioned at the beginning of our session regarding your relationship with your wife?" I ask.

"That's possible. Yes," he says contemplatively. I guess there could be some connection there. Yes, my wife feels that I don't love her, and I think I do. I don't want another divorce, that's for sure. She wants to go to therapy, and I said no, absolutely not. I don't want some shrink telling me how bad I am. And after all, I'm not crazy. No one in my position is crazy. I've accomplished too much."

"I think you have been very successful and I don't think you are crazy. Where do you want to go next?" I inquire.

"What I have so far is a new way to think about the 10-10 issues and guess I have some things to learn, there but that stomach and power thing is too much. I give that a 10% possibility of being true. I can see how my heart problems might be involved with my relationship with my wife and family, but that's about it. Where do I go from here? Ask me a question," he requests.

I say, "I'm wondering if you could use the same perspective of learning in this situation with your wife that you told me about with your friend's 10-10 scale. Is there a way that you absolutely know how to do certain things in relationships, such as provide a wonderful home and social life for your wife and family, but may need some skill-building in the area of expressing feelings or other relationship issues?"

"You drive a hard bargain, madam," he says laughingly.

I laugh too and say, "I do? What do you mean?"

"You ask these little questions, and they have such big answers. I reply to them, and I don't even feel bad about myself, and then suddenly I feel turned around. I could use you in my business! And so yes, I could work with this situation with this new perspective. I could see how this is very similar to being a 10-1 at business. And I imagine that I could be trained to do things differently at home just the way I could be trained to do things at work. Okay, okay I get it. And I guess these things that are happening to me, like my stomach and my heart, could connect to it all. So now what do I do? Where do I learn this other stuff?" he says more seriously.

"What ideas do you have?" I inquire.

"Put it back on me, huh. This is what I pay you the big bucks for? More questions. Oh, I forgot. This is a free introductory session. I guess I don't get answers, just questions for free," he says again in a witty humorous tone.

"When I'm asking the questions, I'm in the coaching role, and when I'm giving the answers, I'm in the consulting role. And I'm fine about giving answers. Not even an extra charge for answers. I've just found that sometimes my clients have better answers than I do. So if you don't know about resources, I'm fine about giving you answers but usually I see what my clients come up with first before I switch into the consulting role," I explain.

"Okay, switch. I don't know how or where to get this training. Well, wait a minute, I guess I do know about the work arena. In fact, I'm bringing in some training for our managers, but I never thought about going to it myself. I suppose I could check it out. And now that I think about it, my wife has been begging me to go to some kind of weekend course about relationships. I said I would never go, but honestly, I don't know anything about it, so I suppose I could at least find out what they are. I see what you mean. I did have some ideas," he states.

"Part of coaching is doing some kind of homework during the upcoming week, and you're way ahead of me. I can see how you've been so successful," I state.

"You got that right. And I must say I've learned something today—much to my surprise, I might add. I do thank you. I really felt up against a high wall, and now somehow I feel that I've knocked it down and can walk over it. Might take some time, but I see a way forward. How do I continue this coaching?" he inquires.

I went on to explain my coaching structure of three scheduled sessions and spot coaching or brief conversations or emails between scheduled sessions if things come up. I told him my monthly fee. He said he wanted to continue, and we set our time for the following week to share our information. I said I truly enjoyed working with him and looked forward to our next conversation.

Over the next several months he transformed some relationship habits, which did improve his connection to his wife, and his stomach discomfort decreased. His heart condition stayed about the same, but at least it did't get worse. At times, he would consider mind-body connections, and when he did and they made sense to him, he was amazed, but sometimes he wasn't interested in somatic or self-awareness. He used to say to me, "What works, works, and I don't have to know all the details! You're in charge of those! I just want the results!" Step by step he saw how those details informed and facilitated his results and his self-awareness grew.

Overview of the Intuitive Structure of Consciousness and Coaching

You might wonder how I chose someone like Arny in the sample session for the Intuitive structure of consciousness. At face value, he seems an unlikely candidate for the use of these tools. It's true that some tools would have been a poor fit, and if I chose them I wouldn't have been meeting my client where he was. For instance, in this first session, I never would have thought to ask him to use a magic wand to come up with some new ideas. And yet as soon as he told me his concerns, energy concepts intuitively came to mind. I immediately began to reflect on the chakra, or energy vortex, system of the body and link his behaviors to their themes. Of course, he wasn't the right client to talk with about energy systems, chakras, or energy currents—especially in the first session. However, knowing about these concepts informed my questions, which he found very helpful. For example, the heart chakra, or energy vortex in the heart area of the body, is linked to love and connection. He had damage and disease in this area, seeming to mirror the difficulties he had in creating loving, lasting relationships. I wondered if he could connect the theme of the heart and his challenges in relating, and if that would help him address the relationship area of his life.

In this chapter, I explain the application of tools that arise from the Intuitive structure of consciousness, but before I present these, let's first look at the structure itself as a way to learn more about this period and understand the basis of these tools.

The Intuitive structure of consciousness preceded the Mythical structure, and with the Intuitive structure people lacked concepts of time and space. We can get a glimpse of this way of being when we dream. We can go anywhere and be anything, and time has no true meaning. We can dream we're falling through space, which seems to last an eternity, but the dream could actually occur in one minute of clock time. Events can happen in the dream state that can't be explained and may seem supernatural. Coincidences and synchronicities naturally occur, and what happens seems related to unseen forces that are real but are intangible and hidden. All these things conjure up the idea of magic and stem from the intertwined, merged, and connected aspects of this structure.

During this period human beings didn't have a defined ego or sense of self: instead there was a group ego or group sense that was sustained by the inseparable bonds of the clan. No clear distinction between the clan and nature existed either. This merged identity allowed a part to be seen as the whole and the whole to be seen as a part, which was the basis for various rituals. For example, a person dressed in an animal skin for a clan dance would not represent but actually *be* the animal, thereby invoking communication and relationship with that entire animal species.

Non-rational knowing, or intuition, was held in high regard and could sometimes mean the difference between life and death. People communicated without words, with each other and with animals. Often certain people in the tribe could predict future events or sense what was wrong with a person and what was needed to heal them. Nature, relationship, and community were medicine.

Things happened without what we now know to be logic or the support of conceptual thinking. Mental understanding wasn't the dominant mode, but other senses were sharp and well developed. Perhaps we can understand this kind of development by analogy with blind people, who may develop extremely keen senses of hearing or smell to replace their eyesight. I can relate to that process since I am on the phone to do my coaching and teaching, and as a result my listening skills have become more developed than they might have otherwise. I have a friend who never used a flashlight at night when living in a remote rural location, and on very dark nights, when he could see very poorly, he said they he could sense something coming up as he walked toward it by almost feeling its energy.

Some people may feel that the Intuitive structure of consciousness is not believable or useful, but actually, much of the wisdom found here has practical application and is scientific— overlapping with the Mental structure of consciousness. Science has begun to shed light on and validate the subtle side of life. Special cameras can take pictures of energy fields around a body. Machines that measure body energy can trace physical changes that seem to be the result of specific interventions. Laboratory research can determine how stress can affect body functions. Quantum physics is answering many questions about this structure of consciousness.

Two Intuitive tools that are used throughout all coaching sessions are walking the talk and intuition. The term *walking the talk* stems from the principles of medicine people or healers in this structure of consciousness, who demonstrated wisdom in order to teach it. Doing that also provides a solid foundation for coaching practice. Also key is *intuition* itself so a portion of this chapter is devoted to how to assess, develop, and use it since it can guide personal life and work. Another powerful coaching skill or tool from this structue is effective use of *silence*.

Especially valuable at the beginning of sessions is an imagined *magic wand* to help clients think of completely new possibilities, separated from the usual limiting assumptions. In the middle of coaching sessions, *energy principles* that arise from this structure of merged unity, spacelessness, and timelessness can be used. I explore this perspective by looking at the energy inside the body, manifested in *energy centers and currents,* suggest *working with the breath*, and use a tool for connecting energy (*tapping*). I assess the energy outside the body by considering group energy fields, which involve the group mind of a species, a class, a family, and more dispersed groups. Tools here are working with the *Law of Attraction* and *powerful questions on family dynamics*.

Several tools can be used for homework during that final phase of sessions. Just as tribes in the Intuitive structure of consciousness used *nature* to heal, you and your clients can tap into this source, whether clients commit to a soothing walk by the water or to lavishing in the aroma of a beautiful rose or other natural sources of beauty. Your client may decide to inquire into *food and nourishment* for healing, through a tool that not only adds input for making dietary changes (something many clients have as a goal), but also uncovers how they nourish themselves in general. Finally, *ritual* is a powerful way to transform a thought, pattern, or situation, and clients can be guided to create powerful rituals to help with changes they want to make.

As you'll see, besides providing a framework for the basic coaching practices involved in the Bark Coaching Institute Model, drawing upon the structures of consciousness also guides coaches if they wish to bring in adjunct methods that they've been trained to practice. I hope you'll be inspired by comments about how and when I call upon these adjunct methods, and by descriptions provided by coaches I've trained, to create a coaching practice that addresses the whole person. You'll begin to know when referrals and resources can usefully be provided.

Anytime during Session:
- *Walking the Talk*
- *Intuition*
- *Silence*

Beginning of Session:
- *Magic Wand*

Middle of Session:
- *Working with Energy in the Body—working with themes related to centers; tapping on connection points; working with currents; and working with the breath*
- *Considering Group Energy—Law of Attraction; powerful questions for considering family and group patterns*

Homework:
- *Spending Time in Nature*
- *Food, Mood, and Nourishment Log*
- *Ritual*

Intuitive Tools Used in All Sections of the Coaching Session

I've divided the tools in each chapter to match the time in a coaching session where they're most frequently used, or by their purpose, for example, assessment; however, some tools, such as walking the talk, intuition, and silence are used so frequently that they deserve their own section.

Walking the Talk

The healers and medicine people of the Intuitive time can teach us about practicing what we preach. It's not that they were perfect, but they studied for many years, learned skills on their own or by being shown, and then taught others directly or through their wise actions. The most powerful way to influence someone else is by modeling the behavior—as Gandhi said, to "be the change you want to see in the world" or "My life is my message."

As a coach, do I walk my talk? Do I practice what I preach? Do I ask myself or have others ask me powerful questions about my mind, body, and spirit that help me reach my potential? Does my lifestyle support health, balance, and wellbeing if these are my values? Is there some way I could do just a bit more without feeling burdened or stressed? How do I deal with my critical voice? Do I avail myself of tools and resources to help me stretch and grow?

I remember a time in the 90s when my intuition was telling me—no, more like screaming at me—to move east. At first I thought that meant Washington DC since I was living in the San Francisco Bay Area and consulting in Maryland. But later, as my inner voice spoke, I realized the move I needed to make was really *east*: China. To move there was the biggest leap of faith I've ever taken, but one question I kept asking myself was, "How can I support people in listening to their intuition if I don't do it myself?" I did move to China, and entered into one of the finest periods of my life for personal and professional growth and adventure.

Mary Perez, RN, Reiki Master
Teaching Self-Care by Caring for Myself

I'm a Registered Nurse working in the postpartum department of a large hospital in New Jersey. After completing the coaching course with Linda Bark, I wanted very much to share what I learned with my colleagues. With my nurse manager's approval I conducted several in-service trainings on self-care and self-nurturing during stressful times.

These in-services provided information on developing one or two stress coping tools as well as learning the importance of giving permission to nurture oneself. My colleagues told me they really benefitted from the tools and also from knowing that to be effective in caring for others they must care for themselves.

My fellow nurses were not the only ones who began to see things differently! As a result of this teaching experience I thought about my own life and habits and was shocked to realize that I do more for my family and friends than I do for myself. Seeing that, I began applying the tools I was teaching to my own life.

Upon awakening I give thanks to my bed and pillows for a good night's sleep and appreciate the new day. While driving to work I listen to music that lifts my spirit and helps me to maintain a sense of serenity upon entering the hospital. When colleagues begin to speak negatively on any subject and I feel myself becoming tense, I put my hands up energetically and say to myself, "I'm not speaking defeat. I declare faith and victory over my life." I've been quite involved in body, mind, and spirit practices. Success in these areas has surprised even me. I've lost 35 pounds and am much more relaxed, even in my stressful work environment.

My new methods don't work all the time but often enough that coworkers ask me what I'm doing. I've come to appreciate the power of walking the talk—being a model. I'm convinced that my personal progress has improved the attendance in the hospital in-services I offer and has drawn clients to my successful and thriving private coaching practice.

Michelle Long, MA
Support for Moms

As I've experienced from both sides, mothers can benefit from the support coaching offers. Mothers can easily lose sight of their own needs in a world of diaper changing, sleepless nights, crying babies, and being overwhelmed with complete love for the children. If there's one thing that motherhood has taught me, it's that I need to take care of myself in order to fully enjoy being a mother. I have to not only acknowledge but also address my own needs in order to be present with my children so that we're all fulfilled. Being coached from an integral perspective helped me in my early stages of motherhood to truly check in with myself on all levels, to understand my own needs, and to then take small steps towards nourishing myself.

For example, I remember a time when I was so run down from lack of sleep and from adjusting to motherhood, that even when I had a quiet moment to rest, I couldn't relax. My mind would take over and I couldn't find peace, but then my coach helped me create a ritual that allowed me to really let go and relax. Each time I found a quiet space in my day I would lie down in silence, place my eye pillow over my eyes, and breathe ten slow and very deep breaths. We did this in a coaching session together, and I found that it immediately calmed my racing mind. Experiencing the benefits of coaching inspired me to become a coach myself.

Combining my skills in coaching, my background in teaching yoga, and my degree in Holistic Health Education, I've started facilitating support groups for new moms. The groups blend coaching, yoga, and meditation, and mothers have a chance to feel supported and part of a community while going through the first phases of motherhood, which can often be isolating. Groups meet twice a month in person, and then between group meetings, I coach individual mothers over the phone.

The most common feedback from mothers in my groups is that the experience helps them regain a sense of self and actually feel into a body that has been forgotten and neglected. Common themes and needs are explored in the groups, and the individual coaching allows moms to look at unique issues and challenges as well as to acknowledge their special skills and achievements. Recently in a coaching session, a mother and I did a dialog (a Mythical tool) where she asked her aching shoulders what she needed in order to feel relief. She actually found the answer in her heart, and all she needed was a little time alone with her husband. Now she makes an effort to find that time each week. It is the little self-care things that truly go a long way, especially for us moms.

220 Chapter 7: The Intuitive Part of Coaching

Intuitive Tool #1	When to Use	Steps in Using	How to Gauge Effectiveness
Walking the Talk	All the time.	Model a life that involves you reaching your goals within the learning framework of fun, taking easy steps, being kind and gentle.	Clients are inspired by your progress and humanness.

Powerful Questions about Walking the Talk
- How do I walk my talk as a coach?
- What could I improve in this arena?

Being Guided by Intuition

What is intuition? The word comes from Latin and means "in to you." It's an internal knowing of deep inner truth. It can come as an inkling or hunch, or arrive as a strong sign or message that runs through body/mind/spirit. Some people actually hear words, see a picture, have a body sensation, experience an intense dream, or sense a symbol. If a person thinks intuition only comes in a certain form, they might be missing the intuitive signals they're receiving in other modes. My intuitive thought or picture is not emotionally loaded, which helps me differentiate it from a wish or desire. Instead, it's more like a neutral news flash that's not connected with an analytical thought process.

Recently I was visiting some friends and had what seemed like an intuitive flash that my friend was pregnant. My thinking mind immediately dismissed it since this was unlikely and had nothing to do with our conversation. However, after dinner, my friend said she was going to have a baby, and I shared the intuitive knowing that I'd had earlier. We all laughed at how sometimes it feels like there are no secrets.

Over my years of working with students and clients I've found that people can improve their intuitive skills—that developing this skill is similar to developing any other: practice.[1] I've seen that the more people listen, the more there is to listen to. Consider developing your own intuition and encouraging clients to tap into theirs. Here are some suggestions:

1. Be open to the idea that you have intuition and that it can be helpful—another lens through which to view your world.
2. Take some quiet time so you can notice what's coming to you.
3. Pay attention to what does come to you.
4. Realize that the symbols, words, dreams, or pictures are your own creation, and you're the best person to assign meaning to them.
5. Cultivate your creativity.
6. Be open to new experiences.
7. Practice using your intuition and see what happens. For example, write down hunches in a journal and see if they are correct.
8. Ask questions, such as, "What's my next step?" and see what comes up from your inner voice or inner senses.

> How does intuition show up in your life—as a hunch, picture, or sensation? Do you feel it in your body, and if so, which part? How has intuition grown in your awareness? What has helped in making intuition stronger? Would dialoging with your intuition facilitate its development?

Here's an example of how intuition showed up when I was coaching Connie. She lived in Wisconsin and said she wanted to develop some wellness practices. Since she was dealing with a chronic illness, her doctors felt that if she made some lifestyle changes her condition would improve. As we were talking, I kept getting the picture of rams bumping heads. I tried to ignore the image, but it wouldn't go away. Finally I said, "This is strange, and I've tried to ignore this, but as you're talking, I keep getting the picture of rams running into each other and hitting heads." She began to laugh and said that was exactly what she felt like when she tried to make changes in her lifestyle. One part of her wanted to change and another didn't. As we continued to learn more about those rams, she realized that the resistance had to do with fear, which actually seemed warranted. In the past when she'd started making changes, she'd overpromised.

This caused stress, her changes could not be sustained, and ultimately her health declined. This time she selected a small step for homework in the exercise area of her life. The step didn't bring up the fear, and she began to see that the fear was an ally to help her move more slowly but more effectively toward her goal.

I've found many applications of intuition in coaching. Once I was working with a man who was choosing among some career options. I asked him to write them on post-its, fold them in half so he couldn't see the words on them, mix them up, and then intuitively pick his first, second, and third choice. His first selection was a surprise to him, but once he explored the idea, it really did become his preference. He found the exercise a bit like magic but very enlightening.

Cynthia Lester, M. Ed.
Accessing Intuition

For more than 30 years I've worked as an intuitive counselor and teacher, helping others deepen their perceptions so they can work with life's challenges, such as transitions, relationship challenges, and illnesses, and as a tool for accessing information about the dying process or about people who have died. The work Linda and I have done together over the years has helped me to refine my career and the directions it has taken.

One of the most simple and effective techniques to develop intuition is to be still and focus on one image, such as a flower. You can visualize and dissolve the same image over and over, and in this way you learn to focus your attention. This simple task can then be expanded into conducting body scans, viewing different times and places, making choices, and also seeing auras, chakras, past lives, or the path of the soul. The simple visualization exercise opens the door by creating confidence, and through practice intuition becomes consistent and accurate.

I teach people that as they develop their intuitive skills they need to be neutral about what they're receiving or visualizing. Acceptance and compassion provides a context for wisdom and insight to arise. Sometimes when I ask powerful questions to help clients tap into their intuition, what comes up for them can initially seem strange, irrelevant, or even a bit disturbing. However, when they assume there's meaning involved, and realize that sometimes our intuitions give us messages in dramatic forms, clients almost always come to see their intuition as a powerful ally.

CHAPTER 7: The Intuitive Part of Coaching

Dawn Preisendorf, MA
Intuition Makes for Extraordinary Coaching

Having spent most of my 17-year business career honing my intellectual and analytical skills, I disproportionally relied on this aptitude when I began coaching. While mental skills are essential in coaching, I've found that if I rely solely on my intellect, I'm using only a fraction of my gifts as a coach, and not able to fully connect with a client's experience.

By using my mental capacities, holding a space of compassion—and most importantly, trusting my intuition, moment-by-moment—I'm tapping into my whole self and can connect with the whole self of the client and be 100 percent present with his or her experience. I've learned—and seen in action—that a coach's intuition can make the difference between an "okay" coach and an extraordinary coach. Key takeaway? Trust your gut.

Besides learning to be receptive to inner wisdom that arises spontaneously or in response to questions and exercises, clients can tap into their intuition by selecting from various decks or objects, such as tarot cards, angel cards, medicine cards, money empowerment cards, or pendulums. Working with these objects helps us access unconscious wisdom or highlights what we already know but hadn't emphasized enough.

I keep several divination decks in my office, and sometimes clients will request that I select some cards for them. I also use them for inspiration at work: my staff and I draw a card from each of three decks, each Monday. This helps us focus our week and is amazingly inspirational.

Markie Stephens, MHR, BSN, RN
Calling on the Angels

My career as a holistic registered nurse has brought me into the world of holistic life coaching. One of my favorite tools is the Angel Oracle Cards written by Doreen Virtue. I've studied with her extensively, learning to connect with the angels again. We've all connected with the angels in the beginning of our lives but have forgotten or been ridiculed and blocked these connections. Card readings are especially helpful when my clients reach an impasse or block—the angels are eager to help and need only be asked.

I have several decks of cards, so sometimes I use one or more decks combined. I choose the deck based on my client's needs. An essential step is clearing the cards—holding them in both hands and asking for the highest good for all, with no attachment to outcomes. An intention is set with the client, asking for one or more answers as I shuffle the cards. The client chooses as many cards as they'd like. Typically, readings are performed with one, three, five, or seven cards, and they're read in order, one at a time. The first card drawn conveys the strongest message, and I encourage my clients to record the card names and short message so they may refer to them later as a personal reference. A picture may be taken of the cards in alignment and then e-mailed to the client. This is especially helpful if I'm performing a phone session.

I never cease to be amazed at the results obtained by using the oracle cards and the accuracy of the readings, confirmed by my clients. For example, while working with a male client, a card representing "father issues" was drawn. I didn't see how that applied to my client, having known him for several years and never having had that come up. When I asked him if this card spoke to him, he said "Very much." He was struggling to decide whether or not to stay with his current job, and he was unclear how to improve his life because of dissatisfaction with his job. This card suggested to him that he was dealing with "father issues" related to his boss. He worked out his problems when he realized his superior was not his father, and ended up staying in his position. In fact, because of his new attitude and behavior, he was given a raise a short time after our session!

226 CHAPTER 7: The Intuitive Part of Coaching

> *How have you used tarot or other cards or types of divination? What happened? What was the takeaway for you in that situation?*

Intuitive Tool #2	When to Use	Steps in Using	How to Gauge Effectiveness
Intuition	All the time.	When you have a hunch, you can ask the client if they'd like to know what's coming to you. Your intuition is a perception you can test with the client. You can also encourage clients to develop their intuition.	Client becomes more aware, which translates into action.

Powerful Question about Intuition
- What part does intuition play in your life?
- What role would you like intuition to play in your life?
- How do you receive intuitive messages?
- What ways have worked for you in developing your intuition?
- What benefits have you found by using your intuition?

Silence

Although the tool of silence in this structure of consciousness is key to intuitive practices and can be seen as part of that process, I've classified it as a separate tool because it has an extraordinary role in coaching, even when intuition is not being used.

Often, especially as a new coach, you'll be ahead of the interaction—thinking of what to say and feeling like you need to provide direction to your clients. You'll be working hard in the "doing" part of coaching. However, remember that the coach is *next to and a little behind* the client (figuratively speaking), and what you say needs to come as a response rather than as proactive leadership. Being silent can provide an atmosphere in which the client can find their own answers, and by waiting quietly you offer support through your presence. If a pause occurs in the conversation, you don't need to rush in to fill it.

Periods of silence in a coaching session slow the pace and allow for deeper responses. For instance, I've been working with Jack for a number of months, and he's fast-talking and fast-moving. He originally wanted coaching to work on a special project. Over time, and after he successfully accomplished his target, his focus changed to looking at his "run here and then run there" behavior. In part, this new goal seemed inspired by the slower pace of our coaching because he saw how he could access deeper wisdom when he used periods of silence. He began to notice how his hectic behavior patterns precluded those moments; he began to miss silence and a slower tempo.

228　CHAPTER 7: The Intuitive Part of Coaching

Silence can be a coach's best friend!

Intuitive Tool #3	When to Use	Steps in Using	How to Gauge Effectiveness
Silence	Useful when client expresses some limitations or when you sense that deepening is possible.	Pause or ask for a minute of silence.	Client moves beyond the limits that were stopping them or goes deeper into issues. Clients find their own answers.

Powerful Question about Silence
- How can silence help with deepening your coaching process during our session?
- Are you willing to just be silent for a moment and see what emerges?

Intuitive Coaching Tools That Facilitate Clarity at the Beginning of Sessions

Unlike the people who were living during the time when the Intuitive structure of consciousness was dominant, we moderns access the Intuitive or Magic most readily in dreams and by using our imaginations. We can tap into the power of this structure through willingness to drop the tendency to value only what's "real," and instead to playfully use our imaginations. Having done so, we might decide to aim for different goals or take steps we hadn't realized were possible.

Magic Wand

The use of an imaginary magic wand is one of my favorite tools. I simply ask my clients to imagine that they have a magic wand in their hands, and with a wave of the magic wand, they can have what they want. It helps my clients explore things that they wouldn't otherwise allow themselves to consider. It breaks through barriers and crosses thresholds into freer and more expanded spaces.

EXERCISE: Using a Magic Wand

Think of an issue in your life and imagine that it's in front of you in some form. Maybe that form takes the shape of a symbol, a picture, a situation, or even a name. For example, "overwhelm." Now imagine that you have a magic wand in your hand, and like a good fairy godmother, wave it over the symbol or words that you've pictured. Remember, there's no limit to what she can create for you—you have none of the usual restrictions. What happened? What came up for you? Is this something you want to consider as a new goal? Was it fun? Did you learn something? What is your takeaway?

CHAPTER 7: The Intuitive Part of Coaching

Intuitive Tool #4	When to Use	Steps in Using	How to Gauge Effectiveness
Magic Wand	When client expresses some limitations.	Invite client to use an imaginary magic wand. Ask how things could change or what new idea, option, or approach appeared.	Client moves beyond previous limits.

Powerful Question about the Magic Wand
- Would you be willing to try a playful exercise, using your imagination?
- What insights arose as a result of using the imaginary magic wand?
- How might these insights add options or change this situation?

Intuitive Coaching Tools to Use in the Middle of Sessions: Working with Energy

When people feel powerless or stuck, or when they can't figure out what's happening or what to do, coaches might look into the sense of life or movement being expressed. Using energy approaches promotes awareness and clarity in coaching sessions. The subject of energy is vast, so I want to limit the scope of my presentation to some simple but important tools I use in my coaching practice: working with the energy that flows in our bodies and the energy that flows within groups.

Working with Body Energy

Gebser discusses a prehistoric cave drawing in Australia that illustrates the energy around the body and was created during the time when the Magic (Intuitive) structure of consciousness was dominant. He said, "...here the aura is clearly in evidence and set in greater relief by the coloring...."[2]

I believe that everything is made up of energy or life force.[3] Very simply speaking, I think about energy as loosely floating around or tightly packed. A piece of furniture in the room and our own bodies are examples of tightly packed energy. We can see them and touch them. In contrast, the energy surrounding our bodies is loosely packed energy that's usually not seen except by special cameras or people who have psychic ability to see this subtle energy. Radio, TV, and internet waves of energy are inaudible to our ears, and again too subtle to see but can be picked up by specialized equipment.

Besides the fact that our bodies are made up of energy, it's been demonstrated that our energy flows in defined patterns called *meridians*. We can think of the energy flow in our bodies as somewhat similar to the electrical system in a building. Traditional Chinese Medicine (TCM) and Ayurveda, the health system of India, especially focus on these for healing. For example, practitioners who use acupuncture (the insertion of very thin needles into specific points on the meridians) or acupressure (the use of massage along the energy routes) work in specialized places in these pathways to change the energy flow. Just as buildings have junction boxes, we have areas in our body that are energy centers.

Larger energy centers are called *chakras* or vortices, and these are present in a central column that runs from the top of our head to the base of our spines.[4] The illustration on the next page identifies the energy centers.

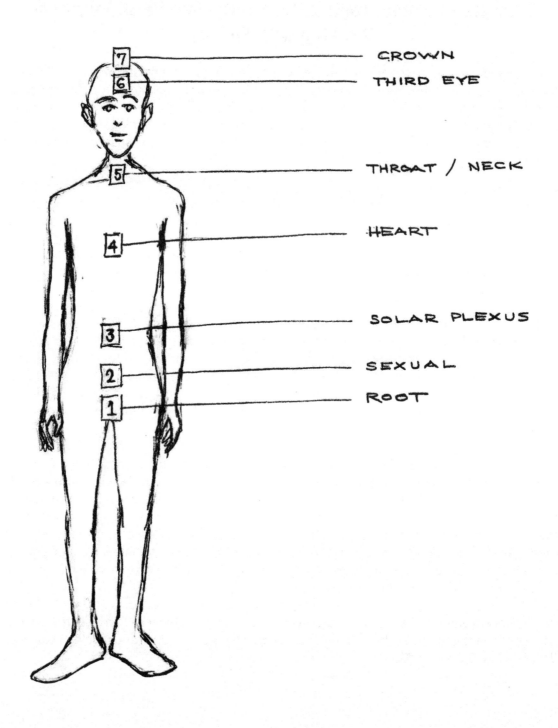

Working with Chakras

The meridian system doesn't inform my coaching practice to a great degree. For example, I'm not very knowledgeable about pressure points that can shift energy in the meridians. However, my knowledge and personal experience with this system does enable me to appropriately refer my clients to acupuncturists and to practitioners who use acupressure, and this resource has proven very helpful with some clients.

I find the use of chakra diagnosis much more valuable in my work with clients. Each of the seven chakras correlates to certain issues and emotions. Knowledge of these correlations informs my powerful questions, such as in the conversation with my client, Arny, whom you met in Sample Session 2C at the beginning of this chapter.

Here is information about each of the energy centers, starting from the bottom of the spine and moving up to the top of the head.[5]

1. **The root chakra**
   - Issue—primal instinct for self-preservation and security
   - Emotion—fear of annihilation
   - Body areas involved in this energy—anus, rectum, descending colon, hamstring muscles in legs
   - Body symptoms—sciatica, colitis, constipation, varicose veins

2. **The sexual chakra**
   - Issue—sensuality, survival of the species, gender
   - Emotion—erotic energy
   - Body areas involved in this energy—bladder, prostate, pelvis, quadriceps, gonads
   - Body symptoms—cystitis, prostatitis, impotence, STDs, menstrual pain

3. **The solar plexus chakra**
   - Issue—power and mastery
   - Emotion—assertiveness, submission/domination
   - Body areas involved in this energy—stomach, duodenum, ileum, pancreas, liver, adrenals
   - Body symptoms—diabetes, indigestion, adrenal fatigue, peptic ulcer

4. **The heart chakra**
   - Issue—love, relatedness, compassion
   - Emotion—security comes from a sense of belonging in community and in the spiritual/religious or transpersonal sense

- Body areas involved in this energy—heart, breasts, lungs, thymus
- Body symptoms—heart disease, asthma, allergies, bronchitis, breast disease

5. **The throat chakra**
    - Issue—creativity, communication
    - Emotion—self-expression
    - Body areas involved in this energy—pharynx, larynx, thyroid
    - Body symptoms—sore throat, TMJ (jaw pain and dysfunction), goiter, laryngitis

6. **The third-eye chakra**
    - Issue—intuition
    - Emotion—intelligence, intuition, discrimination
    - Body areas involved in this energy—sinuses, eyes, pineal gland
    - Body symptoms—insomnia, sinusitis, migraines, visual problems

7. **The crown chakra**
    - Issue—connection with higher power
    - Emotion—meaning
    - Body areas involved in this energy—top of head

I find that knowing the correlations among body areas, illnesses, diseases, issues, and emotions can help me create powerful coaching questions. One thing to remember about energy is that for proper functioning it needs to flow. When energy is stagnant in the body, things go wrong, just as when blood cannot flow in the body, problems arise.

For example, if energy isn't flowing in or through the throat chakra, a client might be more vulnerable to germs and might get a sore throat. If a client has a sore throat, this might alert you to a problem with creativity or communication and could be the basis for a powerful coaching question. You might ask, "Do you feel a bit stifled in the creativity realm, or do you need to say something to yourself or to someone else?" An even more powerful question might be, "What meaning do you assign to this discomfort?" Chances are that exploring these issues may unblock the energy, and the sore throat might heal quickly.

Another example could involve a symptom in the heart area. (In this country, heart disease is still the leading cause of death.) Looking at this from an energetic perspective, if your clients are suffering from symptoms located in the heart, you may wonder if they lack compassion or find loving themselves or others challenging. This was the situation with Arny.

An added source for understanding body messages is Louise Hay's book entitled, *How to Heal Your Life*. She lists physical symptoms, the matching theme, and then an affirmation to help heal the warning sign. For instance, she says that back problems in general "represent the support for life," and that an affirmation to facilitate change is "I know that life always supports me." She becomes more specific, seeing upper, middle, and lower back problems as different indicators. She claims that upper back issues relate to lack of emotional support, feeling unloved, or holding back love, and suggests the affirmation of "I love and approve of myself. Life supports and loves me." The middle back subject matter is guilt, or being stuck in all that "stuff" back there, with pain being a message to "get off my back." She provides the affirmation "I release the past. I am free to move forward with love in my heart." As for the lower back, fear of money and lack of financial support are issues that Hay suggests can be altered by the affirmations of "I trust the process of life," along with "all I need is always taken care of," and "I am safe."[6] The client is really the authority on this kind of reasoning, and things might be more complex than what's listed in a very simple manner in Lousie Hay's book.[6] Of course with any physical condition the client needs to medically check conditions out.

If I think a client is open to looking at body messages from this perspective, I'll ask, "Would you like to see if there's a connection between what's happening in your body and some common themes?" If my client is open to this kind of information, we could explore it. If they're interested in an outside source, I would look up the symptom in Louise Hay's book and read the premise and affirmation and ask if all or a part of that description resonated with my client.

Intuitive Tool #5	When to Use	Steps in Using	How to Gauge Effectiveness
Energy Chakras	The chakra system can help to explore a theme, such as stomach trouble relating to a power issue.	Noticing body experiences in relation to the chakra themes.	Client gains additional ways to understand their symptoms, resulting in modified goals, change of behavior, or homework steps.

Powerful Questions about Chakras
- Where do you feel that feeling, sensation or thought in your body?
- What body symptoms are you experiencing?
- Are you willing to explore themes that correspond to this body location? (If client agrees, move on to specific questions.)
    - **The root chakra**
        Issue—primal instinct for self-preservation and security. Emotion—fear of annihilation. Body areas involved in this energy—anus, rectum, descending colon, hamstring muscles in legs. Body symptoms—sciatica, colitis, constipation, varicose veins.
        - How might safety be a part of this equation?
        - What helps you feel secure?
        - What fears are connected to this situation?
        - What is a symbol that represents this area of your life?

    - **The sexual chakra**
        Issue—sensuality, survival of the species, gender. Emotion—erotic energy. Body areas involved in this energy—bladder, prostate, pelvis, quadriceps, gonads. Body symptoms—cystitis, prostatitis, impotence, STDs, menstrual pain.
        - Is there some way that feelings of sexuality or sensuality affect this situation?
        - What issues about gender might be involved in these circumstances?
        - What is a symbol that represents this area of your life?
        - Which feelings are coming up for you?

    - **The solar plexus chakra**
        Issue—power and mastery. Emotion—assertiveness, submission/domination. Body areas involved in this energy—stomach, duodenum, ileum, pancreas, liver, adrenals. Body symptoms—diabetes, indigestion, adrenal fatigue, peptic ulcer.
        - In what way does power interact with this situation?
        - How might the idea of "power over" be involved with this state of affairs?
        - What might change if you think of sharing power or "power with" in this situation?
        - How would you like to be treated in relation to power issues in these circumstances?
        - What is a symbol that represents this area of your life?
        - What changes are called for in this circumstance, in relation to power?

- **The heart chakra**
    Issue—love, relatedness, compassion. Emotion—security comes from a sense of belonging in community and in the spiritual/religious or transpersonal sense. Body areas involved in this energy—heart, breasts, lungs, thymus. Body symptoms—heart disease, asthma, allergies, bronchitis, breast disease.
    - How might love be playing a part in this situation?
    - How much love do you have in your life?
    - In what ways do you feel loved in your life?
    - How important is love in your life?
    - How connected to others do you feel?
    - How would you describe your network of friends?
    - What is the title of a song that would describe the love in your life right now?
    - I invite you to draw a picture of your network of connections. Put yourself in the middle with those people, animals or things in proximity to you in relation to their importance to you. For instance, the most important are closest to you. What do you notice from drawing this picture?
    - What kind of movement would express love to you?
    - What is the title of a song of how you would like to portray the love in your life?

- **The throat chakra**
    Issue—creativity, communication. Emotion—self-expression. Body areas involved in this energy—pharynx, larynx, thyroid. Body symptoms—sore throat, TMJ (jaw pain and dysfunction), goiter, laryngitis.
    - On a scale of 1-10, how much creativity do you have in your life? How would you like that number to change? How could it change?
    - What is the most creative thing you've ever done?
    - How does creativity affect your spirit or soul?
    - Where does creativity live in your body?
    - What colors support your creativity?
    - How do the arts in all forms stimulate your creativity?
    - What works with your abilities to communicate directly with others? What could be changed? How could that happen? What would be a first step?
    - Who is the hardest person for you to be authentic or honest with? What could happen to change that circumstance?
    - How honest are you with yourself? How could that change? What would be a first step?

- What is the lie in this situation? How could you shine light on this blind spot?
- Do you think that sharing more of your truth with this person would make this relationship more alive and less boring?
- What was the most important thing you've ever said to someone else or yourself?
- What communication is waiting to be expressed? Where does it live in your body? How could your spirit help you deliver this message? What part does "right timing" have to do with this issue?

- **The third-eye chakra**
  Issue—intuition. Emotion—intelligence, intuition, discrimination. Body areas involved in this energy—sinuses, eyes, pineal gland. Body symptoms—insomnia, sinusitis, migraines, visual problems.
  - What is the role that intuition plays in your life? How could this change? What would be a first step in this exploration?
  - What kind of symbol represents intuition to you?
  - How does your spiritual or religious side support or hinder your intuition?
  - How do your mind and intuition interact?
  - What is the most difficult issue for you to meet with discernment? What is the easiest? How might you transfer this discrimination skill in the easy area to the more difficult arena? What would interfere in this experiment?
  - In terms of intelligence, what areas are strong and which are weak? Examples: intellectual, emotional, artistic, moral, athletic, movement.

- **The crown chakra**
  Issue—connection with higher power. Emotion—meaning. Body areas involved in this energy—top of head.
  - What impacts your connection to God or however you refer to a higher power?
  - What hymn or song inspires your connection to God?
  - How does nature play a part in connection to God?
  - What activities improve your connection to God?
  - What is the meaning or sense of purpose in your life?
  - What adds meaning to your life?
  - What would you like said about you at your funeral?

Connecting through Tapping

Besides working with intersections of energetic meaning and body symptoms and coming up with affirmations, clients might wish to physically address charged areas of the body. A variety of healing methods aim to address this, and here's a good place to make a referral (unless you are already a trained professional in a healing modality and wish to switch from coaching to healing).

Like me, most of the coaches I've trained come to this work having been educated in healing, therapy, medicine, or other helpful techniques. Even if not, most have experienced them as patients and clients. Although these methods are not coaching techniques, per se, a skilled holistic coach might bring them in when appropriate, either making referrals or drawing on their own previous training. I'll be mentioning some of these adjunct modalities and how I use them within sessions.

Earlier I mentioned that for health and well-being energy in the body needs to flow, and to assist with this I sometimes call upon Thought Field Therapy, a technique developed by Roger Callahan. [7] You might be surprised to know that a wide variety of tapping techniques can increase the movement of energy in the body. I first learned this from Stina Pope, a colleague at John F. Kennedy University, who was teaching an in-service for nurses. If my client talks about a situation that involves fear or anxiety, I might see if they are interested in the particular tapping exercise I've labeled Intuitive Tool #6. If they don't already know about it and are interested in learning, then I would switch to my consulting hat and teach them this process. If they know the exercise, we might do it together in the session.

I was working with Karen, who had a fear about making presentations in front of groups. I asked if she knew about tapping, and she said she didn't but was interested in learning. I asked her on a scale from 1 to 10, with 10 being the most nervous, how she felt at that moment when she thought of presenting her proposal in front of members of her department. She had worked hard on it, and felt it was going to be well received, but didn't know how she would get through the presentation. She said she was at a 9, even thinking about it. I asked her to say this: "Even though I'm afraid to present my project to my department, I completely love and accept myself."

She repeated it out loud three times. Then I directed her to use her fingers to gently tap places on her face, chest, wrists, knees, and head. After she did that once, she was surprised to find that when she now thought about presenting the material, she was down to a 6. We repeated this two more times until she was at a 1. She was surprised by the effect of the exercise and decided to practice it during the following week at least once a day. Right after she presented her project she called me to tell me that although she was a little nervous, it was nothing like the last time and she had great feedback from her team and even from her manager.

CHAPTER 7: The Intuitive Part of Coaching

Intuitive Tool #6	When to Use	Steps in Using	How to Gauge Effectiveness
Tapping	When client is emotionally stuck about a relationship, situation, or event.	Support tapping if client knows it, and if not, ask if they would like to learn it. If yes, give these instructions. 1. Ask client to give you a number from 1-10 representing how upset they are about an issue. 2. Have client say 3 times "Even though (challenge) . . .I completely love and accept myself." 3. Have client tap: above eyebrows, under eyes, under nose, at chin crease, on chest, under left arm, on wrists, inside of knees, top of head. 4. Check the number representing how upset they are about the issue. Repeat the cycle until the number is 1 or 0.	Number goes down to 1 or 0. (May have to repeat steps several times to get to 1 or 0.)

Powerful Question about Tapping
- Are you interested in using a tapping technique to help you shift your perspective on this issue?

WORKING WITH DIRECTION OF ENERGY CURRENTS[8]

I consider direction of energy flow when working with my clients, based on five energy currents described in the Vedic or East Indian tradition:

1. In and up—nourishing energy.
2. Down—throwing off.
3. At naval—fire and cooking.
4. Up and out—expressing.
5. Centripetal/centrifugal—cohering.

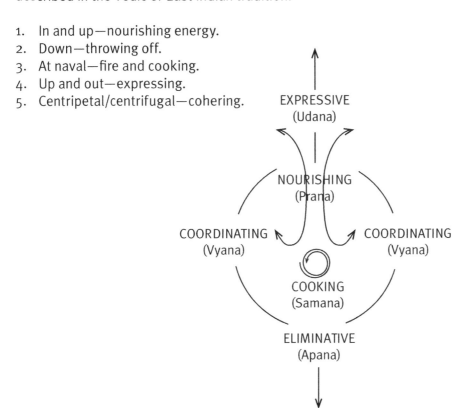

I first learned of this system while enrolled in a course taught by Dr. Rudolph Ballentine in 1990. It seemed interesting but not useful. However, over the years, I've found practical applications for this information in my coaching practice. The most common has to do with the downward current of energy. Sometimes when my clients have headaches (energy might be thought of as stuck in the head and not moving down) or complain of nausea or constipation, I wonder about their downward flow of energy. There are many possible reasons for these symptoms—I'm not a medical doctor and cannot treat illness, and thus I encourage my clients to check out symptoms with their physicians. However, seeing if shifting their energy to a downward flow might help is always an interesting experiment. What happens to the pain in their head if they do what is commonly referred to as *grounding*—using exercises to feel more connected to the ground or earth? That's reinstating the downward flow of energy. If my clients are interested in this type of change, I can change into the consulting role and teach them to breathe in ways that better connect them to the ground, or help them imagine ways to be more grounded, or actually request certain homework in which they sit at the base of a tree or walk in the grass barefoot.

In my first session with Arny, I was intrigued with his acid reflux condition. I hoped that we'd have a chance in a follow up conversation to see if he'd be open to practicing some exercises to help his energy go down. The reflux action can be thought of as a disruption in the down energy. Instead it's going up, and that isn't what needs to happen. In fact, he did sign up for coaching, and I had an opportunity to work with him on this issue. It was a stretch for him, and he was only willing to do it after months of coaching in which he changed many things in his life, but he did learn some ways to release tension and work with that downward energy. It made quite a change in his ability to eat and sleep.

EXERCISE: Grounding Energy

Want to try grounding now? Stand up, take some deep breaths, and spend a few minutes imagining that your feet are like the roots of a tree. Feel really connected to the ground (even if you're in a building). Can you feel any difference? See if you feel heavier or more grounded.

Another current that frequently becomes out of balance is number 5: the one that is kind of like centrifugal force and related to centering. Sometimes my clients report that they feel scattered or just "spread all over." They find themselves leaving things at places they have been. Their energy is not centered.

EXERCISE: Centering

You can try another experiment the next time you feel scattered or spread all over. You could practice now and see if it makes a difference. Stand up again, and this time find your middle or your balance and pull in scattered energy to the center. Take a few deep breaths, and with your feet shoulder-length apart, gently rock forward and backward on your feet just a bit until you find the center on that dimension—the best and most balanced place to stand. Now, without picking up your feet, move side to side and find the center of that dimension. Did anything change?

Intuitive Tool #7	When to Use	Steps in Using	How to Gauge Effectiveness
Energy Currents—grounding, centering, cooking, expressing, nurturing	When the coach hears that the client's energy is not balanced.	Invite the client to change energy now by using energy practices. If the client doesn't have the skills, ask client if they would like you to lead them in an energy exercise.	Client's energy is rebalanced—the client feels more stable and calm if using grounding and centering techniques.

Powerful Question about Direction of Energy Flows
- **In and Up—Nourishing Energy**
    - Is there some way that your energy seems off in terms of taking in nourishment?
    - How are you being nourished in your life right now?
    - How might you want that to change?
    - What would need to happen for that change to occur?

- **Down—Throwing Off**
    - To what extent do you feel grounded or relaxed and settled?
    - What helps you feel grounded?
    - What interferes with you feeling grounded?

- **At Naval—Fire and Cooking**
    - Are there some challenges you're having in terms of your digestion?
    - Digestion is the place where the outside of the world and your inside meet. How would you describe the interaction? What could shift? How could that happen?
    - How would you describe your fire for life—your energy to move forward and/or your appetite for living fully? How would you like it to change? What can help with that change?

- **Up and Out—Expressing**
    - Does the energy that has to do with expressing yourself need to change? For example, do you feel that this type of energy is exhausted just from a day of teaching, or does it feel blocked in some way?

- **Centripetal/Centrifugal—Cohering**
  - Do you find yourself scattered in many directions? How does that feel? How would you describe that experience?
  - What's working and what do you want to change in this situation?

WORKING WITH THE BREATH

It's quite effective to begin energy-related exercises exploring the breath, so let's go into how breathing can help shift energy. Probably everyone has heard or been told to take a deep breath at some time. Something magic happens. A person may release tension, think of a new option, or integrate items in a new way. Why does it work?

Taking a deep breath connects the body and the mind. This is a powerful action and provides new information and perspectives. That deep breath also activates the four higher chakras so that we can use insights from the higher energy centers to explore issues in the lower three chakras, which are more involved with instinctual drives. This new perspective can help us manage actions based on survival.[9]

Breathing deeply is not only powerful but acts quickly. With two minutes of deep abdominal breathing, people can change their brain waves and shift into a relaxed state.[10] This type of breathing is generally misunderstood, so for a full description of how to truly breathe from this part of your body, please go the Rudy Ballentine's book *Radical Healing*.[11] My clients rely on using breath as a change agent. I agree it is key in conscious living and say, "You always have one of the most powerful tools for change right with you, and it's free!"

Looking at how we breathe can also reveal a bigger picture. One of my teachers once said to me, "Show me how you breathe and I will tell you how you live." You may think that is a stretch, but try it. Take a minute to experiment and ponder what your ways of breathing in various situations might tell you.

EXERCISE: Breath Awareness

Take several normal breaths and notice as much as you can about them, and then answer these questions:

- Do you usually breathe deeply or more shallowly? Do you take in just a little air and/or release just a little air? Does that say something about how you live your life? Is there a way that you don't live from deep places? Could you live your life more deeply? What would that look like?
- Do you take in a lot of air and release less? Do you have trouble with letting go?
- Does it seem harder to inhale than to exhale? Is it difficult to "take in" things?
- Without judgment but just with awareness, what else do you notice about your breath that may mirror how you live your life?

Intuitive Tool #8	When to Use	Steps in Using	How to Gauge Effectiveness
Take a Breath	When the coach hears that the client wants a new option, integration, or a more open perspective on a situation, or if the client feels stuck. Another time to use breath is to explore ways clients live their lives.	Invite the client to take a deep breath, and take a deep breath yourself, when you want to help clients see new perspectives. If you want to explore the breath as an example for looking at their life, ask clients to breathe normally and ask questions about the breath, such as inquiring into the depth, rhythm, length of inhale and exhale, etc.	Client has a new idea or way forward. Clients see how their ways of breathing replicate the way they live.

Powerful Questions about the Breath
- Would it be helpful to take a breath and see if something new or different comes up for you?
- How does the way you breathe demonstrate factors about how you live your life?

Lisa Leum, BA, RN
Energetic Support for the Dying

The coaching skills that I've learned from Linda have been an amazing experience for me as a hospice nurse. I've used her skills and translated them into an energetic format that I call *energetic coaching for the dying*. When I'm working with patients near the last two weeks of their life, I've found it very helpful to hold a space of compassion. This space emanates from an area behind my heart, and slightly to the left of my spine. When I move my conscious awareness to that space, I immediately begin to feel and sense a ruby red light radiating out through my energy field and into the room of the patient. This light brings immense peace and helps to soften the fear that's sometimes felt by the family or by the patient. I've observed this as energy needed to clear the room of any lower frequency thought forms or confusion and bring a sense of peace and harmony to the patient.

After this is done, I can then "tune into" the patient and sense, see, hear, or feel what energetic assistance they may need to support them on their journey. For me, this usually comes in the form of "strings of light" or an energy vibration that comes through my body. I may hear words in the form a prayer that they need to hear or receive telepathically. Other times I just sit quietly in the patient's room, holding that beautiful ruby red light. Energy can sometimes speak louder then words! This is one of my ways of energetically coaching the patient to make their journey to the other side.

I would compare this to the setting of an orchestra. The musicians don't just come in sit down and begin to play. They need to unpack their instruments, all of the chairs need to be set up, and each section needs to be divided by instruments: flutes in one section, violins in another, and so on. They're preparing their space to play their "strings of light." I do this same thing as a caregiver. I'm preparing the room or space for these cords of consciousness to be played out to support the patient and family. It's an honor and a privilege for me to assist someone in this way.

Suzanne Koivun, MSN, RN, CCAP, CCAPT, Reiki Master
Equine-Assisted Coaching and Subtle Energy

I have been a nurse for 30 years and now work in postpartum where I take care of mothers and babies. Although the BCI skills I have learned serve me well with my hospital patients—large and small—I'm applying these coaching skills to my newest passion—horse assisted coaching. This is a fairly new specialty but it is growing in popularity and used to facilitate personal growth, team-building, and leadership skills. How does it work? Horses are very sensitive and during the coaching session the horse immediately tunes into the client's energy, reflecting back that person's true state of mind and being. My job as the coach is to provide activities to help my client assess and interpret the feedback from the horse.

For example, in one of my equine-assisted training sessions with my teacher, I was working with a horse named Jake, and I noticed how he kept turning away from me. I didn't understand what was going on, and I became irritated with him. I began to realize during the session how often I drifted off, lost focus, and didn't pay attention to Jake. Because of the powerful questions of my coach, I started thinking about how that played out in other places in my life and grasped the significance of this discovery. The feedback from Jake was key in helping me identify this pattern I wanted to change and then my coach helped me create homework to take action steps in altering the pattern.

Whether I'm working with mothers who want to understand their babies or working with clients who want to learn from the feedback of horses, I am discovering how to be more sensitive to the very subtle energy involved in both of these interactions. It is training me, my patients, and clients to develop the same highly sensitive awareness that comes from deep body, mind, and spirit intuitive listening that I learned in my BCI coach training.

Group Energy in Coaching

I've presented information about our individual energy and how clients can use various resources to help it change and flow to promote wellbeing. Next, I want to address energy from a larger perspective—group energy—and describe how I use this concept in my coaching practice.

A number of years ago, I read *A New Science of Life: The Hypothesis of Formative Causation*, by British biologist, Rupert Sheldrake, a remarkable pioneer in the area of group energy.[12] His concept about species learning immediately made sense to me because I'd always had an inner knowing that the learning of one person made a difference to other people, even though I wasn't able to prove that idea or even know how the phenomenon worked. After reading Sheldrake's work I wanted to learn all I could about group consciousness because I was delighted when my inner knowing was confirmed. Sheldrake has been studying possible mechanisms that could explain learning and sharing of experience among members of groups. His main interest is providing insight into inheritance of biological forms and their self-organization, but his ideas about *morphic fields* might apply to many everyday situations, including education and phenomena considered psychic—for instance, animals that know when their owners are coming home, or how we are aware that we are being stared at.

Sheldrake also describes the curious behavior of birds in England who adapted to the new design of milk bottle tops. They'd been in the habit of stealing milk from bottles left on doorsteps, but when the design of the bottles changed, the birds had to learn a new way of getting into the bottles. After a certain number of birds had mastered it, the skill quickly spread throughout England and further, even though imitation was ruled out as the mechanism. Sheldrake hypothesizes that each species has a collective memory, and among other things, this explains why it's easier to acquire new skills once a significant number of members of a species have mastered it.

How do I use this in my coaching? Clients spend time, energy, and money to change things in their life that no longer serve them or to reach a goal that more fully taps into their potential or reason for living. Sometimes there's smooth sailing, and other times my clients explore and overcome obstacles and resistance. They're willing to put effort into their development because it makes a substantial improvement in their life, but if they feel that their work not only benefits them but people in general, it makes the endeavor even more meaningful.

There's another way that I use the idea of species learning, and it relates to teaching coaching and working with coaching groups. Chris Bache, a university professor for nearly 30 years, has built upon the work of Sheldrake and subsequent researchers. During Bache's teaching career, he became clear that "groups have minds" that are affected by learning, and even more interesting, that a form of "collective consciousness" developed from one semester to the next in his classroom. In his book, *The Living Classroom* he states that "they [classes] show signs of a true consciousness and intelligence. I watched as fields of influence grew around the courses I was teaching, the learning taking place in one semester influencing the learning taking place in subsequent semesters." [13]

Bache shares his own initial resistance to this concept. He asked himself how this group mind could work, since we all have separate brains. However, as the years progressed and his understanding evolved, he realized that group consciousness was real. He encourages his readers to think of looking through two eyes: one eye sees what most would call the regular reality of separate beings and the other eye sees "the exquisitely intricate patterns that weave these separate lives into larger wholes."[14]

As he became increasingly aware of a collective group mind, Bache began to work consciously with it, first by preparing the field of consciousness for new classes. For example, during his daily meditations, he reviewed his purpose for teaching a course and then began to screen the field of consciousness, asking for students who would benefit from the class to enroll. Once a class began, he worked to nurture the field by using meditative practices, such as Tonglin, a process in which he would imagine drawing from the students any dark energy representing pain or conflict.[15] He also worked with the students in class on exercises that invited them to recognize the energy that connected them. The last part of his conscious work with the group was designed to close or end the group's energetic connection so that students could leave and have their energy freed up to go on to their next class.[16]

I've been teaching coaching for about 15 years and been involved with other long-standing groups, and my experience is that group mind does exist, as can be seen, for example, in accelerated learning. A current class does seem to benefit from the work done by previous classes, and later classes can learn things more quickly. Like Bache, I've wondered about the cause of this phenomenon. Was the basis of this accelerated learning a demonstration of group mind, my becoming a better teacher, or the development and improvement of my content? Upon reflection, my teaching skills and curriculum refinements probably account for a portion of the accelerated learning but don't seem to explain the entire effect.

So what does this mean for you? Chris Bache says, "I tend to view these fields as connected to individual professors because of the highly personalized nature of teaching. . . .For these reasons, I tend to give more weight to the professor as the anchor of these learning fields than the course itself, though clearly there is overlap here.[17] Perhaps you will be switching into the educator role or the consultant role, or will teach groups, and can explore group learning and practice building, nurturing, and closing the group field.

You may be beginning a coaching practice with individuals or groups, or adding coaching skills to your current role. As your practice experience grows, your clients will benefit from the work of your former clients. Perhaps you already have a rich background of working with people in a learning, growth, or healing manner, and this also will benefit your clients or students. I think we unconsciously realize the power of prior group learning, because we tend to go to people who have experience.

LAW OF ATTRACTION

Group energy may be the basis for the recently publicized idea of attracting what you want—not a new idea but popular again. How does it work? An individual's energy can be described in terms of *vibration*, which is easiest to think of in terms of quantity, with "lowest" being experienced as most negative (quality). We are energetic beings who are connected with one another and tend to be drawn to (or grouped with) those with similar energy to that we send out or experience, whatever its vibration. This suggests that there's no coincidence that events come together in seemingly magic ways. Such happenings are meaningful—*synchronicities*—rather than random, and held together by a similar energy.

The Law of Attraction is a principle of energy that says that whatever you focus on—thereby adding energy to—will expand or become larger. Therefore, if you focus on the negative in your life, it increases. You can use this principle in your own life and help your clients do the same. Finely tuned manifestations skills can occur at any age. My five-year-old granddaughter lives on a ranch a long day's drive from my home and has wanted to come to visit me on the train for about a year now. She's been talking about it as if it were just a matter of time before it happened. I go to her home or see her almost every month, and one month ago when I was at the ranch, she announced to me that she could come home with me now for the visit. At first, I laughed to myself about her plan but marveled at her clarity and her "of course, this could happen now" attitude. Immediately I thought of all the reasons the trip wouldn't work. I suggested that she visit me the following year. She said, "That is sooooooooo far away." I realized that to her one year was one fifth of her life, and if I translated that into my years of experience it would be like someone saying to me, "Let's do that in 13 years." I began considering how it could work, and almost like magic, she did drive back with me and then we took the train back to her house. She was delighted, and I was impressed about her materializing her wish. As we were walking down the street to go to dinner the first night, I asked her how she got the trip to happen, and she said, "First I asked myself if I could go, and I said yes, then I asked my dog, Sally, if I could go, and she said yes, then I asked you if I could go, and you said yes, and then I asked my Mom if I could go, and she said yes, and then I asked my Dad if I could go, and he said yes, and then I asked Sissy if I could go, and she said yes." She shrugged her shoulders and added, "So then I got it in my life! That's how you have your dreams come true." "Great job!!" I exclaimed, and as we continued to walk down the street, I wondered how I could remember that attracting what I want in my life can be easier than I sometimes make it.

Today I worked with a client who's starting a private practice in coaching. He has a strong meditation practice and in his time of contemplation has been asking for information about what steps to take to attract clients to his new business. In his reflection yesterday, he had the insight that he should work less and prepare more. I thought this was an interesting approach and asked him about the implications. He said this means that he needs to hold the most positive energy possible, including readiness for clients to come and confidence that he can provide a valuable service. He felt if he did that kind of preparation, he would need to do less work because clients would be drawn to him.

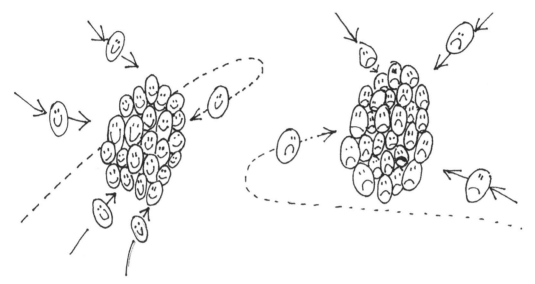

Clients can learn to harness the power of the Law of Attraction, using tools mentioned earlier in this chapter.

Intuitive Tool #9	When to Use	Steps in Using	How to Gauge Effectiveness
The Law of Attraction	When clients want to meet a goal that relies on their ability to hold a positive energy that it will happen—like building a coaching practice, changing a relationship, etc.	Help the client connect to the energy of attaining the goal and find ways to stay connected to that energy: • Visualization • Affirmations • Tapping into the power of doing what others have already done.	Goal is reached.

Powerful Questions about the Law of Attraction
- How would you describe your energy when things are working well for you?
- What is an example of when things seemed to flow naturally and easily while working toward a goal?
- How do you stop your forward movement?
- How do you get unstuck when you lose traction?
- How does setting an intention affect your level of success?
- Where does your attention focus when you just let it wander?
- How does seeing the positive in life, or the "glass half full," affect your daily life?
- What happens when you concentrate on the negative or the "glass half empty"?
- In terms of the people around you, what are their values, aspirations, levels of success and sense of purpose?
- How do the people around you affect you?
- What adds to your energy?
- What drains your energy?

Darlene Hess, PhD, AHN-BC, PMHNP-BC, ACC
Manifesting Your Goal

When my clients want to manifest something in their lives, I encourage them to think and feel as though they already have what they want. Some clients believe there's not enough for everyone or that they deserve only so much. They believe there's a finite source of abundance, when actually it's infinite. All spiritual traditions speak of a source of infinite love and abundance that's not bound by economic theories based on competition for limited resources. Limiting beliefs are always important to explore because they're often the key to what's stopping people from realizing their goals. I encourage my clients to move out of the mental, linear, three-dimensional reality and discover new ways of perceiving and thinking.

For example, one of my clients wanted to increase her annual income from $70,000 to $125,000. She believed that abundance was limited, so we explored this concept. One question I asked was how this belief served her. What was a benefit to thinking this way? She said that two answers came to mind—believing in limited abundance kept her from getting too egotistical, and the limit stopped her from finding out if she really was talented enough to obtain her goal. Staying with her limited 70K kept her business small, and she didn't have to see if she could run a larger company.

This client believed that some of her desires were good and some were bad, so that became another avenue of exploration. She thought that she should cut off her desire for money. She could feel her stomach noticeably tightening as she thought about bringing in $125,000 this year and realized she had held an unconscious belief that money was evil. During one of our sessions, she realized that having money wasn't evil but that having it could enable her to do work that would benefit many other people. She began to see money as a means to an end rather than the end itself. She spent time discussing what she wanted to do with the money and how she could even share it with others.

By the end of our work together, my client could imagine herself looking at her bank statements and seeing large balances and not feeling guilty or thinking she was a greedy or bad person. Later she saw money coming to her in "chunks" as she called it—some were large and others smaller, and they were coming to her in a caravan of vehicles. There was a steady stream that seemed to flow unendingly. As she talked, she began to see images of trucks that came from side roads, hit the vehicles and stopped the flow, but she quickly realized the trucks were representations of her doubts. She easily came up with a way to deal with these disrupters of financial abundance. When she saw one coming from the sidelines, she said, "Oh, those are only insubstantial doubts, and as I dismiss them, the trucks disappear and the flow of money is reestablished." I recently heard from this client, and she told me that she had not only reached her goal but had surpassed it.

Group Energy and Family Dynamics: Powerful Questions

Coaching can be done in groups, and you can experiment with adapting any of the tools in this book. You may have noticed places where I suggested how to use the tools with groups—plenty of other ways exist. Working in groups adds the benefit of built in support for participants and the chance for them to learn from one another.

You may have been trained in methods for working with groups and can adapt those methods to group coaching. I suggest that as with healing modalities you carefully consider the underlying principles of adjunct methods to ensure they're compatible with coaching's emphasis on partnership, clients leading, learning and growth—and that they facilitate a whole person (integral) perspective. It's also very important that you don't bring in adjunct methods that you are not professionally credentialed to practice.

I'd like to describe a method for group work that's compatible with a coaching orientation and very much in harmony with the concept of group energy. Even though most coaches won't be trained to use the method, I offer this so that you can see the power of considering family dynamics. I provide powerful questions you can use for working with your clients.

Just as classes and generations of classes have a group mind, so do families and generations of families. Over the past 25 years another application of Sheldrake's pioneering species learning theory has evolved, called Family Constellation work, developed by Bert Hellinger, a German psychotherapist.[18] Hellinger has applied the concept of morphic fields to changing dysfunctional family relationships and patterns, and this work is one of the fastest growing forms of family intervention, practiced in more than 30 countries.[19] While training is required to practice using this method, how it works will be of interest to coaches who work with groups.

Family Constellation work is routinely conducted in groups of 15-20 people who usually don't know each other and meet together for a day or more. The trained constellation facilitator works with one individual, whom I will call the *constellation client*, who selects people from the group to represent her or him, as well as other family members. The constellation client carefully positions the representatives in the center of the circle in such a way as to illustrate their relationships. For example, the mother and father may be close and turned facing each other, or perhaps one of the parents is more distant from the other and turned away, looking off in the distance. Siblings or grandparents may be part of the inner family group and are also positioned in relation to each other.

Interestingly, the chosen representatives usually begin to feel into their roles, even knowing nothing or very little about the people they are representing. As explained by the theory of group energy, they become aware of the part they are representing and act accordingly. The somatic positioning may also play a role.

During the process the constellation facilitator often asks the representatives if they feel right about moving to change the relationship to others in the composite family, asks them what they are feeling, or asks them if they feel a need to say something to others in the group. The process may take an hour or more. During that time new people from the outer circle may be brought in to represent earlier generations or other current relatives to help with the family re-patterning.

From my experience in being the constellation client whose family is being worked with, or in acting as a representative in another person's constellation, often situations that have been forgotten, unknown, or misinterpreted by the constellation client become apparent, causing a change in feeling, thinking, and acting. The new acknowledgment and integration allows for a change in relationship among the composite family members in the inside of the group. The theory and my experience support the idea that once this realigning has occurred in the therapeutic constellation environment, the actual family members benefit by the shifts and act differently toward each other because of the group learning and growth that occurred with the representatives. The constellation work can access the actual family field of energy.

When I hear clients say that they are behaving in a way that's repeating a multigenerational pattern, I may shift into a consulting role, explain constellation work, and ask if they'd be interested in a referral to a constellation facilitator. Sometimes they attend a Family Constellation workshop, feel a change in themselves, and also find a shift in the family dynamics. As we continue to work together, clients can select homework that facilitates continued and increased change in their actions in other areas of their life, including work situations. Patterns are often widespread, and once people change a basic dynamic, they can see how that old pattern was present in multiple life arenas.

Whether or not clients would like to be referred to a practitioner that does Family Constellation work, you can ask your clients the powerful questions presented here. Another approach would be to explore a related tool from other structures of consciousness, such as delving into behavior patterns or the 1-10 scale.

256　CHAPTER 7: The Intuitive Part of Coaching

Pattern passed down from generation to generation, affecting the current generation.

Intuitive Tool #10	When to Use	Steps in Using	How to Gauge Effectiveness
Powerful Questions about Family Patterns	When the coach hears a specific pattern that is being repeated from a previous generation.	Ask questions that encourage clients to consider how their issues relate to larger patterns of family and group.	Client connects to a sense of membership in family or group and sees issues as not just personal. Changes in client bring change in groups s/he is a member of, such as family.

Powerful Questions about Family Dynamics
- In what way might this pattern be inherited from your ancestors or culture?
- How can you change it?
- What kind of support from your network would be useful?
- What would the title of this situation be if it were a movie or book?
- What rhythm would represent this pattern?
- What part could a cartoon or storybook character play in this situation?
- If you were to act this out in movement, what would be the action?

Intuitive Tools As Homework

Any of the Intuitive tools presented for work in the middle of sessions could instead be homework—depending on client interest—or used in situations where not enough time is available. The homework phase is also a time when you can make referrals for adjunct modalities that you've found effective and your client is interested to use. Some referral options related to this structure of consciousness include herbs, aromatherapy, homeopathy, and essential oils.

Kamron Keep, RN, BSN
Aromatherapy as An Adjunct to Coaching

In 2005, I began offering aromatherapy classes and personal consultations through the oncology integrative medicine program where I work. At the time, I was also working as a nurse in the chemotherapy infusion center and was excited to offer aromatherapy as a potential intervention for patients who were struggling with the side effects and symptoms of cancer treatment. It worked so well in this situation that I wanted to figure out how to use it in my coaching practice.

It's common for people undergoing chemotherapy to experience a heightened sense of smell. Sometimes they respond well to aromatherapy, and sometimes the smells are too intense. If they can tolerate low dilutions of oils, I might suggest an essential oil such as bergamot that has a pleasant aroma and can mask smells that bring nausea. Personal inhalers allow patients to choose scents they enjoy, that have positive associations for them, and these can be used to overcome unpleasant tastes and smells, in various medical situations. I've found citrus to be the most preferred scent.

Besides masking unpleasant scents, essential oils can help shift emotional state. One patient chose a lavender aromatherapy personal inhaler and called me after a few months to let me know how much it helped her manage her anxiety through her radiation therapy treatment and MRI tests. She said the aroma helped her to relax and stay calm, even through the claustrophobia she felt during her MRI. They are also useful for pain and inflammation.

Essential oils are powerful distillations of the oils produced by plants, and using them brings a sense of connection with nature. When my coaching clients are considering homework steps and want to find ways to become more grounded, relaxed—or uplifted—focused, or balanced, I might refer them to an appropriate reference and suggest they try working with the oils. I might share with them some research about how the oils can pass the blood-brain barrier and what the sense of smell can mean to human beings. I love essential oils for how they evoke beauty and life, and my clients do too.

The more my clients learn to shift their own energy in positive directions, the happier I am as their coach. Sometimes they may want help with changing their energy that requires referrals. I've had some training in Homeopathy and energy healing methods, such as Therapeutic Touch, Reiki, and Touch for Health, and in my experience any of these interventions can be extremely helpful. If my clients are interested in pursuing any of them, I help them find qualified practitioners.

One adjunct modality I do use in coaching, since I've had training and have used them successfully myself, are Flower Essences. They're made by putting a flower in water for several hours, and some part of the flower infuses into the water. Energy, or more particularly a "vibrational imprint," thought to be a form of information from the flower, flows into the water. Alcohol is added to preserve the water holding the flower energy, and this seems to evoke the positive qualities that help my clients attain their goal. Clients can take some drops of an essence several times during the day or add it to a bottle of water that they drink intermittently over the day.

It may be a stretch for clients to think that some preserved form of flower water could inform their being, but it can work. I've found, for example, that trumpet vine flower essence and mountain pride have helped me work with large corporate clients. The trumpet vine flower helps me project my voice, and the mountain pride assists in feeling confident and substantial. There are hundreds of types of flower essence preparations that can be found in most health-food stores and online.

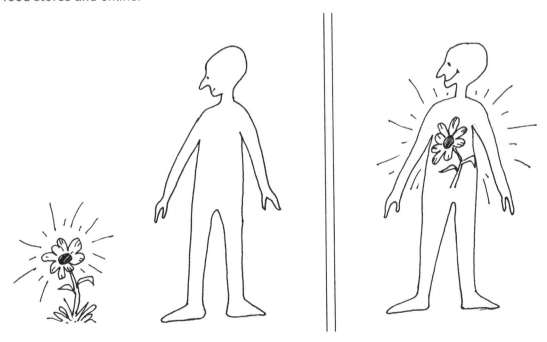

Besides suggesting adjunct modalities as homework, you can work with several coaching tools from this structure. Drawing upon *the healing power of nature* is a tool that taps into the Intuitive structure of consciousness and offers so many benefits. Working with *nourishment* through considering relationship to food is another beneficial practice. Coaches can also bring in the magic power of *ritual*.

Drawing upon the Healing of Nature

The role of nature in this structure of consciousness was central. There was little separation between people and nature during this time in history. People felt a part of nature, and nature was a part of people. Even today—and perhaps especially for those who live in urban areas—experiencing our connection with nature brings numerous benefits. In my coaching practice my clients often build encounters with nature into their plans.

Currently we're more interested in nature because we're sensing that our connection and even our survival rests with nature. It's not uncommon that clients will focus on this connection and their fears and hopes about sustainability. This may be the subject of a project or life change that they want to accomplish. On the facing page is a contribution from a graduate who is contributing to a blueprint for national sustainable energy production, and she finds that her coaching skills serve her well as she helps to grow her company.

EXERCISE: Take a Walk in Nature
Spend some time outside. Let go of tension in your body. Take some deep breaths. What do you notice? What can nature teach you about how to live your life? How much connection do you feel/think/experience between the health of other species/the planet and yourself? What changes have you made? What empowers you to make changes? What is the next step in moving toward more sustainability and planet wellbeing? What would the world be like if human sovereignty would be placed above national sovereignty, but national sovereignty would be respected and supported as well? What would be different in your life if the rights for all species would be the primary concern of society, and the connection among them would be understood?

Ruth Backstrom, PhD
Facilitating Sustainability

I work in a small nonprofit started by two couples who are friends. We're working on putting together a consortium to develop a national energy plan. Naturally, both working with our spouses and working as friends, can sometimes be very challenging. I find that my background in coaching is really helpful in letting me step back and look more objectively at any situation from multiple perspectives. My training as a coach gives me tools to confront most problems that arise in this sticky situation. I feel confident now in addressing challenges that I probably would have ignored before.

For example, the men in our group don't like to contact other people, and yet contacting people is the lifeblood of a nonprofit, so we've had a lot of friction around that issue. My coaching experience allowed me to neither push this issue under the rug and pretend it wasn't a problem, nor become totally frustrated. I was able to continue to confront the issue and have dialogues so that we were able to resolve it. Before learning to be a coach, I think I would have ignored the issue, but it would have been a continual simmering source of irritation.

I've also been able to examine our organization from a more objective frame of reference, imagining what it would be like to work together in a more formal setting where we aren't connected in more intimate relationship ties. I've also been able to consider patterns in how we all relate that might be holdovers from how we're used to relating at home or even in our original families. This has allowed me to openly confront issues as they arise, while maintaining good feelings between everyone concerned.

Sometimes we're building our airplane while flying it, so we have to establish procedures as the needs arise. The experimental nature of trying to do an organization in this way requires a lot of flexibility and fluidity. I have more patience with this approach because my coaching has allowed me to make more careful distinctions and to recognize how to, and when to, tweak a problem so that it doesn't grow to be disastrous. This makes our organization much more effective, fun, and smooth.

Nature fills so many of our basic needs, from the air we breathe and the food we eat that support our wellbeing, to more subtle requirements for inspiration and beauty. For example, when noticing the intricacy of a flower, my mood shifts in an instant. One of my clients uses a nature walk to de-stress after a busy workday, which not only helps her relax but often produces a new idea for a current work project. Another client told me that nature heals, and he didn't know why. He said maybe it's the larger patterns, cycles, the time for everything, and that things aren't wasted—yesterday's vegetables transform into compost for the ones we'll soon plant. Last spring's seeds will be used for next year's crops, and things seem to continue despite challenges and bad weather. I see people walking their dogs in urban areas and think of something my cousin said to me years ago. She and her family live in Manhattan and have a dog, and one day when it was time to take the dog out, she said "We need our dogs to take us for walks." We laughed, and now I always see the dog walking the person rather than the other way around.

As homework clients often consider ways to spend more time in nature, once powerful questions have uncovered a need for the nourishment and relaxation this might bring.

Intuitive Tool #11	When to Use	Steps in Using	How to Gauge Effectiveness
Spending Time in Nature	When clients want to become more relaxed, more connected to beauty or to something greater than themselves.	Help client become aware of their degree of connection to nature, and the benefits of increasing it. Explore options for spending time in nature.	Client is more relaxed, inspired, connected.

Powerful Questions about Connecting with Nature
- How can nature help you relax?
- In what ways do you feel connected to nature?
- How does beauty calm, inspire, or renew your spirit?
- What song, movement, or art form mirrors your feelings of nature?
- What is the most sacred place in nature for you?
- What movement in nature speaks to your soul or spirit?
- How does watching nature change your life?
- What lessons do you take from nature?
- What kind of sustainability practices help with the health of the planet?

- How does the health of our planet affect you?
- How do you deal with the idea that we as humans might be moving toward the endangered species list?

Barbara Hannelore, BA, MHE, MT
Women in Harmony with Nature

In my program, I show girls and women a positive approach to their monthly cycles. It's possible to be in harmony with our own natural rhythms, and I use the cycles of nature as a guide to inspire this connection.

Everyone can see the balance in the cycle of seasons, the moon, and the regular passage of day into night. I show women how to balance their own lives in the same way, with optimal energy, time for themselves, and a welcome period of renewal that their cycle brings to them each month.

The coaching skills I've learned from BCI have given me tools to help each woman to make this process her own. While I do have a curriculum and ideas I want to share, I use the core competencies of building trust and intimacy; deep active listening at a body, mind, spirit level; powerful questions about my clients' connection to the rhythms of nature; and holding the space for discovery, as each woman learns where she needs to heal, and how to integrate these ideas into her life.

I teach a very feminine process, and these coaching skills are feminine as well, enhancing a woman's ability to move more deeply into herself.

Food and Nutrition: The Food, Mood, and Nourishment Log

Nourishment in general, and the kind that comes from food in particular, are so important to wellbeing that I'll talk about them here in this structure of consciousness because food is a gift from nature. If your experience is like mine you'll work with clients who'd like to lose weight or to eat more healthfully because of a diagnosis from their doctor or simply because they want to feel better.

Dea Daniels, RN, CWW
Healing and Nourishment

As an RN with over 40 years of experience in health care, I've worked in my own practice doing what I consider to be the core of nursing. I'm a health and wellness advocate, coach and educator, empowering people with confidence, awareness, and tools to help them take charge of their own health. I blend my extensive background in Traditional Chinese Medicine, The Arvigo Technique of Abdominal Massage, Reiki, Deaki,* Native American Medicine, nutrition, healthy cooking, herbs, flower essences, Homeopathy, Yoga, Qigong, and lifestyle coaching into a unique blend of teaching that I call "The Seven Directions of Health."

My passion is feeding the human need for nourishment, especially related to love—of self and from others. People's issues around food and eating are often the expression of a larger need for nourishment, and my intuition seems especially tuned to this. Using coaching tools, I sense, hear, see, or touch where they have the greatest difficulty nourishing themselves. Powerful questions also help. The need may be for physical, emotional, mental, or spiritual nourishment. It could relate to how they move in their life—their activity—or it may be an issue of rest and receiving or elimination and releasing.

An example is a client I'll call Alice. She was referred to me for nutritional consultation. She ate only about five different foods because she said she didn't tolerate other things. She experienced indigestion, nausea, vomiting, and malaise, and had been this way for about fifteen years. She was afraid she was making herself sick. Yet she was also terrified to make any changes, take supplements, or keep a food and mood log. In fact, any aspect of focus on her food intake created a near panic attack. She'd tried working with psychotherapists and nutritionists, without success.

Alice's conflict about receiving nourishment came out in stories and dialogs she created with parts of herself. As she considered how she breathes, she noticed that though she would exhale "normally," she almost resisted beginning to inhale again. On a very deep level, I felt in my heart how she'd shut out available love and blessing, convinced she was not safe in this world. The key to her healing would be about reconnecting with the refuge of her heart.

During the year we worked together, we seldom spoke about food. She experimented with being present with herself while eating, but that was difficult for her. She moved

> into history and judgment more often than not. She became aware of her judgments and to feel her kindness no matter what she choose to eat. She was willing to begin the practice of writing down the things she was grateful for on a regular basis, and little by little began to be aware of sources of nourishment and satisfaction she'd previously ignored. Slowly Alice was becoming less fearful and less anxious about food, to feel pleasure in eating, and even to enjoy her "bad" food choices.
>
> * The name I've given the blend of energetic bodywork that I use with my Seven Directions of Health theory.

Good coaches are ready to refer clients to high-quality written materials on nutrition and dieting as well as to nutritional consultants that specialize in areas clients need help with, beyond coaching. Given the complexity of this field it's best to avoid temptation to make specific dietary recommendations, though coaches can provide resources. But there are ways that coaches can offer support with the process of change around food and eating, even when they're not experts in nutrition.

One of the best tools I know of is encouraging clients to keep a *Food, Mood, and Nourishment Log,* which aims at increasing awareness around food, nourishment, eating patterns, and other issues. This provides useful information and also helps people understand that they have unique nourishment needs and responses to what they eat. They learn to pay attention to the cues from their own body/mind/spirit instead of simply following dietary prescriptions. The Food, Mood, and Nourishment Log can also inspire awareness of larger issues related to taking care of themselves.

Coaches can ask if clients want to keep a record of when and what they eat and drink, and how they feel before and afterwards. You might provide a worksheet like the one here.[20] Please feel free to reproduce this worksheet for them to use. Alternatively, they might like to write about food, eating, and nourishment in journal form, perhaps writing there at one or more specific times of day.

Food, Mood, Nourishment Log

Time	Food, Beverage, Supplements	Activity	Hunger Scale Rate from 0 – 10 0 = Starving 5 = Neutral 10 = Overfull	Mood	Rate from 0 – 10 Note any activities that nourish you. Example, petting my cat, feeling the warmth of the sun, hearing a baby laugh

List 5 things to be grateful for today....

1. _____
2. _____
3. _____
4. _____
5. _____

Intuitive Tool #12	When to Use	Steps in Using	How to Gauge Effectiveness
Food, Mood, and Nourishment Log/Journal	When client wants to explore nourishment issues or change how they eat.	Give clients the worksheet and explain how to work with it. Use powerful questions to help them understand and integrate what they uncover.	Client knows more about patterns related to food, mood, and eating and uses this information as input for achieving nutritional change or goals related to nourishment.

Powerful Questions about Connecting with Nature
- What's working in your diet and nutrition? What's not, how could it be changed, and what is the first step in that direction?
- What feeds your soul?
- How would you describe your intake of all kinds of things in relation to your letting go of all things? Are they equal? Do you take more in than let go of things or vice versa?
- How would you explain the relationship of activity and rest in your life? Are they balanced or is one more prevalent than the other?

Paula Szloboda, RN, NI, MA, MBA, Therapeutic Chef
Health Education and Health Coaching, the Dynamic Duo!

I've provided health education as an expert, in my position as a registered nurse, and also from the position of health educator/health coach and therapeutic chef specializing in nutrition. In this realm I find a combination of coaching and consulting to be most effective. The following story illustrates these concepts.

I received a phone call from a client, calling from his hospital bed. "Help! I'm in the hospital and all they'll feed me is green jello and hydrolyzed beef broth!" Larry (not his real name) was hospitalized after a medical procedure went awry and a hole was accidently poked in his bowel. Working as a multidisciplinary team, including the client, surgeon, physician, nurses, dietician, and health educator/coach, we were able to create a plan for using food to help the client's bowel to heal.

Larry was hospitalized for fifteen days, and after his discharge, he and I continued to work together. Using a combined coaching/consulting model, we were able to identify the information that would be most useful to him as he made the necessary changes to augment his body's healing process.

In this model, the client identifies his goals, and as the coach/consultant, I function as a "choice architect," offering a selection of suggestions to the client and inquiring about his interest level in learning more about any of the approaches. He selects the topic that's of most interest to him, and we co-create a plan. If he has no interest in the suggested topics, we move on to a new selection of possible approaches.

After the client identifies his goals, I help him to identify all of the ways in which he's already supporting his health, paying careful attention to the actions he's taking currently to support the new goal that he's identified. This enables the client to shift his perception and begin understanding that health ultimately comes from within. Beyond this initial realization, an ultimate goal of the work that we do together is to build *response-ability* so that as new health/life challenges emerge (as they inevitably do), the client can meet them and respond in ways that continue to build a healthy, joyful life.

Larry's bowel healed and our work together was completed. A year later, he called me to work on another health issue. I inquired about how his past year had been, and he replied, "This has been the best year of my life!" I was astounded to hear this proclamation and asked him to tell me more. Although the nutrition information and practical skills he had garnered as a result of our previous work together were very helpful in both healing his bowel and also increasing his energy and vitality, the most profound change that Larry had experienced was related to the coaching experience we had around reconnecting to activities that bring him joy and a sense of meaning in his life.

In a whole person model of health coaching, the psyche, soul, and spirit are addressed as well as the physical body. They need nourishing also! Part of the coaching work we had done in the previous year had to do with helping Larry to develop a plan for surviving fifteen days in a hospital environment. As a retired art teacher, Larry identified that he'd be much happier in his hospital room if he could create art. He asked family members to bring in his art supplies and transformed his hospital room into an art gallery. Noticing the positive impact that the impromptu art gallery had on all who entered the room, Larry decided to volunteer his services as an art teacher in a hospital environment, once he was well enough to do so. In the past year, he had begun a volunteer position at a local hospital, which had become a part time job that brought tremendous joy and meaning to his life.

Creating Rituals

Rituals are powerful enactments reflective of this structure of consciousness of merged unity: one part can represent the whole, and the whole can be represented by one part. Rituals can be used to help ensure safety, to consummate connection or separation, to acknowledge power, and to honor places or objects or people.

Remember that the effect of a ritual is stronger if it's witnessed by the tribe or people close to the one doing the ritual. Its power comes not from the mere actions of the people, but the subtle energy that it engenders. For example, a wedding (ritual occasion) can include numerous rituals, such as exchanging a round ring, which many represent a commitment or love unending. The bride and groom might feed each other the cake, perhaps mirroring a commitment to love and cherish each other. The relatives and friends of the couple act as witnesses and support for the binding relationship.

You probably participate in specific family rituals around holidays, with special meals, songs, and events.

RITUALS

Sometimes my clients don't know how attached they are to a ritual until there's a change in it, causing distress. When I lived in China, it was hard for me to celebrate Thanksgiving when I couldn't have the foods that were part of my Thanksgiving ritual. I celebrated this holiday on the traditional day, and was with people I really enjoyed, but the food was "not right." Thus, it didn't feel like Thanksgiving.

Besides considering cultural or traditional rituals and how they affect us, in coaching we can encourage clients to develop powerful rituals to help with change. Here's an example of how I used it.

I was coaching Leslie, who lived in the South. She wanted to move and change not only her job but her field of work. She felt this was a very important transition and wanted to acknowledge it. During one of our coaching interactions, she designed a gathering of her friends to help create her new life. She asked each person to bring something that would signify a talent she had that would help her with this move and something very small she could take with her to remind her of that person in her new home, such as a picture or event ticket. She also asked a couple of her friends to bring one of their friends that she didn't know. She wanted these strangers to represent the new people that she would find in her new life. Her friends were very responsive, and the gathering was very special for Leslie. She felt officially launched into her new life by her friends, and her gifts were genuine reminders of the talents that would help her during her transition.

Here's an example from my personal life, involving ways to mark an age-based life transition. When my daughter turned 21, I wanted to create a ritual to acknowledge the very special event of my daughter becoming an adult. Traveling to some distant country felt like one way to do that, so I told my daughter that we could travel to any place in the world. It represented a journey for both of us: my daughter into a new chapter of her life as an adult and for me a new period as the mother of an adult child. My daughter chose Australia, and we had a one-month adventure into unchartered territory for both of us, staying in hostels and enjoying the people and the countryside.

Intuitive Tool #13	When to Use	Steps in Using	How to Gauge Effectiveness
Ritual	To establish transitions and celebrate successes.	Clients can be supported in creating rituals. Involve a community of some sort to witness the ritual.	Client feels a sense of completed transition.

Powerful Questions about Rituals
- How could a ritual help in shifting this situation to one you prefer?
- What is the purpose of the ritual?
- How could it be created?
- If you had a magic wand, what would you like to happen?
- How would including art add to the event?
- What movements are key to this change?
- What symbols are crucial to this process?
- How could spirit, spirituality, or religion add to the success of this transition?
- How could you involve part or all of your community in witnessing this ritual and supporting your change?

Further Thoughts about Accessing the Intuitive Structure of Consciousness

This structure of consciousness offers much to coaching. How could we do without it? Yet, often it gets thrown out because it's not based in the scientific framework of the Mental. The Mythical—well, stories are okay and entertaining, even if not too useful—but tapping into this structure of consciousness with all the subtle energies that seem like magic, that's over the edge.

Of course, Mental scientific methods are beginning to give legitimacy to tools that arise out of this structure. But even before things have been fully substantiated by science (or even if they can't ever be) how can the experience of the Intuitive be denied? When I use my intuition in coaching, or encourage my clients to use theirs, and something is discovered and explored that's exactly right, how can that be thrown out? When my clients say that they're inspired by the way I live my life and that's why they chose me as a coach, I know that walking my talk not only helps me feel authentic and empowered, but it even helps me attract clients.

When I work with energy principles, such as focusing on the positive (which is not about denying the negative), I find that positive events or perspectives increase. This structure is not actually so strange. If you spend time with a five-year-old and praise them for the positive things they do or the way they are being, guess what—we all know that those behaviors increase. How can this be thrown out?

I talked with a client who'd been sick with a sore throat that just didn't seem to go away. She'd been to the doctor, who gave her more antibiotics and suggested giving it time. We worked on the possible message of the throat chakra: what she was needing to say to herself or to someone else. She got clear, and that afternoon she started to get better. I know you could say that her improvement was due to something else, but when I've had years of experiences like this, I can't deny the impact of a repressed feeling or realization at a body level. Sometimes people say things like "This is not just in my head, you know." I agree it's not just in your head; it's in your head and your body and your spirit. Changing things at less conscious levels might seem like magic because we might not be able to easily see how the body, mind, and spirit can shift, but change it does.

If my clients are new to these approaches, they might wince in the beginning but give me the benefit of the doubt about creating a ritual or shifting an energy pattern. But once they experience the power of these tools, they can't throw them out either. Isn't it great that we don't throw out everything that we can't clearly understand?

1. You can also study with teachers and learn from books such as this: Mona Lisa Schultz, *Awakening Intuition: using Your Mind-Body Network for Insight and Healing* (New York: Three Rivers Press, 1998).
2. Jean Gebser, The Ever Present Origin, trans. Noel Barstad with Algis Mickunas (Athens, OH: Ohio University Press, 1985), 55.
3. An excellent reference if you'd like to know more is this: Cyndi Dale, *The Subtle Body: An Encyclopedia of Your Energetic Anatomy* (Boulder, CO: Sounds True, 2009).
4. Energy centers continue beyond the head and foot.
5. Rudolph Ballentine, *Radical Healing: Integrating the World's Great Therapeutic Traditions to Create a New Transformative Medicine* (Honesdale, PA: Himalayan Institute, 2011), 410-446.
6. Louise Hay, *You Can Heal Your Life* (Santa Monica, CA: Hay House, 1984), 154.
7. Gary Craig, The EFT Manual (Santa Rosa, CA: Energy Psychology Press, 2011), Roger Callahan and Richard Trubo, *Tapping the Healer Within: Using Thought-Field Therapy to Instantly Conquer Your Fears* (Chicago, IL: Lincolnwood, 1975).
8. Ballentine, *Radical Healing*, 412.
9. Personal conversation with Rudolph Ballentine, Ballentine, South Carolina, April 2010.
10. Here are a couple of good resources: Jon Kabat-Zinn, Full Catastrophe Living: *Using the Wisdom of Your Body and Mind to Face Stress, Pain, and Illness* (New York: Delta, 1990) has a great chapter on the stress-relieving power of working with the breath. Another good one is this: Dennis Lewis, *Free Your Breath, Free Your Life* (Boston: Shambhala, 2004).
11. Ballentine, *Radical Healing*, 430-432.
12. Besides that book, which he's recently updated, he's written many others you might find interesting and less technical, such as these: *Dogs that Know When Their Owners are Coming Home, and Other Unexplained Powers of Animals* (New York: Three Rivers Press, 1999) and *The Sense of Being Stared At, and Other Aspects of the Extended Mind* (New York: Three Rivers Press, 2003). On his website www.sheldrake.org, he offers a chance to participate in research projects that shed light on morphic fields and species learning.
13. Christopher M. Bache, *The Living Classroom: Teaching and Collective Consciousness* (Albany, NY: SUNY Press, 2008), 1.
14. Ibid., 33.
15. Ibid., 109.
16. Ibid., 116.
17. Ibid., 53.
18. There are a number of books in English by Bert Hellinger that can be ordered in the United States.
19. You can find out about training and information from www.hellingerpa.com.
20. This worksheet was shared with me by Paula Szloboda, a nutritional consultant and professor at John F. Kennedy University.

Chapter 8
The Archaic Part of Coaching

Sample Session 2D—The Sacred Friday

"I'm just not going to do my life the way I've always done it. I'm done. I'm not going to pressure myself to work too much and drive myself the way I have in the past. No more! And I need help with this. The way I've done things is second nature, and everything around me supports me pushing myself. I see other people doing their lives differently but here I am. . .working, and more than that, working hard and fast. What kind of life is this anyway?" Sally says with exasperation.

"You're so clear. Congratulations. What a wonderful place to start. I know that you're done with your old way of being—driving yourself past what's comfortable for you. You see some real differences between yourself and others," I say.

"Yes, that's it," she says and then quickly adds, "But I'm not really interested in how others got to where they are. I'm only interested in how I'm here—working, working, working."

"I hear what you don't want to do. What's the new pattern?" I inquire.

Sally says, "That's a good question. I've been so focused on what not to do; I don't know that I'm as clear about what I want, but that's my goal for our session."

"I am glad that you understand your objective for our time together. What would be a good way to clarify your new way of operating?" I ask.

After a minute, Sally says, "I think I know why I don't have a clear plan for my new life. I don't want to plan it. I want it to happen. I want to stay present and tune into what feels right at the time."

"You want to be spontaneous," I paraphrase.

"No, I don't want to be spontaneous! That feels too irresponsible. Oh, I don't know what I mean," she says with frustration.

"What is happening for you right now? I ask.

After a period of silence, she says, "Okay, I have it now. 'Spontaneous' is a very emotionally loaded word. Even as a kid, I think I yearned for this, but I was always told to be different, and so I have been. I've planned things to the nth degree, and this responsibility thing is part of it. I think I have to work and work and work. And where is time for me—all of me? I've gotten left behind."

"What parts are not getting what they need?" I ask.

"I'm so confused. I don't know what to think!" she says emphatically.

"Would it be helpful to take a deep breath?" I ask.

"Please!" she responds.

We take another minute breathing deeply, and then Sally says, "This breath thing really works. It allows me to go deeper into myself. I'm going to use this when I want to slow down or ask myself what I want. It stops my automatic response and action. Thanks."

"You're very welcome. I use it too, and it does the same for me," I reply.

"What I understood this time, and what was shocking to me to realize, but really shouldn't be such a surprise, is that most of me doesn't get any time and attention. I'm busy taking care of others or busy at work, and there's no time for me. Again, this is not such news, but I feel that I got it at such a deeper level this time. It's as if I'm crying out and saying, 'Pay attention to me. I deserve time too,'" she says quietly and begins to cry.

After a minute and when she stops crying, I say softly, "Humm, sounds like you're speaking from deep within yourself and having some very important awareness. Please feel free to cry. It's just fine. I'm right here with you." She spends a couple minutes crying softly, without any comments from either of us.

"Whew, I didn't know that was going to happen. I can even breathe more easily now—and more deeply. This deeper thing is also a part of what's been bothering me. I spend so much time in my day-to-day life on the surface—taking this action here, and that one there, and getting this project completed, and making the next proposal. That's got to stop, and time for me has got to start," she says strongly.

"I know you don't want to plan time for yourself, but what needs to happen so that personal time takes place?" I ask.

"This very moment, the answer seems simple. I want Fridays for me. I don't want to plan the day. I just want it to be mine. It will be my day! I may take walks in nature, or even naps, or read some of my devotions that I've never had time to look at in the morning. During that time I want to go deep and feel connected to God. Is it alright to talk about God in my coaching session?" she inquires.

"Of course," I say quickly. "I explore body, mind, and spirit issues with my clients."

"Okay, that's great because I think this is a big part of my problem. To me God seems multi-faceted. I see God in nature and in myself. I used to have conversations with God, but I don't do that much anymore. I miss that connection," says Sally, and then she's quiet for a minute or more. I stay with her in the silence. She continues, "Now I can explore it during my Friday time. I do go to church off and on, but even there I'm running around organizing this and baking for that. I suppose I could do it differently, but right now, I just want my Fridays." She begins to cry softly again and says, "now these are different tears. The other ones were of longing, and these are happy tears. I'm just so relieved to know how to go forward with this. I want to live my whole life like this, but starting with one day seems like a good beginning," she says cheerfully.

"You've already selected your homework. I'm wondering if it's too big a step, but you know best. What do you feel deep down?" I ask.

"That question helps me continue to explore what is best for me. Maybe I need to start with four hours this next week. It will take some time for me to organize my life around this 'Friday to myself' time, but I definitely want to start it now. As I think about it, I don't know who will support this change," she states.

"What kind of support do you need?" I query.

"That's a good question. Another moment of silence, please," she requests, takes some time, and then adds, "This is why I need you. Although my family and friends will say they support this, when it comes right down to it, they'll probably want me to do something with or for them on that day. But you know what? I do want some time with my husband and me on a Friday night. I don't think it will happen every Friday night, but I also want time for us to be together in a deep way. I think that's really important to our relationship, and after I have time to myself, I'll really be in a wonderful place to connect with him. In fact, I think I'll be able to connect with everyone in a more significant way. Perhaps as my family members experience a new way for us to connect, they'll see the benefit and be less demanding during my Friday time. That might be a dream—let me take another breath with that one." She's silent for a couple of minutes and then says, "What I get is that some will and some won't. I think my family will, if I explain it clearly and am consistent with my request for my Fridays. As I contemplate my friendships, I see that some people don't want to go that deep, and quite honestly, I don't want to spend time without this depth anymore. I suppose those friendships will fade away, but that's okay. It leaves more room for me."

"So support for this may come from your family as they experience the benefits of this change, and some friends will champion this adjustment and others may drift away," I summarize. Then I ask, "How do you want me to support you with your sacred Friday?"

"I want you to keep doing what you did today: give me lots of room to go deep and help me hear what comes up for me. That's extremely helpful. I feel so touched by your support with this. It brings tears to my eyes again," she says softly.

"I have tears myself. Thank you for sharing with me at this level. I feel your commitment, and it's inspiring," I say gently.

We ended our session and set up our next appointment. Sally did start taking half of her Friday for herself and then moved to a whole day most weeks. It made an extraordinary difference in her life. Her ability to live from a deeper, fuller, more satisfying place grew and grew, not only changing things for herself but for her family and some of her friends as well. She was right that some of her friendships dropped off, but she was firm in her desire to be around others who shared her passion and had skills to deeply relate. She realized that the people she had in her life were so valuable because they reinforced her determination and supported her desire to live a richer and more fulfilling life.

Overview of the Archaic Part of Coaching

My experience with Sally isn't unique. Many of my clients go to that deep place inside of them and consider their relationship to source or God, or how ever they relate to that aspect. I want to introduce the Archaic structure of consciousness, which holds and supports a deep connection to Source.

The Archaic structure of consciousness began with the inception of human beings millions of years ago.[1] Gebser named this period *Archaic* not because this was a primitive structure of consciousness, but rather referring to the Greek derivation of the word, meaning origin.[2] This earliest way of being represents the One Mind without separation and escapes definition and understanding, which create limitation. The All, God, Goddess, the Divine, Mohammed, the Force, Allah, Brahman, the Higher Power, and the Tao are some of the ways it's named.

The coaching tools that I present in this chapter incorporate methods to help reach this original consciousness—this innate state. Gebser said that this consciousness is ever-present, or always with us, though perhaps our experience of it (as a species having developed through the other epochs) is different from how it was experienced by human beings so long ago. For us, accessing it may require skill and practice.

If Gebser were sitting with me today as I write, he might say that the Archaic is a pure, innate consciousness, and that what I feel when I think of God or touch that spiritual place is a combination of that innocent consciousness along with my adult wisdom, experience, and mental concepts. Even naming God, causes a separation from this structure of consciousness. However, I want to leave the issue of what is that pure consciousness to the theologians and philosophers. Based on what I've heard and read, and on my own experiences, I assume that people can access it to some degree. All the people I've worked with in a spiritual or religious space can identify with some level of the Archaic structure of consciousness, so that's my starting point. I want to focus on how this sense of God—by all names—fits into my coaching model, both for me and for my clients when they want to go there.

I experience this mysterious, intangible state of being, this heart-warming state, this innate sense that "all is well," when I participate in various kinds of religions, including those that think their way is the only way. I see it in the eyes of strangers on a subway, friends, students in class, family members, and colleagues. I'm especially aware of it when I watch my grandchildren as they sleep, when five-year-old year old Madison gives me a kiss and says she loves me so much that it will never stop, or when seven-year-old year old Mackenzie gives me a new present she has made for me about every two hours on my birthday. A walk along the shore next to my office also puts me in this state—my heart opens, I breathe slowly, feeling my whole body, especially my heart, and sometimes tears of joy come from my eyes.

I start my courses in the same way I've written this book—with the Mental—because it's familiar to everyone. I make sure we include body, feelings, and spirit, and students are pretty comfortable with this recognizable way of being and thinking. Then, as we explore the Mythical, people start to experience their own personal stories, to use imagery, to hear how language impacts their progress toward their goals and life in general, and to see how to work with the Mythical tools in coaching. Next, of course, is the Magic structure of consciousness, where we move the learning into even more subtle interconnection and realms of intuition and energy. The Archaic seems to be the subtle of the subtle, and I'm always glad that we've had preparation for this state of consciousness.

> *What helps to open your heart? What brings tears of overflowing joy to your eyes? How do you arrive at this state that "all is well"?*

My talented illustrator, Bob Boisson, and I spent a great deal of time creating the graphic for this chapter. How can you draw something that can't be defined or described? We brainstormed hundreds of ideas, even considering a blank page, but instead, settled on the picture of the lotus blossom because it has roots that reach down into the water, and some think that water represents consciousness. For me the lotus illustrates the blossoming that results from rooting deep into the consciousness represented by the water. It's also a very beautiful flower, and now that I have lotus blossoms growing in a lagoon by my home, I see that they have a long gestation period. It can take time to blossom in the way of the spirit.

So what part does the Archaic play in coaching? When I'm teaching my course and describing the states of consciousness, I always say each one is my favorite, and then I remember how much I like the next one or the previous one. As I write this chapter, it's happening again: I feel that this *is* my favorite one, and the true foundation of coaching.

Love is the foundation of coaching: love of self, spirit, work, play, mystery, ideas, and body—being present to life in all of its manifestations. It's difficult to write about this, and I fear you might think I'm saying that religion or spirituality is the basis of this coaching model. Well, yes and no. This ever-present way of being is so basic and so deep that being able to live from this place does inform my coaching practice. This isn't to say that I'm able to come from this position all the time, but certainly when I feel I've done my best coaching, and my clients support that with "this was an amazing session," I feel I'm more or less in this special place. It seems to be a state of no work, of simple being, where the words flow from everyone involved— our hearts are warm and open. Amazing insights arise and actions are taken or planned that feel perfectly in alignment with my clients' wellbeing. This state is part of the "being" of coaching. Here are some things I do that foster finding this space. First, I've designed my office as a sacred, healing environment. Often I'll light candles in my office, find a comfortable, upright, almost meditative position at my desk, slow my breathing, practice abdominal breathing, and set my intention to be as open-hearted, compassionate and non-judging as I can be. Another way I move into the Archaic is by meditating on a client before working with her or him, or upon waking, some insight or idea will come up about a client situation. Like all the tools, I use them for my own development as well as with clients.

The ever-present awareness gives rise to tools used during sessions and as homework. During every aspect of sessions it gives rise to the deep compassion (for self and other) that shapes coaching work.

> ***Middle and Homework Part of Session:***
> - *Meditation/Prayer/Contemplation*
> - *Being Present*
> - *Working with a Sense of Life Purpose or Meaning*
> - *Compassion*
> - *Three Faces of God*

Archaic Coaching Tools for Clarity and Awareness During Sessions and As Homework

Some of my clients are interested in ways to include and nurture a sense of compassion and connection to something larger than themselves. Having an internal, experiential sense of the Archaic is a foundation for working with the tools arising from it, which I'll describe in the sections to follow.

My clients may want to explore the issues related to suffering, pleasure, joy, and pain, and accessing the Archaic can help them get to the deepest levels. My practice is varied in terms of the age and the health of my clients, and I've worked with people who are in the dying process. Life's big questions often rise up during this experience, but certainly someone doesn't have to be dying to consider these issues.

> *In what way, if any, do these deeper aspects of being interest you? What supports you experiencing these states? How could work with them benefit your clients?*

Let's look now at some tools from the Archaic. These can be included during sessions and as homework: *meditation/prayer/contemplation, being in the present moment, cultivating a sense of life purpose or meaning, compassion,* and the Three Faces of God.

Meditation, Prayer, Contemplation

My clients are sometimes stressed and overwhelmed when they call me. A sense of wellbeing and calm can occur when my client and I tap into the Archaic consciousness during our time together. Numerous types of prayer, contemplation, or meditation practices can take us to the Archaic, and most of them work by focusing, which quiets the mind. Breathing or movement can also be used to achieve this state, and these can go along with meditation or visualization.

Being in a peaceful state positively affects scores of body processes, such as blood flow, heart rate, blood pressure, body chemistry and immune function. Research has demonstrated that as people change neurological patterns, changes can happen in the brain, causing actual physical remodeling. Besides relaxation and peace of mind, reasons for doing these practices include becoming more conscious and more aware of different states of consciousness, building character, coming from wisdom or compassion, and uncovering a sense of origin. The latter seems to be the basic goal of major religions and traditions.

Clients who want to reduce stress and reconnect to a deeper sense of life may want to start or return to mediation.[3] When people want to explore this tool, I encourage them to try different options so they can find out what's best for them. A sitting practice doesn't work for all people. Moving meditation (a practice that involves slow walking or specific movement, as in Taichi) may suit people who have trouble sitting still. If a client wants to learn mediation, there are numerous resources, ranging from in-person classes, to workshops, retreats, and even online programs. Sometimes using biofeedback equipment is helpful, and today this equipment is small, portable, and convenient. Using this type of technology can demonstrate how people can shift out of this calm state almost immediately by having a negative thought.

Archaic Tool #1	When to Use	Steps in Using	How to Gauge Effectiveness
Meditation/Prayer/Contemplation	To help clients maintain a peaceful state of being or to help them become clear on an aspect of their life.	Ask the client if they want to have a practice that has a single focus, such as the breath, a mantra, a prayer, etc. May want to do it in the session and/or later.	Client feels more grounded, pleasant, peaceful, connected, and/or has more clarity.

Powerful Questions about Meditation/Contemplation/Prayer
- What kind of a focus helps you relax, find peace, experience healing, discover answers to your question?
- Do you practice meditation, prayer, or contemplation, and if so, what kind and how often? How does it impact your life? Are you interested in changing anything about your practice? How could you do that and what would be the first step?

Fay Daley
A Closer Walk with God

I grew up in Jamaica and learned about traditional healing practices from my relatives and culture. After high school, I started experimenting with fasting as a way of cleansing, but after moving to New York City began to use it as a spiritual practice. In 1991 I started leading fasts for people in my congregation at Abyssinian Baptist Church in Harlem. Over the years I led numerous fasts, but the most popular and successful has been the Lent Fast, with its weekly scripture readings, guided meditations, discussions, and prayers. The physiological body cleaning not only allows for cellular rejuvenation but also facilitates a less cluttered mind that gives rise to inner peace, clarity, and a closer walk with God.

When I took this coach training in the mid 90s, I saw how to use coaching in my work with the people in my fasting groups. Linda helped me as I started a Wellness Committee at church. I soon realized that I could branch out from the fasts and work as a life and health coach.

I find that God is my inspiration and help in both the fasting groups and in my coaching practice. I usually start each coaching session with a prayer that I lead or my client leads, calling for His help and direction in our work together. For me coaching is about a partnership that includes God.

My clients have great success in achieving their goals. For instance, in my fasting groups people learn that the small movement of their hand from their plate to their mouth is one of the most powerful behaviors, and having control over that specific action says a great deal about motivation, self-care, and commitment to their body as their temple. Skill and success in nutrition can spread to other parts of their lives, and soon a whole new lifestyle can be created. Seeing that happen and being a part of that process is a blessed event, and I thank God for my ability to help others in that way.

Author's Note: Fay passed on November 25, 2010. The celebration of her life was attended by hundreds of people who knew, loved, and were supported by her. I've never witnessed such an outpouring of love for someone who will be so sincerely missed. During that day, in various services, people shared the impact she had on their wellbeing at all levels. I was so struck by the extraordinary result one good coach or perhaps one good person could have on such a very large nationwide community. She wrote a soulful book entitled *A Call to Fast: Taking the Spiritual Journey*.

Being in the Now—the Present Moment

One skill that can facilitate a level of the Archaic state (and also more satisfying meditation or contemplation) is the ability to be in the here and now, and yet we're often preoccupied with the past or future. This ability to be present is a foundation skill for coaching, and when I'm very present in the moment, my clients feel it and appreciate it. It helps me stay open and allows me to be right with them. My ability to be present can rub off on my clients—and their ability to be in the present moment also helps me!

Being in the present is also effective at reducing stress caused by too much busyness, and therefore this might be a skill clients want to develop. One exercise that I've used for many years is called "Now I am aware." How about practicing it now?

EXERCISE: Now I Am Aware

Sit, lie, or stand in a comfortable position. Close your eyes and take a couple of deep breaths. Then complete the following sentence:

Now I am aware....

This is how I (Linda) would finish this sentence at the present moment:

Now I am aware...of the clock ticking in my office.
Now I am aware... of a car driving by.
Now I am aware...of an airplane flying.
Now I am aware...of a dull pain in my right leg.
Now I am aware...of the need to straighten my back.
Now I am aware...of the dryness of my lips.
Now I am aware...of the sun streaming in my window.

By doing this exercise, I am brought into the present instant. What happened for you? How could this be used personally and professionally?

288 CHAPTER 8: The Archaic Part of Coaching

Much has been written about being in the present moment.[4] Coaching applies this concept of present awareness and then takes it a step further, mirroring the Nike ad "Just do it." In the beginning of my experience of being coached I became aware of a feeling and was then astonished when my coach asked me if I could shift that feeling immediately. During therapy I had never heard that request, and in my training as a therapist was not taught to make it of my clients. Thus, I was shocked to find that I could change my thinking and feeling quickly in that moment. I've found that my clients can also access the present moment, which is the only time in which changes can happen!

Archaic Tool #2	When to Use	Steps in Using	How to Gauge Effectiveness
Being Present	When the client seems distracted.	Ask if the client wants to bring their attention to the present moment. May want to ask them if they want to feel their body/breath.	Client is more present, which can allow for instant action (Do it now) or other changes in the future.

Powerful Questions about Being Present
- On a scale of 1- 10, with 10 meaning being present almost all of the time, how would you rate the amount of time that you are present?
- How does being in the present moment influence your daily activity and your life?
- What kind of changes would you like to make in terms of being in the present moment?
- How would movement increase your ability to be present?
- What kind of music would help with being in the moment?
- How could you change that thought or feeling now?
- Now that you have changed that thought or feeling, what new action is possible now or in the future?

Working with a Sense of Life Purpose or Meaning

It's not unusual for clients to hire me to help them uncover and/or strengthen their sense of life purpose. Sometimes they don't know if that's the missing piece they've been searching for, but if it is, sooner or later, it will be identified. When people lack an overall direction that's connected to some belief about being a good person, making a difference, or changing the world, they can feel lost, empty, or too separate. Sometimes a simple question about sense of meaning or life purpose can be the opening to explore this arena. Deep listening can assist clients as they survey and discover this terrain. This can be heart-warming and soulful coaching that can impact clients at the depths of their being. Certainly my work with Sandra (Sample Session 1A & B) was along those lines.

Archaic Tool #3	When to Use	Steps in Using	How to Gauge Effectiveness
Sense of Purpose or Life Meaning	When the client is not connected to life purpose.	Ask if the client wants to explore this area.	Client becomes connected to life purpose and is able to move ahead with situations that align with life meaning. Client may become calmer and more joyful.

Powerful Questions about Sense of Life Purpose or Meaning
- What brings you great joy?
- When do you feel most alive and vital?
- What makes getting out of bed in the morning worth it?
- Who do you admire? What is that person's life purpose?
- How would getting more connected to your sense of purpose change your life?

Merla Olsen, RN, PhD-ABD
Meaning Comes from How We Live

For me "how" something happens—the process—is as important as what happens. At my age of 86, I'm still interested in living with a sense of meaning and purpose and in working with people to help them live healthier, happier, and more conscious lives. I often ask clients to concentrate on the process, whatever is going on. The *how* is filled with rich information that allows people to know what attitudes, beliefs, and values drive their actions. For instance, I work at a fitness center, and a person there talked with me about his interest in pursuing a new career. He was not aware of his process. He had never considered it before. I asked these questions: How did he want to go about changing his career? Did he want to move slowly or perhaps quickly? Did he want to gather factual information about what was available? Did he want to come from the intuitive part of himself as he considered new options? Did he want to ask for advice, help, or support? Did he want to run over others to climb to his goal? What was really going on in his current job that was pushing him to a career transition? Was he feeling pulled toward something? Perhaps it was a combination of factors. How does he act when he feel pushed or pulled? Is one more comfortable than the other? Is one easier than the other? How will his sense of purpose affect his future decision? Considering how we live is sometimes the key to success.

Compassion

Sometimes people connect with their life purpose through the expansion of a self-sense that comes with practicing kindness and compassion toward others. I have a personal example to share about compassion. During one of my coaching sessions, my coach asked me how I could feel differently about a person I thought had betrayed me and who was a great source of consternation to me. I suddenly realized that I could have compassion for the person, realizing that he knew he had not kept his word, which in the long run could undermine his self-worth and cause suffering. However, then I realized I was actually pitying him rather than having compassion.

The next step was realizing that he was a human being with things to learn, just as I have skills to develop. Compassion is not about feeling above someone or something; it's about feeling like the other.[5] Because of my coach's emphasis on doing it now, I realized (with a jolt!) that I could shift back and forth between stress and compassion. In those few minutes I was gaining the ability to consciously choose how I wanted to feel about the situation. I realized I was building some kind of compassion muscle or some type of new nerve pathway. It was a fascinating experience. I've found that my clients can shift in and out of stress and compassion as well.

At a conference I learned even more about compassion when a Buddhist monk related this story. He was going to attend a three-month meditation retreat, and he asked the Dalai Lama what he should practice during the time. The Dalai Lama said to start with Loving Kindness meditation. Then the monk said, "What should I do in the middle?" and the Dalai Lama replied, "Loving Kindness mediation." "Okay," the monk said, "and what about the last part?" The Dalai Lama smiled and said, "Loving Kindness meditation." When I heard the story and thought about the state of many parts of the world, I felt that was great advice and began to practice this type of mediation more often myself. Compassion is the heart of all coaching.

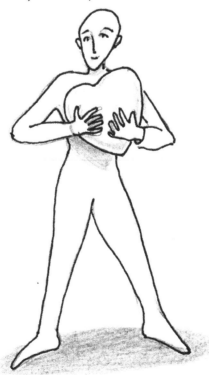

EXERCISE: Boundless Love (Loving Kindness Meditation)

This is a meditation about boundless love that I've been taught by various spiritual leaders. The basic idea is to become settled, grounded, centered, and comfortable and then begin to remember and experience a time when you were very happy and filled with joy.

Send these loving, kind thoughts, and energy to yourself by saying, "May I be happy and feel love." Stay with this as long as it seems helpful.

Next think of someone you love and care for, and send this loving-kindness message and energy to that person.

Slowly move to expand this message and energy to your family or closest friends. Next send it to the people in your building, your neighborhood, etcetera. Keep expanding the message and sending the feeling to a larger and larger area, including all people and all beings, until it encompasses the entire planet or universe or all universes. Notice how your heart energy feels.

Archaic Tool #4	When to Use	Steps in Using	How to Gauge Effectiveness
Compassion	When the client wants to cultivate love for self and others.	Ask the client what helps them feel more love, what opens their heart. Loving Kindness Mediation is one way for people to experience added love.	Client experiences additional love and joy of living.

Powerful Questions about Compassion
- What opens your heart?
- How do you view and define compassion?
- How could you shift into compassion?
- If you felt compassion in this situation, how would you change? Given this change, what new action could you take?

Working with the Three Faces of God

Clients can connect with their compassion through inquiry into their relationship with God or spirit, however they define it. (For simplicity, I'll use the word *God*, but please replace it in your mind as you read if you use a different word for a creative force or higher power.)

Ken Wilber, a preeminent philosophical thinker and writer of our times, talks about the *three faces of God*, or experiencing God from the first, second and third person. Although this is a mental conceptual framework about God, I added it to this chapter because I've found it very useful as clients explore this realm. Wilber reminds us that the *first person* in grammar is the person speaking, the *second person* is the one who is spoken to and the *third person* is the one or thing that is spoken about.

Wilber suggests we can think of God in the first person when we realize that God is in each one of us. We can identify with God. The same God that looks out your eyes, looks out my eyes, and looks out your neighbors' eyes too. Some call this the ever present, which is present now, was present when you were born, was present before you were born, and will be present after you die.

The second face of God, or God in the second person (the person who is spoken to), is the aspect expressed by spiritual masters, living or dead. Connecting with this face of God might occur when we talk to, pray to, or ask forgiveness of Jesus, Mohammed, or Buddha, or when sitting across from a living spiritual teacher that's part of a lineage established hundreds or thousands of years ago.

Examples of experiencing God in the third person (the thing that is spoken about) might be when you sit viewing Yosemite National Park, contemplate another beauty of nature, see things from the great web of life, with everything being connected, or revere Gaia, the Goddess of the earth.[6] Thich Nhat Hanh, a well-known and celebrated Vietnamese Buddhist monk and peace activist, has written about this third aspect of connection:

> If you are a poet, you will see clearly that there is a cloud floating in this sheet of paper. Without a cloud there will be no water; without water, the trees cannot grow; and without trees you cannot make paper. So the cloud is in here. The existence of this page is dependent on the existence of a cloud. Paper and cloud are so close. Let us think of other things, like sunshine. Sunshine is very important because the forest cannot grow without sunshine, and we humans cannot grow without sunshine. So the logger needs sunshine in order to cut the tree, and the tree needs sunshine in order to be a tree. Therefore you can see sunshine in this sheet of paper. And if you look more deeply ... you see not only the cloud and the sunshine in it, but that everything is here: the wheat that became the bread for the logger to eat, the logger's father ... the paper is full of everything, the entire cosmos. The presence of this tiny sheet of paper proves the presence of the whole cosmos.[7]

Not all clients will be interested in connecting their life purpose with a larger sense of sacredness. Some clients don't believe in God. They might feel that there is no organizing pattern or force, and think that things happen randomly. You can ask people if they believe their personal life purpose is connected to a larger one, and what they call it (God, Source, spirit, etc.). If they think it is, you can ask powerful questions such as the ones on the next page (replacing God with the word they prefer).

Archaic Tool #5	When to Use	Steps in Using	How to Gauge Effectiveness
Three Faces of God	When the client wants a way to become clearer about their spiritual relationship to a creative force or power.	Ask how client sees spiritual or religious being: • In the first person when client feels that God is inside client. • In the second person when God is outside of client as a living or deceased spiritual being. • In the third person as seeing God everyplace in the great web of life.	Client becomes clear about their relationship to something larger, which allows for deeper connection to the sacred and usually results in more purposeful action that leads to peace and joy.

Powerful Questions about Relationship to God
- How do you view God, or whatever name the client has for a higher, creative, or larger power?
- What is your relationship to God?
- How do you partner with God?
- What is the influence of God in your life?
- Where does God live in your body?
- How do you see part of yourself as God?
- What influence do spiritual leaders have in your life?
- In what ways do you feel that God is part of the web of life or part of all of life?
- How would you like to alter your relationship with God?

A Few More Comments about Drawing from the Archaic

The tempo of modern life constantly pulls our attention outwards and sometimes ratchets up the pace to an almost unbearable level. Many people yearn for a slower speed, one that is less hectic and at least allows them time to *see* the flowers, if they don't actually take time to smell them. Those desires can also represent a craving to spend more time in moments of contemplation and appreciation, by themselves and with others, participating in experiences that can bring the sacred more fully into their lives.

Sometimes people come into coaching unaware of the depth of their need for these things. Yet as they begin to explore this realm by starting with something as simple as a yearning for a slower pace or an organized desk, they find that their desires expand to touch the Archaic that they want to embody and experience. The focus shifts to examining their relationship with how they use their time, and this requires understanding what's meaningful and important. This might lead them to explore the sacred in their lives and to reacquaint themselves with forgotten parts of themselves that hold meaning for them.

The Archaic realm also holds the promise of bringing people a deeper experience of the underlying unity of life. Escaping isolation is another secret longing within our modern "caved" lives, where perhaps we go from our cars to our cubicle at work to our enclosed homes and finally to bed in our enclosed room. Even within our broader spheres we may see the same people day after day, and in the same ways, digging ourselves into ruts that we are not even aware of. Contact with the Archaic can revitalize us and bring us more empathy and insight into others by familiarizing us with how to operate on a deeper level that brings significantly more meaning and energy to our lives. It can deepen our connections with the sacred and magnificent aspects of life, in ourselves, in others, and in our world.

[1] Gebser, *The Ever Present Origin*, trans. Noel Barstad with Algis Mickunas (Athens, OH: Ohio University Press, 1985), 44-45.

[2] Ibid., 43.

[3] There are many meditation courses, offering a range of practices, for a wide variety of purposes from healing to spiritual development. Rudolph Ballentine shares mediation practices in his book, *Radical Healing: Integrating the World's Great Therapeutic Traditions to Create a New Transformative Medicine* (Honesdale, PA: Himalayan Institute, 2011), 468-470.

[4] You may already be familiar with very popular books by Eckhart Tolle and Thich Nhat Hanh, about living in the present, with practices for helping you do so.

[5] Meditation and generating compassion can be the subject of homework. Clients might want to learn to feel compassion for someone else or for themselves. If someone wants to develop compassion there are a plethora of practices, such as the Buddhist Loving Kindness mediation.

[6] Online (e.g. YouTube) you can find Ken Wilbur discussing the three faces of God.

[7] Thich Nhat Hanh, *Being Peace* (London: Rider, 1987), 45-47.

CHAPTER 9

The Integral Part of Coaching

Sample Session 2E—Putting It All Together

This sample session is presented in a different format because we're now entering the integral structure of consciousness, putting together tools and principles in our holistic and integral approach to coaching. I'd like you to see the Bark Coaching Institute Approach in action one last time. What my client and I actually said is on the left, and the right rail adds my inner thoughts and/or how I've integrated the tools from the previous chapters.

Helen says, "I found you on the internet because I was looking for a coach to help me with school. I'm a nurse and have started working toward an advanced degree, and I saw that you're a nurse with graduate degrees, so I want to see if you could help me with school. I saw that you have a holistic approach, and I don't know what that means exactly, but I guess that you consider more of me than just my brain, and that sounds helpful. I'm new to this graduate program, but I can't seem to make progress. I've lost my enthusiasm for my courses and I think I'd better do something now because my grades are going down! I might not even get passing grades this quarter. This is so unlike me—I do have a good brain—and I usually get mostly "A's. I don't know what's wrong with me. I've talked to my friends and they just tell me to work harder. My partner doesn't know what I should do and suggested I talk with someone. Can you help me?"	*I'm listening with my body, mind, and spirit to her concern. I hear a great deal of stress in her voice, and I begin to feel tension in my jaw. I don't want to mention these things to her, as she says she knows little about a holistic or integral approach, but these feelings inform me, and I begin to feel compassion. I understand how hard it must be for her to be confused about her motivation and inability to utilize her student mastery. She sounds really desperate.*
Linda: "I'd be happy to give you a free session to see if my coaching could be of value. What do you want to achieve in this session?"	*I realize I don't want to promise a result since I truly don't know if I can help her, but from my sense of compassion, I want to offer her a free session.*

Helen: "I want to figure out what is going on about school, why I am so disengaged, and what to do about it."	*I'm delighted to hear her clear goal and realize how setting an intention at the beginning of a session can lead to a successful interaction.*
Linda: "How would you like to do that?"	
Helen: "I want a suggestion because what I've been trying is not working."	
Linda: "What comes up for me intuitively is to invite you to tell your current school situation as a story, and that might be a stretch, but there's no wrong way to do it. Would you be game to explore in this way?"	*I realize that she probably needs a new approach, so suddenly the intuitive flash of asking her about her story comes to me, and so I ask her if she would like to use it. It's a tool from the Mythical, but an approach that's not unknown to the average person. She says she's bright, so I think she can do it, and this might be fun for her. My thinking reinforces my intuitive hunch.*
Helen:" What have I got to lose?"	
Linda: "Okay, you could start with 'once upon a time there was a nurse named Helen, and she started a graduate program, and....'"	
Helen: "Okay. She started a graduate program that she thought was going to advance her—help her find a job in which she could thrive and help patients, and then after the second quarter, her legs gave way, and she just couldn't walk along the path anymore. She wanted to, and she got crutches, but her legs wouldn't move, so she just sat down," she says with discouragement and a deep sigh.	*I'm pulled right into her story and realize that she's using a kinesthetic approach and she mentions her body as well. Interesting, I think.*
Linda: "That's great, what happens next?"	*I'm fascinated by her story and wondering what she'll say if she continues it.*
Helen: "I don't know."	*I sense her "stuckness" and intuitively I want to go to a dialog tool.*

Linda: "Well, here's another stretch, but could she talk to her legs and find out what happened to them?"	
Helen: "Okay, you're right. This seems odd, but I'll try it since none of my other methods have worked. I know that mental drudgery hasn't helped. My brain is exhausted. Okay, I'll add to the story. So then after she sat down, she said to her legs, 'What's wrong with you!!!? Why don't you keep going?!!!'"	*I see that she's coachable at this moment and could probably be in the preparation stage of Prochaska's Stages of Change.*
"Helen's Legs scream: 'Nothing is wrong with us. We're going the wrong way, and we know it, so why don't you know it? Why do you blame us and keep making us use these crutches? We're throwing them away. So take that!!'"	*I feel her frustration again in my jaw but also in my stomach. I also feel sad. I sense her anger now. I feel very compassionate toward her.*
Helen begins to cry: "Why won't you help me? I need to find a new job. You know how much I hate my job now. Rush, rush, rush. Stress, stress, stress. I can't do it anymore. I want to give good care but it feels impossible. I hate going home and sometimes waking up in the middle of the night wondering if I gave the right pill or remembered to chart something. Why don't you help me? You're my legs. I need you to take me to a new place—to a new job."	*This is such a common theme in coaching—people feel stuck in a situation they hate.*
"Helen's Legs: 'Sorry we yelled at you, and yes, we know you want to have a different kind of job, but that's why we absolutely can't go on this path. It's not that we don't want to help. We think we are helping, but you don't see it that way. We're trying to	*I hear her compassion for herself. I also notice her willingness to be truthful to herself with me listening. I applaud her courage. She's doing fine with the dialog. I don't want to say anything to interrupt her. It seems like she's venting*

tell you that this is not it. This is more of the same and won't get you out of your stressful situation. It will be like moving the deck chairs on the Titanic. Honestly, this won't help.'"

Helen: "Then what will?"

"Helen's Legs: 'We don't exactly know that part, but we do know that this isn't it, and if you stop trying to make us work, maybe you could figure out a different path."

Helen: "It just seems too hard, and I'm tired, but what you say does seem right to me. I just don't know where to go now. So, Linda, what do I do now?"

Linda: "Would it be helpful to take a breath together?"

Helen: "Okay, great idea," and we both take some deep breaths.

Helen: "That helped. My legs are right. I hadn't put it into words, but this line of study doesn't feel right to me. It doesn't excite me. I feel fed up. It is more of the same. It won't get me out of my misery. I hate to admit it, but this is true. I really hate to admit it. I've told everyone about my program, and people are happy for me. I went through all the trouble of getting admitted—you know those essays and references and transcripts—and it was a job just to do that. And for what? Now it feels like a waste of time and I should have known better."

a volcano. There's so much built up pressure and stress. I hear a request for a change. I wonder what she'll do with the suggestion. She's picking up on and is connected to her inner knowing. Great!

I resist coming up with an answer to her question because I really have no idea what she should do. She's been able to tune into her inner voice, so I suggest that we take a breath, which will help her come from her higher chakras and connect her body and mind. I know it's not my job as her coach to find the answer even though I want things to change for her. I take a breath with her so she feels my presence and that we're in a partnership.

Linda: "It seems like you've added a piece to your story: 'and then Helen realized she wasn't on the right educational path, and she started beating herself up.' Is that right?	*I hear her critical voice and I want to acknowledge it.*
Helen laughs and says, "Yes, that's right. 'But then she realized it and stopped beating herself up and. . .'—I don't know where to go from here.'	*I am delighted that she sees it too and can quickly change her thinking, at least in the story.*
Linda: "No problem, would you like to take another breath and see if a little more of the story comes to you?"	*Seems like a breath could help here.*
Helen: "Yes...and then a handsome prince came up on a white horse and scooped her up, and they rode off into the sunset and lived happily ever after."	*I'm continually surprised and pleased with the result of a deep breath.*
Linda: "Wow, amazing."	
Helen: "Well, I guess it doesn't really go that way, but it's interesting that a handsome prince came to rescue me."	*I think this is a surprise ending and wonder about the meaning but before I have time to ask a question, she starts exploring it.*
Linda: "In what way?"	
Helen: "I feel like I need to be rescued. I feel that I've lost my confidence with this school thing and my unsatisfying job. Well, maybe I can't say totally unsatisfying. I do love working with my patients, but much of the rest is so stressful. I don't want to talk about that anymore. I think you get the picture, and I certainly do get it. I see it clearly, and so I guess I could	*Her exploration seems rich and significant. Again, I don't want to interfere with her examination.*

go back to the story and say that 'she realized that she needed to be rescued from that school, so she jumped on her horse—which she had not noticed was standing next to her—and galloped to the school to resign. Then her legs immediately became stronger, and she jumped off her horse and registered at an oasis that she hadn't noticed was right next to the school, for a week of rest.' The end for now," she says with glee.

Linda: "You sound so much stronger. I can feel your strength. My whole body position changed with that ending, and I'm sitting up straight and breathing deeper and feeling the tension drain out of my shoulders and jaw."

Helen: "Me too. It's as if you can see me. That's exactly what happened. I almost feel like my old self. I don't know what to do, but the week of rest at the oasis sounds just like what the doctor ordered."

Linda: "Part of coaching is to pick some kind of practical step—some real movement toward a goal. Homework is about some fun and easy next step that feels just right, not too big, not too small, but something you could do in the next week that would show you that you were moving forward. Would you like to select a next step?"

Helen: "I know my next step. Drop out of this school. Did I really say that?" questions Helen, and a minute of silence takes

She seems like she is reaching her goal of knowing what to do about school. I'm so fascinated by her process and her conclusion.

I'm pleased that I can share my physical shift and that she feels my presence and partnership.

I want to bring in the homework part now and figure that the story told her steps but want to see if those steps are what she really wants.

place. Then she says, "I do need to talk this over with my partner and a couple of friends, but honestly, this needs to happen. I really do know this program is not for me. So that will be my next step, and I know they'll support me in this because they've seen how miserable I am. Oh, I really need to drop out! And then find that oasis. I don't have the money to go to an oasis—or in this day and age, I guess it would be a spa—but I could take a long weekend. I think I deserve it and I'm ready for a break."	
Linda: "You sound like a different person than the woman who started this call. I'm very happy that you're so relieved. Congratulations on your being courageous and so honest with yourself about your true feelings and inner knowing."	*I start thinking that she is a great coaching client: she can observe her behavior, she's honest with herself, she readily used several coaching tools, she feels my connection, especially when I mention my physical shift. I wonder if she is a kinesthetic learner.*
Helen: "I am even happier than you are about this clarity. This is exactly what I wanted today. I know what to do now. Thank you!"	
I say she is very welcome and ask, if she's interested in continuing coaching. Helen wants to know how it works. I explains about her three scheduled sessions a month, with the addition of spot-coaching, we agree on a fee, and select our next appointment.	*I think she might be unstuck now and able to move forward on her own and not need more coaching. I am a little surprised when she wants to continue but delighted to realize I will have more time with her.*

From Helen completing my welcome packet that I send to new clients, I learned that she was a kinesthetic learner (easy for me to sense from her first session) and was Kapha dominant, in terms of personal constitution. That made sense to me when I thought back on our first conversation when she talked about her legs.

I also found that she usually avoided the gap at all costs. She had the next job or relationship or approach before she let go of the current one. After I saw that, I was surprised that her story ended with a trip to the oasis. I wondered if the long weekend was the gap time, and if so, would she would be interested in moving forward with a new plan in our next session.

In looking at Helen's lifeline exercise, I realized that she'd experienced fewer than average transitions and that she found support during changing times from her partner or a couple of friends. I wondered if her Kapha or Earth-like constitution was out of balance often and if she could easily become stuck. If that was the case, I understood why she signed up for more coaching. If she'd had a Pitta-dominant constitution, she might have been fine to continue on her own after one session. In her description about her loss of enthusiasm for her coursework, I was curious about that stuckness, which seemed to be a useful message. I wondered if sometimes she didn't move forward because she had too much Earth, so to speak. I also was curious when she didn't mention more friends, since Kapha types usually attract many people who like to be around them.

Helen called to say she wanted to start coaching a month later because she'd decided to finish the quarter, and she needed time to raise her grades and take her finals. She found that making the decision to drop out of the program was the right move, and having made that decision she had enough energy to complete the quarter.

In her next session, she was ready to figure out her new path. I explained the three-stage Bridges theory of endings, the gap, and new beginnings. She described her reluctance to take time in the gap because if she did, she thought she wouldn't move out of it. This reminded me of her Earth-dominant constitution, and I explained this concept. She said the description really fit her.

During our next sessions, Helen became even clearer about her needs and began imagining getting a better job. She used the affirmation, "I now have a well-paying, satisfying job in which I can use my nursing skills to the fullest." She put a post-it on her mirror in the bathroom that she'd read when she was there. We worked with the negative messages that came up for her as she practiced the affirmation when she first woke up and at the end of the day, just before falling asleep. Most of those messages revolved around feeling that she didn't deserve a fulfilling job, and belief that those kinds of jobs don't exist. As she worked with her ability to allow herself pleasure and fulfillment, she began to notice that there actually were satisfying jobs right next door to her, just as she'd seen the horse and the oasis close to her in her story. After several months, a door opened up for her at work, and she was promoted to a new position in which she felt she could use her potential and find fulfillment.

Helen continued with coaching to work with accepting pleasure, especially relating to friendships, and even in her romantic relationship. My awareness of her not having a larger group of friends had some truth to it. Again, just as her story portrayed, with the horse and the oasis, it wasn't that people weren't there, but that she didn't take in their friendship and attention. She yearned for comfort and pleasure (very much a Kapha characteristic) but again believed she didn't deserve it. As that began to change with regard to looking for a more satisfying work situation, it also danced into other areas of her life, with equal benefits.

Overview of the Integral Structure of Consciousness in Coaching

As you work with the BCI Model you'll find out how appropriate and timely such an Integral approach is. Many feel that as a species we're moving out of the Mental way of thinking/being and moving into a new structure of consciousness—the Integral way—a combination of all the other structures of consciousness. The Integral brings together the core consciousness of the Archaic, the vital consciousness of the Intuitive, the imaginational consciousness of the Mythical, and the rational consciousness of the Mental.[1] We're entering the land of *and*: we want to act from all the ways of being. For many of us, this requires a reawakening of latent, dismissed, or undervalued structures of consciousness. Look around and you'll notice this happening.

Consider the interest in re-owning the Intuitive structure of consciousness, with the extreme popularity of Harry Potter and increasing value and interest placed on magic, intuition, healing environments, Feng Shui, Acupuncture, Yoga, Qigong, and sustainable use of natural resources and herbs. Notice how the Mythical is coming back, as people seem to be using more imagery and storytelling. Take a look at the growing number of classes in meditation, compassion, spiritual practice, and personal mission statements that help us revitalize our Archaic way of being.

According to Gebser, coming from the Integral structure of consciousness requires that we practice the efficient form of each structure of consciousness. The structures manifest in an efficient form and over time slip into a deficient form as they begin to make way for the next structure.[2] Since we're moving out of the Mental structure of consciousness, examples of the deficient Mental abound.

For instance, research adheres to a randomized double-blind process referred to as the "gold standard." This means that two groups that are identical except for the aspect being studied are compared to each other. This *may* work for very simple situations like those in biology (where this method was developed), when scientists investigate plant-growing techniques by designing experiments with identical seeds planted in identical soil but exposed to different amounts of sunshine. But even then, how do we know the seeds and soil are identical, allowing comparison? When research involves looking how one intervention or approach affects people we must wonder even more about the assumptions behind the method. No two people are identical, and it's difficult for the interventions under investigation to be separated from a multitude of influences. The double-blind experiments are based on a deficient form of the Mental, which emphasizes knowing by breaking into parts without being able to see the interrelation. The kinds of divisions we make in medical practice can also come from deficient Mental. I remember when I was working in surgery, and a veteran had terrible deep boils from the toxic chemical, Agent Orange all over his body. Surgery was so specialized that he needed to have three different surgeons work on the different parts of his body. The surgeries were to be done at the same time, and it took weeks to find a time that all three surgeons could be available for the operations. In the meantime, the soldier suffered excruciating pain and experienced deteriorating health.

Efficient Mental, on the other hand, is a process of proceeding to a conclusion by reason, using skills of discrimination, evaluation, and analysis of all that's relevant.[3] For example, efficient Mental would take into account feedback from the body as something to add to the process of reasoning.[4]

We're ripe for a mutation beyond exclusive use of the Mental to the integral structure of consciousness (but remember the hallmark of Integral—include, embrace, and transcend). We're moving toward the Integral, but include the Mental in our thinking and being. Never before in the history of human development have we had access to as much information and connection to all the structures of consciousness as we do now. Most of us are not limited to the facts known in our local village by our neighbors or our wise elders. Using the internet and other avenues we can find out about almost anything in the world. We can explore the anatomy and physiology of the human immune system, learn how to reduce our stress levels, read about how people in a foreign country worship, investigate chaos theory, and discover ways to develop our intuition.

With more information and connection, we have a bigger, more whole picture. This allows us to see deeper patterns and repeating themes, which can expand our perceptions. We can look through different lenses and might say, "Oh, this is the way people in other countries use Mythical thinking," or "this is the way that someone else defines success or satisfaction. Hum...I never thought of it from that viewpoint." This expanded whole picture can increase our Integral perspective. It opens us to new ideas, solutions, and actions from all the structures of consciousness.

310   CHAPTER 9: The Integral Part of Coaching

Here the person is using a kaleidoscope that has combined the colors in the strips of glasses that represent different structures of consciousness, providing a totally new look of the Integral with lots of options.

The result of bringing together many possible perspectives is more than the sum of it parts. One example is the process of putting a picture puzzle together. I can see each piece individually, but when I've placed all the pieces together correctly, a whole new picture emerges. Baking a cake is another illustration. You add together flour, eggs, yeast, water, and heat, and the result looks quite different from the pieces that went into it.

A restructuring happens with the Integral structure of consciousness: combining the structures brings results beyond the sum of the parts. Imagine someone wants to lower an elevated blood pressure. The patient might reduce salt intake, and the blood pressure might drop a few points. Next, the patient starts to walk a mile three times a week, and again the blood pressure goes down a couple of notches. When the patient sets some limits at work and reduces stress, a few more points are shaved off the number. Then, let's say that the patient adds a relaxing and fun new hobby to life, and bingo, the blood pressure drops into the normal range. It's as if there's a cumulative effect—the build up of small changes leads to a big change. This is the advantage of combining different approaches. I see this synergistic affect all the time in coaching: skillful combination of approaches helps my clients reach their goals more quickly and with less effort.

An objection might be that determining the whole picture or putting all the pieces together requires more examination and may take more time. I'd say yes, perhaps that's true. However, not seeing the connections and not joining the pieces can hinder real growth or make lasting change less likely. I sometimes scratch my head when I see landscape companies using those leaf blowers to move the leaves from one piece of property into the street or to the next property. Often the city street sweepers don't pick up the leaves right away, so they blow back onto the property or onto the neighbor's land. If the object really is to clean the streets, more needs to be considered than just getting the leaves and debris off one place. Seeing the connections and coordinating operations may take a bit more time, but the result could be worth it. Piecemeal approaches are less effective than whole-Integral approaches to reaching a goal.

The person using Integral thinking and being is aware of the entire spectrum of consciousness, and in so doing moves a step beyond any one of them. Accessing this structure you may wake up and begin by creating a plan for your day (Mental), then shift into an awareness that you'll be functioning in the role of parent (Mythical) during the day. You may suddenly intuit the need to check in with a person that day (Intuitive). The next second, you may want to spend time in a meditative space (Archaic) to lower your stress. At a deeper level you witness all this happening, without losing yourself in any of these shifts. Thus, the sum is greater than the total of the parts.[5]

It's important to remember that we don't actually become lost in the former structures because we've evolved, just as an adult doesn't turn back into the four-year-old who believes in Santa. However the adult is able to capture that sense of wonder and belief in the context of the Integral.

When we look at coaching with Integral eyes, listen with Integral ears, and sense with an Integrally-alive body, we look at all levels of the person as well as at ourselves. We look at who we are, and we investigate who our clients are. We can call on all the tools of the structures of consciousness. Here are some considerations of an Integral coach:

- Drawing upon the Mental—How can progress be measured? What are the next steps to the goal?
- Drawing upon the Mythical—What images and stories support or limit the change?
- Drawing upon the Intuitive—How can intuition help with the change? What parts of

nature could support movement? Is the body sending signals about limits or progress? What groups support or limit the change?
- Drawing upon the Archaic—Does compassion play a part in the journey toward the goal? How can a contemplative or meditative process help achieve an aim? What larger meanings provide a foundation for the movement?

What are the advantages of listening, sensing, and seeing from an expanded whole picture while working with your client? The more you can understand about your client and yourself:
- the more you can co-create a coaching agreement that's realistic and successful;
- the better you're able to establish trust and intimacy;
- the more effectively you can listen from a body, mind, and spirit perspective;
- the more targeted your powerful questions can become;
- the more likely that your partnership functions with clear, direct communication that your client can transfer to other relationships;
- the more effectively you can help your client manage progress toward their goals.

Okay, you may say, I understand how the whole picture is helpful, but how do I pull all the coaching tools together in working with my clients?

Now comes the fun part of this coaching model—putting these tools together by using the one that feels the best, given your client and your skills, and doing it in a way that flows naturally from one tool to the other based on your client's needs.

Let's imagine you have a client named Sam, who's a visual learner, has a fiery constitution, is experiencing high stress, has a high-status professional position, likes to feel that he's not alone, isn't very connected to his feelings or body sensations, tends to procrastinate, and doesn't acknowledge his successes. As his coach your approach might be as follows:

- Use visual metaphors along with your paraphrasing (Mythical).
- Help him create clear, detailed, purposeful, and quick steps toward his goals, which also provides feedback if he's on track or off track (Mental).
- Co-create his sessions and contact to fit his busy schedule—perhaps using 20-minute sessions with some email contact (Mental).
- Share an occasional example from your own life, if he's interested, that mirrors his situation so he realizes that others have the same issues (Mythical).
- Listen to see if building a few closer relationships would help him feel more connected (Archaic).
- Explore his religious or spiritual practices, if he's interested, to see if that would help him feel more connected to something beyond himself (Archaic).
- Ask if he's interested in learning how to identify and express feelings (Mythical).
- Find out if he wants to benefit from his body wisdom (could be all structures of consciousness).
- Listen and ask about his process for accomplishing goals and setting priorities (Mental).
- See if he would be interested in using a Ta Da list to acknowledge and celebrate his accomplishments (Mental).

We'll look at the assessment, beginning, middle, and ending parts of the coaching session as we have in other chapters and see how to apply the tools from an Integral perspective. You'll be able to read about how other coaches are applying an Integral perspective, drawing upon all of the tools. But before we put it all together, I'd like to introduce some ideas from a philosopher whose work focuses on defining an Integral approach.

Wilber's Integral Approach

I can't discuss the Integral structure of consciousness without touching on the four-quadrant framework of Ken Wilber, a prominent thinker of the integral evolution, who's brought remarkable clarity to this emerging paradigm. Wilber's four-quadrant framework provides an integral or whole perspective through which to experience, view, and interpret anything.[6] The quadrants are one aspect of Wilber's model—the others are developmental stages, lines, types, and states.

The *four quadrants* refer to the subjective and objective, individual and community realities present in every situation or that come together to form every being.

Individual Subjective "I"	Individual Objective "It"
Plural Subjective "We"	Plural Objective "Its"

Thinking about a person, the upper left quadrant represents the individual and subjective aspect, or the "I." This includes feelings, attitudes, sensations, values, thoughts, and all the person's ideas, such as the ones they hold about their health.

In the lower left quadrant, the plural subjective lives, or the "we": a person's values, practices, and responses as a member of a culture or family, work group, state, or nation. As sons and daughters, employees, and citizens, we share certain traditions and collective views, such as those we hold about health, types of illness, how people behave when they're sick, and so on. The other two quadrants—right side, top and bottom—are the objective perspective: aspects of a situation or person that can be seen from the outside. The top right is the individual, objective aspect, or the "it." Applied to health, this would represent lab values and MRI images or behavior.

The bottom right describes the objective, or the "its." This section includes collectives or systems, and a person's interactions within the health industry fit here. Systemic factors such as economic status play a role in people's health. We'll apply the simple four-quadrant framework in integrating coaching tools, but first a little refinement.

According to Wilber, each quadrant can be further sub-divided, giving us *lines of development*. Think about the upper left (singular, personal, the "I") quadrant. We can think about the lines of development as multiple intelligences—cognitive, moral, interpersonal, physical, and emotional, to name a few.[7] The development of these lines occurs in *stages* that are progresive and permanent landmarks along the growth pathway.[8] One stage is transcended, but the skills or capacities gained in earlier stages are not lost, but integrated, or turned into components of the next stage, which is characteristic of developmental models. The idea of lines of development explains why most of us are not equally developed in all aspects of ourselves. Think of someone you know who may be very developed in interpersonal skills but not in cognitive ability, or alternatively, you may know people who have extreme dexterity in physical talent but lack moral development.

Lines of Development in Individual Subjective "I" Quadrant

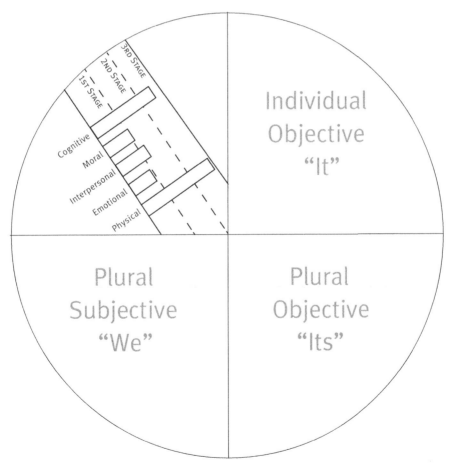

This illustration could describe a professional athlete who is intelligent with lower levels of moral, interpersonal and emotional development.

CHAPTER 9: The Integral Part of Coaching

Gebser's work on structures of consciousness can be seen as fitting into the lower left quadrant, as he was talking about collective human development.

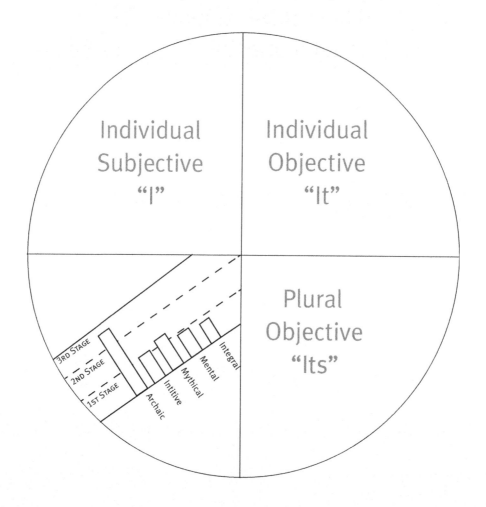

Lines of Development in Plural Subjective "We" Quadrant

This illustration above portrays development of a group of people, like a company, which functions mostly in the Mental and Mystical structures of consciousness with little behaviour in the Intuitive and Archaic structures of consciousness, and even less in Integral structures of consciousness.

These concepts are very useful in coaching. For example, when I was coaching Deborah, she lacked confidence and felt she had limited skills. From my understanding of lines of development, I was able to ask powerful questions about many lines of personal development (cognitive, moral, interpersonal, physical and emotional), and she soon realized that she was only considering one aspect of development—the cognitive or mental—and could see that she was very strong in the others. This more extensive map of her skills and development helped her create a realistic picture of herself and helped her map a plan to develop her cognitive ability. Again, an expanded whole picture served her well.

Most lines have three to nine stages of development, depending on the model used. For instance, moral development can be staged in three parts: egocentric (focus of concern is on the individual); ethnocentric (focus is on the individual's group); and worldcentric (concern is for the entire world.)[9] Stages build upon each other in concrete ways, and can't be skipped. However, before a stage is permanent, we can sample or taste it in peak experiences or passing moments.

Even though I won't go into detail, another aspect of Wilber's model is interesting to explore. The stages of development can be further separated into what Wilber describes as *types*, such as gender.[10] Carol Gilligan says that boys develop through asserting independence and emphasizing fairness, and girls develop through acting in ever-larger circles of connection. For example, she tells a story about a boy and girl trying to select a game. The boy says, "Let's play pirates!" and the girl suggests that they play neighbors. When neither wants the other's game, the girl offers a new idea: "Let's play pirates who are neighbors!" and that seems to satisfy both of their needs.[11]

This concept of gender differences can be relevant to your coaching practice. In 2000, two UCLA researchers, Shelley Taylor and Laura Cousin Klein, challenged the notion of fight or flight as a reaction to stress. Until that point, experts accepted that people either fight or leave when stress becomes intense. However, in their lab the UCLA researchers noticed differences between men and women. When the department was under stress, the men did take flight, isolating themselves in their offices, but the women didn't do that: they cleaned up the lab, made coffee, and befriended and bonded with each other. When the researchers realized that 90 percent of the stress research had been done with men, they knew they were onto something. After conferring with other scientists, they conducted experiments that have been verified by subsequent studies, showing that the sexes can respond differently to stress.[12] You might be on the look out for different ways that clients experience stress, based on gender.

Although gender does affect how the developmental stages express themselves, Carol Gilligan maps an Integral stage of development in which men and women can embody both independence and connection. An Integral framework of lines and stages of development, modified by types, doesn't imply that we're all alike: quite the opposite. Having achieved an Integral perspective we're aware of useful, profound patterns that can help us understand each person's uniqueness. We're able to see and value the entire spectrum of possibilities, including the strengths and wisdoms we've individually and collectively gained by passing through the structures of consciousness: Archaic, Intuitive, Mythic, and Mental.

Powerful Questions for Aspects of Ourselves Described by the Quadrants

Putting together the quadrants with coaching goals allows us to generate powerful questions. You'll start to notice that some clients respond better to those that focus on the objective rather than the subjective side, or that they tend to consider individual feelings and values rather than those from culture.

Let's look at how the quadrants schema might play out with specific issues: physical fitness, work-life balance, and starting a business.

Physical Fitness Goal

Individual Interior—the "I"—internal personal, singular	Individual Exterior—the "it"—the view of the internal from the outside
How do you feel in your body at your current level of physical fitness—what energetic sensations do you have as you move or when you are sedentary? How does being physically fit relate to what you value in life? Tell me a story about how your body would feel as you changed your fitness level. What do you need, related to physical movement or fitness?	What's your current physical fitness level, defined in measurable terms? What's your metabolism rate? How can you change any measurable indicators of fitness? What kind of goal do you want to have about fitness: Are you focused on being healthy, on being a certain size, on fitting into an outfit for a class reunion, or some other objective? On a scale from 1-10, how close are you to your goal?
Collective Interior—the "We"—the internal plural	Collective Exterior—the "its"—the view of systems, organizations, groups
How do members of your culture, family, friends, and or your significant other view physical fitness? What kind of family rituals support or interfere with your change? What do others say about you that contribute to your attaining your goal? Would your goal be furthered if you were to ask for support from your family?	What types of organizational supports would you find helpful to move along your path? How could they help? What type of fitness programs have you used? Would you exercise more often by joining a gym or class or by exercising in a structured environment?

Work-Life Balance

Individual Interior—the "I"—internal, personal, singular	Individual Exterior—the "it"—the view of the internal from the outside
How would your sense of yourself be different at the end of six months if your life were balanced? How can you use your knowledge of personal constitution to assist in progress? Is there anything that the deepest, oldest part of you is aching to do? How are you using empowered language as a statement of your ability to improve your work-life balance?	What body system frequently lets you know you are out of balance, and what are the specific ways it does so? What behaviors and observable signs tell us that a person is in (or out of) balance with work and the rest of life? What behavior patterns promote and inhibit balance?
Collective Interior—the "We"—the internal plural	Collective Exterior—the "its"—the view of systems, organizations, groups
How does your current family feel about work-life balance? What is the perspective of your colleagues about work-life balance? What kind of work ethic does your family of origin hold? How does your nation support or inhibit balance? How would your supervisor and significant other rate your ability to balance your life? What would other central observers of your life say is key to more balance? How could you mobilize group energy to help you promote work-life balance? How can your spiritual/religious community support your balance?	What groups or companies have desirable behavioral patterns of work-life balance that you could learn from and align with? What myths in your industry need to be changed before you, as well as others, can enjoy more work life balance? What behavior patterns, such as breaks, vacations, time off, etc., act as catalysts for movement toward your goal?

Starting a Business

Individual Interior—the "I"—internal personal, singular	Individual Exterior—the "it"—the view of the internal from the outside
How ready are you to start your business? What internal myths about business or being a businessperson do you need to eliminate or create in order to be successful? In terms of your personal constitution, what strengths do you have that can also become a liability? How does this business feed your deepest sense of purpose? What qualities do you have that will make you a success?	What part of a business plan will be helpful at this stage of development? What kind of start-up money do you think you need? What kind of personal financial reserves do you have for the start-up period? What kinds of observable behavior patterns have been successful in the past when you have completed a project?
Collective Interior—the "We"—the internal plural	Collective Exterior—the "its"—the view of systems, organizations, groups
How does your family feel about this start up, and how would succeeding here impact your family and other important roles? What kinds of family or company myths impact your success? How does the success of your significant groups impact your own potential? What kind of energy work do you need to do to draw the right products, people, market, finances, and physical office area to you?	How can groups such as SCORE, a free non-profit retired businessperson organization, help you create a business plan? What other groups can help with this vital step, and in what specific ways? How could you align with other groups that share your deep commitment and sense of purpose? How could social media help you promote your business?

The Integral Coach in the BCI Model

The Integral structure of consciousness contains all the previous ways of thinking and being: remember the theme of the Integral is include, expand, and transcend. When we take all the coaching tools that match the four structures of consciousness (Mental, Mythical, Intuitive and Archaic), we have a broad spectrum of approaches that can truly assist people in moving toward their goals. People move more quickly, and their choices are more in alignment with their whole being. Using this perspective is easier and more fun for both the coach and the client.

I hope the power of an Integral approach is becoming too obvious to dismiss! Just in case you need more persuasion, please consider these illustrations. In the first below, you can see that the client on the left, and the coach who is next to and a little behind the client, both live in the Mental. You can see such items as the calendar, the clocks, and other forms of measurement.

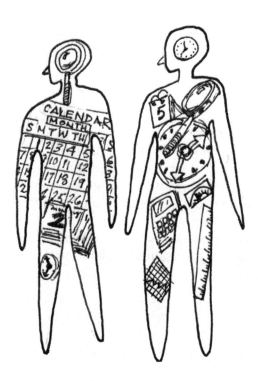

Figure 1. Both Client (left) and Coach are in the Mental.

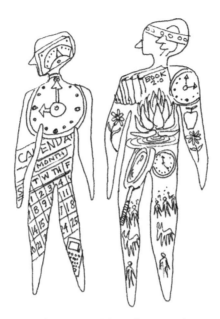

Figure 2. The Client is still in the Mental but the Coach can operate in the Integral.

The illustration above portrays the coach after training now able to function in the Integral. The illustration below shows the client's process in learning to embody the four structures of consciousness. Of course, this change happens over time, and not all clients learn to consciously inhabit all of the structures of consciousness, but most are open to them when they see how it benefits them.

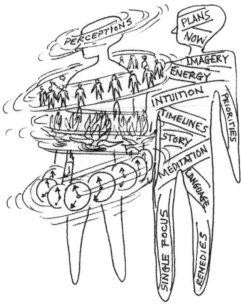

Figure 3. The client is now learning how to come from the Integral.

324   CHAPTER 9: The Integral Part of Coaching

Illustration four shows both the coach and the client operating in the Integral structure of conscious. Once that happens the pictured sequence can start again, with the coach as well as with the client now impacting the lives of the people they contact. This is the ripple effect that causes cultural change. I once saw a bumper sticker that said that first something new is ridiculed, then it's violently opposed, and finally it is accepted as self-evident[13] (and/or those who originally opposed it, think it is their idea).

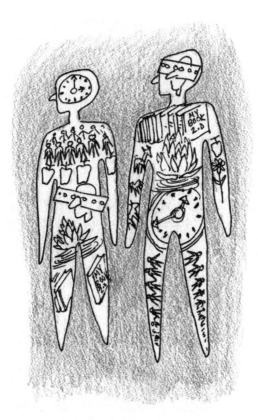

Figure 4. Both now can be in the Integral Structure of Consciousness.

Where do you think you are with the idea of the Integral structure? Are you comfortable with the Mythical but not the Intuitive, or with the Mental but not the Archaic? How would you explore a structure that was not familiar?

The Integral Coach in Action

So let's put together the coaching tools introduced throughout the book. How does the Integral coach in the BCI Approach decide when and how to use the tools?

Here's a guide—and only a guide—for how to organize the tools when you're first working with the BCI Model. *The more practice you have with coaching, the more you'll realize that these tools can be used in many different places in the session, and you'll become more masterful in staying in the moment with your clients and noticing what tools surface from your deep listening.* However, in the beginning, these tables may be useful. Please don't be overwhelmed, as each tool or each quadrant will not be used in each session!

For Use All the Time

Some tools can be used all the time because they're so foundational to coaching that it's impossible to limit them to only one part of the coaching session. This table identifies the structure of consciousness, the tool and where in the book it was presented, the timing (just a guideline), the steps to using it, and the way to measure the effectiveness of the tool.

Tools to Use All the Time

Structure	Tool	When to Use	Steps in Using	How to Gauge Effectiveness
Mental	Coaching Grid (CHAPTER 1)	All the time	Act from the coaching role where the coach and the client are exploring new territory unknown to both parties, or act from the consulting role when requested by the client and it seems appropriate to the coach.	Client reaches the goal.
Mental	Critical Thinking and Decision-Making (CHAPTER 5)	All the time	Model analysis, inference, discrimination, and evaluation and ask powerful questions that take clients through the process so they can learn it.	Client makes decisions that are effective and successful.

Intuitive	Intuition (CHAPTER 7)	All the time	When you have a hunch, you can ask the client if they would like to know what's coming to you. It's an assumption or perception that you can test with the client.	How it's received by the client—on the mark or not.
Intuitive	Walking the Talk (CHAPTER 7)	All the time	Model a life that involves you reaching your goals in the framework of a fun, easy, kind, and gentle growth model.	Clients are inspired by your progress and your humanness.
Intuitive	Silence (CHAPTER 7)	All the time	Pause or ask for a minute of silence.	Client moves beyond the limits that were stopping them or goes deeper into issues. Clients find their own answers.
Archaic	Compassion (CHAPTER 8)	All the time	Come from the place of understanding, empathy, and kindness as much as possible when working with clients.	Client senses your caring and trust and intimacy grows.
Archaic	Being Present (CHAPTER 8)	All the time	Come from the present moment and convey the feeling that all is well.	Client feels empowered and moves toward the goal.

For Use in Assessment

You want the assessment tools to help you answer this vital question: who is your client? Remember, the Mental part of coaching helps you evaluate learning types and readiness for change, while the Mythical part of coaching offers an appraisal of personal constitution and empowerment language, with the Archaic providing a way to understand your client's relationship to source, God, or whatever form this connection takes.

Don't forget to put yourself in this equation as well. For instance, does your learning type or personal constitution match your client's? If so, how will that help with your work together and what blind spots might you discover? If not, how do you need to adjust your style so your interactions can be effective?

Tools to Use for Assessment

Structure	Tool	When to Use	Steps in Using	How to Gauge Effectiveness
Mental	Learning Types (CHAPTER 5)	In working with a client, lead to their learning style.	Visual—drawing, imagery, and symbols. Kinesthetic—physical—movement. Auditory—verbal conversation.	Client feels understood, and communication seems easy, like you and the client are speaking the same language. Client owns a new concept or behavior and increased awareness. Client is ready for more effective action.
Mental	Mental Map of Stages and Styles of Change (CHAPTER 4)	When beginning to work with clients or beginning a new phase.	Notice cues that suggest where client is with regard to process of change.	Client feels met with appropriate processes and tools.
Mental	Coaching Readiness Gauge —Prochaska's Stages of Change CHAPTER 4	When beginning to work with clients or beginning a new phase.	Notice cues that suggest where client is with regard to process of change.	Client feels met with appropriate processes and tools.

Mythical	Personal Constitution Types—Vata (Air), Pitta (Fire), and Kapha (Earth) (CHAPTER 6)	When listening to a client, the coach may hear words or issues that relate to personal constitution, such as the client is spacey and unorganized (Vata), or too busy and easily frustrated (Pitta), or stagnating (Kapha).	Ask client who has unbalanced personal constitution if specific interventions might be helpful. Coach uses knowledge of personal constitution to inform powerful questions and supports strenghts.	Client experiences more balance and the positive characteristics of their personal constitution.
Mythical	Empowerment Language (CHAPTER 6)	When a client uses any language that indicates lack of personal power.	The coach invites reframing language from powerlessness to language that expresses choice and empowerment.	Client starts to feel more choice about actions and therefore more power.
Archaic	Three Faces of God (CHAPTER 8)	To help understand client's relationship to God.	Ask the client if s/he experiences God in self, in a revered spiritual teacher, and/or in the web of life.	Client and coach understand client's perspective on God.

For Use at the Beginning of Coaching Sessions—Where Does Your Client Want To Go?

At the beginning of sessions you might "contract for completion" with your client. This simply means that you discuss what the client wants to obtain from time with you. Is the session's goal to change an attitude, gain a new perspective, develop a clear vision of a goal, identify resources to help accomplish a next step, or what? The second consideration is how you and your client will know that the session goal has been reached. For example, if a change in perspective or attitude is the desired goal, your client will probably feel relieved, relaxed, excited to take new actions, or experience some other feeling. You may want to determine baseline measurement of progress toward a goal. For instance, you may want to ask your client (using a scale of 1-10) where they think they are now and where do they want to be by the end of the session.

Some clients prefer less structured sessions and may not want to "contract for completion" for every session or at all. They might like more of a "let's see what comes up" approach. It's important to let the client guide the session, but if telling a long story or moving from one issue to another doesn't produce concrete results, it's important to point that out. For example, you might say, "I notice that when you tell me all the details about your homework and it takes half our time, you don't have enough time left to select a next step for the week." Or "When you spend half our time going from one issue to another, it seems that you don't have time to look deeply into one area and move closer toward your goal." You might also wonder about and ask if this behavior is a pattern that the client might be experiencing in other areas of her or his life.

Here's a table that can help you to select tools for use at the beginning of sessions:

Tools for the Beginning of Sessions

Structure	Tool	When to Use	Steps in Using	How to Gauge Effectiveness
Mental	Contracting for Completion Using Scale of 10 (CHAPTER 5)	When the client wants or needs a structure for the session.	Ask client what they want to achieve by the end of the session. When that's been established, ask how the client will know they've achieved that goal by the end of the session—for example, they might feel relieved or excited.	Client arrives at the goal by the end of the session and experiences a feeling or another way of knowing that the goal has been completed.
Intuitive	Magic Wand (CHAPTER 7)	Useful when the client expresses some limitations.	Invite the client to use an imaginary magic wand. Ask how things could change or what new idea, option or approach appears.	Client moves beyond their limits.

Tools for Use in the Middle of Sessions

In the previous chapters, many tools have been provided, and the ones that I generally use in the middle part of the session are listed below. Notice which ones are your favorites and which ones are not as familiar. In one training that I conducted, a participant realized that the tools she found herself using were the ones she'd practiced in class. See if the tools you haven't used need review or more practicing so that you have more options when you work with clients.

Tools for the Middle of Sessions

Structure	Tool	When to Use	Steps in Using	How to Gauge Effectiveness
Mental	1-10 Scale (Chapter 5)	When client has made some progress on a goal and wants to become clearer about the goal or the steps required to obtain the goal.	Have the person place themselves on an imaginary 1-10 scale, looking back to see what helped them get to their current number. Ask about moving forward, identifying body/spirit/mind experiences at each step.	Client has insights that help them feel that they can get to the goal or can identify what helps them get there, or learn how to tune into body, mind, spirit information regarding the goal.
Mental	Pie Chart (CHAPTER 5)	When working with limitations, like 24 hours in a day.	Have the client portray the current way time is used in a pie diagram and then see what needs to be expanded or added and what to be reduced or taken out.	Client puts together a realistic plan for change that satisfies current needs.
Mental	Choosing Between Options (CHAPTER 5)	When client is deciding between or among various alternatives.	Invite client to experience each option in an assortment of physical places in a location. If there	Client sees new aspects of options, creates a new option, or becomes clear on which option

			are two points of decision, ask client to move to a new place in the area to consider a third scenario. Ask body, mind, spirit, and energy questions.	to select—or becomes more skilled in accessing body, mind, spirit, and energy knowing that leads to action toward a goal.
Mental	Lists—To Do and Ta Da (CHAPTER 5)	When client feels overwhelmed with tasks or lacks confidence.	Ask the client to list all the things needed to get done on To Do List and then use Ta Da list to celebrate the things accomplished.	More things are accomplished and more things are celebrated.
Mental	Observing Behavior Patterns (CHAPTER 5)	When a client wants to replace or change a behavior pattern.	Help your client learn the triggers that initiate a behavior and all the steps in the pattern, including the reward or benefit from the behavior. Then create a new behavior to satisfy the benefit. If this step is not accomplished, lasting change is unlikely.	Reduction in use of the problem behavior and increase of the new behavior.
Mythical	Story (CHAPTER 6)	To help stimulate a clearer vision of the present and the future.	Ask client to make up a story when more information is desired—how they would like something to happen or how things are happening now.	Client has increased awareness that leads to effective action.

Mythical	Imagery (CHAPTER 6)	To help a client see goals or change mood or stress level. To explore next steps in their examination of a pertinent metaphor or simile that they used.	Provide space for the client to create an image that represents the client attaining the goal.	The client deepens her or his understanding and finds the imagery useful.
Mythical	Dialog (CHAPTER 6)	When the client needs more awareness and there is an identified situation or part of the person that is resistant or helpful in movement toward the goal.	To identify a part of the body or part of a process and establish a conversation with it.	Client's awareness is broadened to include new approaches or parts of a situation.
Intuitive	Divination—I Ching or tarot, angel, medicine cards, etc. as an aid to Intuition (CHAPTER 7)	When you or the client would like a more concrete way to access intuition about a situation.	Ask if you can draw one or more cards for clients and discuss results.	Client is inspired to consider messages from their intuition and applies them to achieving their goal.
Intuitive	Energy Chakras (CHAPTER 7)	When you can see a theme or pattern, such as stomach trouble, with possible power issue.	Noticing body experiences in relation to the chakra themes.	Client integrates symptoms with life issues and goals.
Intuitive	Tapping (CHAPTER 7)	When client is emotionally stuck about a relationship, situation, or event.	Support tapping if client knows it, and if not, ask if they would like to learn it. If yes, give these instructions:	Number goes down to 1 or zero. (May have to repeat steps 1-3 times to get to 1 or 0.)

			1. Ask client to give you a number from 1-10 representing how upset they are about issue. 2. Have client repeat three times: "Even though (challenge), I completely love and accept myself…" 3. Have client tap: above eyebrows, under eyes, under nose, at chin crease, on chest, under left arm, wrists, inside of knees, top of head. The number of times depend on how upset they are about the issue. 4. Check for changes. 5. Repeat the cycle until the number is 1 or 0.	
Intuitive	Energy Currents —grounding, centering, cooking, expressing, nurturing (CHAPTER 7)	When the coach hears that the client's energy is not balanced.	Invite the client to change energy now by using energy practices. If the client does not have the skills, ask client if they would like you to lead them in an energy exercise.	Client's energy is rebalanced
Intuitive	Power Questions about inherited energy patterns (CHAPTER 7)	When the coach hears a specific pattern that is being repeated from a previous generation.	Ask questions like these: "In what way might this pattern be inherited from your ancestors or culture?" "How can you change it?" What kind of sup-	Client sees issues as part of larger patterns rather than personal. Changes in client have impact on their groups

			port from your network would be useful?	
Intuitive	Taking a Breath (Chapter 7)	When the coach hears that the client wants a new option, integration, or perspective on a situation, or if the client says they feel stuck. Another time to use breath is to explore ways clients live their lives.	Invite the client to take a deep breath and take a deep breath yourself when you want to help clients see new perspectives. If you want to explore the breath as an example for looking at their life, ask them to breathe normally and ask questions about the breath, such as inquiring into the depth, rhythm, length of inhale and exhale, etc.	Client has a new idea or way forward. Client sees how the way they breathe replicates the way they live.
Intuitive	Law of Attraction (Chapter 7)	When clients want to meet a goal that especially relies on their ability to see it happen—like building a coaching practice, changing a relationship, etc.	Help the client connect to the energy of the goal and find ways to stay connected to that energy.	The goal is reached.
Archaic	Work with Sense of Purpose or Meaning (Chapter 8)	When the client is not connected to life purpose.	Ask if the client wants to explore this area.	Client becomes connected to life purpose and able to move ahead with situations that align with life meaning. Client may become calmer and more joyful.

Tools for the Ends of the Sessions (Homework)

In this component of the interaction, you'll want to ask questions that help your client create a clear, measurable and observable next step. A clear understanding of the exact commitment is most useful. For example, your client might decide to begin an exercise program by starting to take her or his dog for an extra 20-minute walk on Wednesday after work. Goals can also be more subjective, such as becoming ten percent more aware of a behavior pattern during the week.

If you've "contracted for completion" at the beginning of the session, you'll want to ask the client if the goal has been accomplished and the "how will we know you reached the goal" objective has been reached. Intermittent evaluation periods are central to identifying client satisfaction with the coaching process in general. It's helpful to establish a ritualized evaluation conversation once a month, once a quarter, or at the end of the year. Here are tools you can use at the end of sessions:

Tools for Ends of Sessions

Structure	Tool	When to Use	Steps in Using	How to Gauge Effectiveness
Mental	Plans and Timelines (CHAPTER 5)	When trying to get to a goal. Use for setting up homework.	Have clients create small, steady, reasonable, fun steps toward their goal.	Client meets their goals and feels empowered. They have learned about patterns, values or perceptions about meeting their goals or not meeting the goals.
Mythical	Affirmations (CHAPTER 6)	To help accomplish a goal in which the client has negative self-talk. For example, the client may want a better paying job, and there	Jointly design a statement that claims a new perception or goal is now in existence. Next look at the obstacles that come up as they say the affirma-	Client moves towards the new goal, overcoming newly uncovered obstacles.

		is a part of the client that doesn't think that's possible.	tion. Consider the truth of the negative assumptions.	
Intuitive	Spending Time in Nature (CHAPTER 7)	When clients want to become more relaxed, more connected to beauty or to something greater than themselves.	Help client become aware of their degree of connection to nature, and the benefits of increasing it. Explore options for spending time in nature.	Client is more relaxed, inspired, connected.
Intuitive	Food, Mood, and Nourishment Log (CHAPTER 7)	When client wants to explore nourishment issues or change how they eat.	Give clients the worksheet and explain how to work with it. Use powerful questions to help them understand and use what they uncover.	Client knows more about their patterns related to food, mood, and eating and uses this information as input for achieving nutritional change or goals related to nourishment.
Intuitive	Ritual (CHAPTER 7)	To establish transitions and celebrate successes.	Client can be supported in creating a ritual. Involve a community of some sort to witness the ritual.	Client feels a sense of completed transition.
Archaic	Meditation/ Prayer/ Contemplation (CHAPTER 8)	To help people maintain a peaceful state of being or to become clear on an aspect of their life.	Ask the client if they want to have a practice that has a single focus, such as working with the breath, a mantra, a prayer, etc.	Client feels more grounded, pleasant, and/or clear.

Some Final Comments

Ken Wilber states that "In any field of interest—such as business, law, science, psychology, health, art, or everyday living and learning—the Integral Vision ensures that we are utilizing the full range of resources for the situation, leading to a greater likelihood of success and fulfillment."[13] Coming from the whole picture in coaching means not viewing one quadrant or one structure of consciousness as the truth but considering all of them as correct—just different—which mirrors Wilber's enthusiasm for the integral perspective. Inspired by the classification of the tools and the maps presented in this book I hope you'll consider new things and make sure you don't inadvertently overlook powerful options or any aspect of situations and people. From this wide range of perspectives one tool or approach can intuitively float up at the right moment in a session and inform your coaching comments and powerful questions. This can move coaching from good to great, offering you and your clients an easier, more congruent process, aligned with deeper values—leading both you and your clients to more joy, health, and success. Enjoy.

Coaching Graduates Working Integrally

All of the contributors included in this book practice from an integrative/integral perspective but have chosen to write about their experience with a specific tool or concept. The following graduates share the ways they've incorporated this new holistic/integral mode of operating in their professional practice and in their lives.

Roxanne Taracena
The BCI Approach in Action

I'm an office manager for a dental office and also the treatment plan coordinator. I've used coaching in many aspects of my job, and it's been extremely useful on various occasions, both in working with patients and with staff. We take our work seriously and our office mission statement expresses our commitment to providing exceptional dental service because we know that dental health is a very important aspect of whole health.

One powerful time I apply my coaching training is when a patient is diagnosed as needing treatment. When I first meet a patient, I like to do a new patient interview, which helps me get to know them a little and find out what they're looking for in our practice. I often use the magic wand. Some patients come in very apprehensive, and it's hard for them to express their hopes and concerns, so I ask, "If you could have any dental wish granted with the magic wand, what would it be?" Most everyone lightens right up, and their hopes and fears come pouring out.

I also gauge each patient's readiness on a scale from 1-10. Once I find out what level they're at, I ask powerful assessment and clarification questions to see what they really want and what are their expectations for the treatment. At the same time as I'm asking powerful questions, I also like to get a feel for what personality type they have so I know how to approach them and how much time I have with them before they lose interest.

We really like our patients to "own" their treatment plan and not see it as just doing what's recommended. That way they're more likely to complete treatment, which brings me to another useful tool—the timeline. We co-create milestones together so that when patients do reach a goal, they experience a sense of accomplishment and pride, and we also reinforce their goal with encouragement and praise. This tool also gives them the incentive to complete treatment.

After taking the coach training, I'm better able to relate with patients and with my staff. It taught me how to open up and tune in to people with something as easy as asking the right question. Since using these methods, I've noticed a huge increase in treatment acceptance, success in building a healthy collaborative office culture that supports teamwork, and more confidence in speaking with people. This coaching method has not only made me effective on the job, but a more effective communicator with my family members.

Judith Gruber, MSW, LCSW, CCET
Money As an Integral Issue!

The integral coaching model in this book aligns with my own training and beliefs about how to be in life and how I approach my work as a therapist, as a life, business, money, and career coach, a seminar facilitator, and teacher. While I work with people on a great many issues, the dynamics of money profoundly impact people's lives on the physical, emotional, mental, and spiritual levels. We explore how we use money as a reflection of our beliefs, attitudes, and behavior with money, such as overspending, under-earning, compulsive shopping, hoarding, or acting in an obsessive-compulsive manner. This helps clients to transform self-defeating behavior patterns into positive ones.

A woman I'll call Jane came to me for coaching. She wanted to pay off her credit cards. When Jane talked about what kept her sleepless and full of anxiety, it was her worries about money, and she told me she felt the worry most in her belly and head. Jane was very ungrounded, so we worked with techniques to ground her energy. I asked her to stand up and use her breath and voice while stamping her feet. This helped to create more awareness and clarity in her mind and she felt more present in her body.

We looked at behaviors around money. I asked some powerful questions to help Jane understand her pattern of spending and the unconscious force behind it. For example, "What's happening in your life when you find yourself overspending? What's the experience you're looking for?" Jane kept a journal of her spending and the feelings that were present at the time. This was a powerful exercise that helped Jane see her behavior patterns so that she could begin to change them.

We then came up with a strategy for paying off her debts. Jane worked with visualization and inspirational affirmations from my Abundance and Prosperity Cards. This helped her to connect to her body and to believe more in her ability to reach her goal. She used many of the cards, and there were two that she most identified with: "Money has only the power that I give it," and "Budgeting allows for my dreams to become reality." Jane continued to take action that changed her spending patterns, which resulted in Jane paying off her debt in a short period of time, as well as giving her a new sense of empowerment.

Kathy Moehling, RN, AHN-BC, ND, LCPC, LMT
So Many Applications for Coaching Tools!

I began learning about health coaching in 1999, when working as a holistic health practitioner for a freestanding holistic center connected with a local hospital and health system. After completing my initial health coaching courses with Linda, I saw a wide range of adults at that center—staff from the health system, and professional and lay people from the community. As I also have experience as a registered nurse and as a counselor, I couldn't help noticing that individuals seemed more open to attending coaching sessions than to attending traditional counseling sessions.

Beginning with the very early coaching sessions, I incorporated guided imagery with individuals who are open to that modality—to assist them in becoming more centered, calm, and relaxed. I also invited people to use imagery to tune in to their bodies and feelings and for seeking intuitive or spiritual guidance. I especially remember one man who said he wasn't particularly religious but had an image of Jesus as his guide in his session and was surprised and perplexed about that. However, previously, he'd told me he was accustomed to only accepting guidance from the "highest authority." His image seemed like a pretty high authority to me, and he laughed and agreed when I pointed it out.

A woman with esophageal cancer told me that the coaching sessions helped her to re-connect with her spirituality. The receptionist at the center said she noticed this client looking very tired and haggard when she arrived for the sessions, and when she left she often "just glowed." Another woman recovering from breast cancer said she'd been very fearful of her cancer returning when she began the sessions, and was much less fearful by the end of the series. I encouraged her to trust her own thinking and to use whatever methods of healing that made sense to her. I honored her feelings and encouraged her to do so and gave her ways to release those feelings in a healthy way—crying, laughing, shaking, and verbally expressing anger.

Our center also had an Ornish program for reversing heart disease, which included classes and experiential sessions—an integral approach to cardiac health. Participants were involved in aerobic exercise, strength training, Yoga with a brief period of meditation, group support sessions, and sharing a meal of low fat vegetarian food. Several people from that program who were making a major lifestyle change said that my coaching facilitated their acceptance of the lifestyle changes they needed to make. I appreciate how coaching can so easily be integrated with other approaches, enhancing their benefits.

I've also seen several people for health coaching in my private practice, and have used a wide range of the coaching tools with them, including "underpromising," which is very effective.

In addition to the tools, I use a variety of handouts, cassette tapes, CD's, VHS tapes, DVD's, and books with clients. As mentioned above, I almost always use some guided imagery. As I have an energy work background—Therapeutic Touch and Healing Touch—I frequently add energy work to the coaching sessions when my clients request it, which seems to help people integrate and more readily utilize information for healing.

In the past year, I've seen several individuals with food and eating issues, who seem to respond quite well to the coaching format. Another certified chakra instructor and I will be starting a monthly chakra-based group this fall, called "That Food Thing," for people with food and eating issues. I'm really looking forward to facilitating this group and intend to use many coaching tools.

I've also coached people with anxiety issues, with general personal growth issues, and with other health challenges. Each person and each session is different, which makes the work challenging, enjoyable, and usually productive. Health coaching has given me great joy and satisfaction in my work. Being a coach continues to be very meaningful and rewarding and a way to integrate the perspectives from my nursing and naturopathic medicine approaches.

Steve Friedman, DDS
Coaching Tools for Service in a Dental Office

The culture of our dentistry office has changed after we adopted many of the coaching principles of the Bark Coaching Institute—especially deep respect for each other and for our patients. That's been the foundation of our teamwork and the key to our success. I wake up wanting to come to the office, but it's taken some time to get here.

I used to feel under-supported and overwhelmed at work. That's changed, but let me be perfectly honest—I still do have moments when I feel weighted down. When I do, my staff and I shift into a new process that involves one or all of the following: we maximize our resources, realign relationships, re-evaluate our mission, and look to system readjustments. My whole team has co-created our mission as well as our team agreements, and each person helps corrects what's out of sync. We realize that we create our reality, and therefore, we can change it.

One focus of our communication is to eliminate the word "if." For example, we don't say "if this changes," we say, "when this changes." Using empowerment language makes a very big difference. As in coaching, we rarely use blame but think about results as feedback. We remember that each team member is coachable—and wants feedback to improve. I've set up a profit-sharing model so everyone really sees and is rewarded as we increase our revenue. Our work culture is less about adapting or coping and more about creating and expanding our capacity. We're partners.

I feel really fortunate to have what I call the "A Team." We have a positive attitude and fun—difficult to believe, but we really do have fun. Being in our office is energizing, for us and for our patients. Our culture, or way of doing and being, can be felt by those who come into our office. Most want to come back. Yes, it's hard to imagine, but most want to come back to the dentist!

I've learned to listen so much better to my staff and my patients, and that's helped establish deeper trust between us. I'll never forget Linda playing my role and dressing up as the dentist, with one of my staff as the patient, as I looked on. She acted out me talking to a patient, standing almost behind my patient in "my costume" of mask, special magnifying glasses that make me look like a bug, and my white coat. That playful method helped me really see how little I was actually relating to patients as people. That wasn't the kind of interaction I wanted to have with my patients or the respect that I wanted to show. I really care about my patients as people and want to provide the best

> service possible. I've set up a different way of talking and listening to them. I've also learned to listen to my gut more often, and find that it doesn't let me down in sizing up a situation or a person.
>
> My staff and I have all taken the BCI training, along with having ongoing phone meetings with our coach and site visits from Linda and a colleague, Laura Boone, who's trained in the BCI Method. We use the tools all the time. Honestly, I never thought I'd have the kind of supportive team that sees change as good and wants to move forward as much as I do towards an even higher level of service and mission. My question continues to be, "How good can it get?" and so far I haven't found the limit!

---

[1] Jean Gebser, *The Ever Present Origin*, trans. Noel Barstad with Algis Mickunas (Athens, OH: Ohio University Press, 1985), 116-122.

[2] Gebser's book, cited above, also gives information on how structures of conscious manifest in efficient and deficient forms: 92-94, 125-126, 142, 299.

[3] Gebser, *Ever Present Origin*, 142.

[4] Private conversation with Rudy Ballentine, March 29, 2pm, 2011, Ballentine, SC.

[5] Gebser, *Ever Present Origin*, 299.

[6] Ken Wilber, *The Integral Vision: A Very Short Introduction to the Revolutionary Integral Approach to Life, God, the Universe, and Everything* (Boston & London, Shambhala, 2007), 16-17. Ken Wilber has written over 20 books on philosophy and the integral perspective, however, this book is an excellent synopsis of his ideas presented in a easy to understand format with numerous color illustrations that depict multifaceted concepts. A companion to this book that applies all his theories to everyday living is entitled *Integral Life Practice: A 21st-Century Blueprint for Physical Health, Emotional Balance, Mental Clarity, and Spiritual Awakening,* by Ken Wilber, Terry Patten, Adam Leonard, and Marco Morelli (Boston & London, Integral Books, 2008).

[7] Ibid., 38.

[8] Ibid., 30-37.

[9] Ibid., 34-35.

[10] The personal constitution breakdown is another kind of typing scheme.

[11] Wilber, *The Integral Vision*, 47.

[12] S.E. Taylor, L.C. Klein, B.P., T.L. Gruenewald, R.A.R. Gurung, and J.A. Updegraff, *Female Responses to Stress: Tend and Befriend, Not Fight or Flight*, Psychological Review vol. 107, no. 3 (2000): 411-429.

[13] Wilber, *The Integral Vision*, back cover.

Made in the USA
Middletown, DE
24 November 2020